12 $\frac{50}{}$

4/4

The Secession Movement
in the
Middle Atlantic States

The
SECESSION

William C. Wright

MOVEMENT
in the
MIDDLE
ATLANTIC
STATES

Rutherford • Madison • Teaneck
Fairleigh Dickinson University Press

Associated University Presses, Inc.
Cranbury, New Jersey 08512

Library of Congress Cataloging in Publication Data
Wright, William C   1939–
    The secession movement in the Middle Atlantic States.

      Bibliography: p.
      1. Secession.   2.   Middle Atlantic States—Politics and government.
I.   Title.
E440.5.W96   973.7'1   72-424
ISBN 0-8386-1152-4

Printed in the United States of America

to
my mother and father

CONTENTS

Acknowledgments   9

1 INTRODUCTION   13

2 MARYLAND   21

3 DELAWARE   74

4 NEW JERSEY   98

5 PENNSYLVANIA   125

6 NEW YORK   164

7 CONCLUSION   206

Appendices   213

Notes   222

Bibliography   242

Index   265

ACKNOWLEDGMENTS

To the various archivists and librarians who gave of their time and abilities helping me with my research, I wish to express my appreciation. In particular I would like to thank the staff of Cornell University Library, University of Delaware Library, Maryland Historical Society, New Jersey Historical Society, Pennsylvania Historical and Museum Commission, and Rutgers University Library.

I would also like to express my appreciation to the following institutions for their permission to quote from their manuscripts or publications: Columbia University Libraries; The Cooper Union For The Advancement of Science And Art Library; Cornell University Library; Historical Society of Delaware; Hall of Records of Delaware; Eleutherian Mills Historical Library; Lancaster County Historical Society; The Library of Congress; Hall of Records of Maryland; Maryland Historical Society; New Jersey State Library; The New York Historical Society; The New York Public Library; The New York State Library; Pennsylvania Historical and Museum Commission; The Historical Society of Pennsylvania; The Pennsylvania State University; George Peabody Department of the Enoch Pratt Free Library; The University of Rochester Library; Special Collections Division of Rutgers University Library; The Historical Society of Western Pennsylvania; and Wyoming Historical and Geological Society of Wilkes-Barre, Pennsylvania.

I am also grateful to the following for permission to quote from their books or manuscript: Doubleday and Company for permission to quote from *The Lincoln Papers* by David C. Mearns, © 1948 by David C. Mearns. Reprinted by permission of Doubleday and Company, Inc.; The Catholic University of America Press, for permission to quote from Brother Basil L. Lee's *Discontent in New York City: 1861–1865,* © 1943 by The Catholic University of America Press. Reprinted by permission of The Catholic University of America Press; Philip S. Foner, author of *Business and Slavery: The New York Merchants and the Irrepressible Conflict,* © 1941, by The University of North Carolina Press. Reprinted by permission of Philip S. Foner; Harold B. Hancock, and the Historical Society of Delaware, for permission to quote from *Delaware During the Civil War,* © 1961, by The Historical Society of Delaware. Reprinted by permission of the Historical Society of Delaware and Harold B. Hancock; Tradition Press for permission to quote from J. Thomas Scharf's *History of Maryland;* and Julius W. Pratt for the use of his Master of Arts thesis, "Public Opinion in the East from the Election of Lincoln to the Firing on Fort Sumter."

This book could not have been written without the cooperation and encouragement of the chairman of my doctoral committee, Professor James M. Merrill. I also would like to express my thanks to my committee: Professor George F. Frick, Professor Stephen Lukashevich, and Professor John A. Munroe.

To those many other people who assisted me in this work, I wish to express my special thanks.

The Secession Movement
in the
Middle Atlantic States

1

INTRODUCTION

i

THIS IS A STUDY OF THE SECESSION MOVEMENT IN THE FIVE MIDDLE
Atlantic states: Maryland, Delaware, New Jersey, Pennsylvania, and
New York. An adequate study has never been made either of the people
who opposed the use of force against the South before the firing upon
Fort Sumter or of those northerners who wanted their states to leave the
Union. Historical writing during the Civil War and immediately after
noted the existence of these men. As the years passed, however, historians
came to accept the view that Lincoln had the full support of the North
prior to the attack on Fort Sumter. This was simply not true.

During the secession crisis the South hoped to receive support from the
North. John A. Logan, a Union general who wrote *The Great Conspiracy:
Its Origin and History* in 1886, stated that

> the Rebels hoped for Northern assistance in case of Secession, is very
> clear from many speeches made prior to and soon after the election of
> Mr. Lincoln to the Presidency—and from other sources of information.[1]

He cited as one example a congressman from South Carolina, L. M. Keitt,
who in November said:

> Let me tell you *there are a million of Democrats in the North who, when
> the Black Republicans attempt to march upon the South, will be found
> a wall of fire in the front.*[2]

Governor John Letcher of Virginia addressed the Virginia Assembly in
December 1860, predicting the end of the Union and the formation of
four separate nations.

> Not two, but four political entities would replace the Old Union. The

13

New York-New England area and the Pacific states would each form a separate nation, and the deep South would form a third entity. The rest of the old Union, the border states, Pennsylvania, New Jersey, and the northwestern states, would be the mighty fourth force that would entice Louisiana, Texas, and Mississippi away from the deep South. Finally this growing giant would wrest Pensacola from the dwindling cotton kingdom, and a rough equilibrium would be established.[3]

While Governor John Letcher was pessimistic about the future of the Union or the Confederacy, he nevertheless prophesied that secession would spread to every state. Horace Greeley, editor of the New York *Tribune* and an anti-slavery Republican, expressed a similar view but envisioned only two nations.

> Throughout the Free States, eminent and eager advocates of adhesion to the new Confederacy by those States—or so many of them as might hope to find acceptance—were widely heard and heeded. . . . [excluding New England and Northwestern states] The remaining States and parts of States, it was assumed, might easily and wisely fit themselves for adhesion to, and acceptance by, the Southern Confederacy by expelling or suppressing all "fanatics," and adopting the Montgomery Constitution, thus legalizing slaveholding as well as slavehunting on their soil. Among those who were understood to urge such adhesion were Governor Seymour, of New York, Judge Woodward and Francis W. Hughes, of Pennsylvania, Rodman Price of New Jersey, etc., etc.[4]

Jefferson Davis, President of the Confederate States of America, concurred with Greeley that there were northerners who supported the South. He, likewise, showed bitter disappointment at their change of attitude.

> It is a great mistake, or misstatement of fact, to assume that, at the period under consideration, the Southern States stood alone in the assertion of the principles which had been laid down in this work, with regard to the right of secession and the wrong of coercion. Down to the formation of Confederate Government, the one was distinctly admitted, the other still more distinctly disavowed and repudiated, by many of the leaders of public opinion in the North of both parties—indeed, any purpose of direct coercion was disclaimed by nearly all. If presented at all, it was in the delusive and ambiguous guise of "execution of the laws" and "protection of the public property."[5]

After the firing upon Fort Sumter, Davis was shocked to see such a remarkable change of opinion.

> No *new* question had arisen—no change in the attitude occupied by the seceding States—no cause for controversy not already existing when these utterances were made. And yet the sentiments which they expressed were so entirely swept away by the tide of reckless fury which soon

afterward impelled an armed invasion of the South, that (with a few praiseworthy but powerless exceptions) scarcely a vestige of them were left. Not only were they obliterated, but seemingly forgotten.[6]

Jefferson Davis was bewildered by this change in attitude, and historians have never explained it. He laid down a challenge that has not yet been taken up:

> I leave to others to offer, if they can, an explanation of this strange phenomenon. . . . in times of revolutionary excitement, the higher and better elements are crushed and silenced by the lower and baser—not so much on account of their greater extent, as of their greater violence.[7]

This work is an attempt to answer this challenge, to study the people who supported the South prior to Fort Sumter and to explore their attitudes immediately after the firing upon that Fort.

The five Middle Atlantic states exerted influence and power, and they present an interesting case study. The United States Census Bureau in 1860 referred to this area as the "Middle States." The Bureau recognized a unity of interest in this geographic area. Over 26 percent of the population of the entire United States, including the Confederate States, was located in this five-state area. More significantly, over 29 percent of the white population lived in the Middle Atlantic region. About 5½ percent of the people who moved into this region came from the eleven southern states that were to make up the Confederacy. These people who moved from the South were about one-half of one percent of the total Middle Atlantic population.

The states of New York, New Jersey, Pennsylvania, Delaware, and Maryland were leading manufacturing states when compared to the United States as a whole. They possessed 42 percent of the annual value of products manufactured in the United States, and they owned 43 percent of the total capital invested in manufacture. In agriculture, they had over 27 percent of the cash value of farms. No matter how one looked at this region economically, it was significant in the national economy.

Within these five states there were three types of secessionists: first, those who wanted to join the Confederacy; second, those who wished to form a central confederacy, that is, to join with the other border states and divide the United States into three separate nations; third, those who preferred to allow the South to go in peace rather than to use force to save the Union. Many individuals who did not want a war with the South refused to admit the right of secession.

The secession movement was prominent in the five Middle Atlantic states,[8] and each of the five states reacted differently to the secession crisis: Maryland was ready to join the Confederacy, while elements of her population strongly favored the Union. A small state like Delaware was dependent upon its surrounding states and had to wait for their actions. Of the five, Pennsylvania, the most pro-Union state, had a Democratic party led by the President of the United States, James Buchanan, that actively supported the South. New Jersey, with relatively few slaves and strong economic and social ties with the South, had many supporters of the Confederacy as well as the central confederacy. New York was divided between upstate regions that supported the Union and the Hudson Valley and New York City areas that had ties with the South. Fernando Wood, Mayor of New York City, proposed that New York be made a free city.

This study discusses those individuals and groups as well as geographic areas within the states that supported some form of secession. Together, the advocates of secession weakened the Lincoln administration's ability to react to the Confederacy. At the same time, they offered the South hope of northern support if war broke out.

ii

With the end of the Mexican War in 1848, vast areas of territory had been added to the United States. The future status of this land was questioned immediately: would it be slave or free territory? The gold rush in California the next year greatly increased that state's population, making its admission to the Union necessary. Debate on these issues reopened the territorial question that supposedly had been settled with the Missouri Compromise of 1820. A new compromise was now necessary, and since the one finally arrived at by the United States Senate included the admission of California as a free state, the balance in the Senate was upset. Free-state senators were now in the majority. The Senate also enacted a stronger fugitive slave law for the capture of runaway slaves. Yet few people either in the North or the South accepted the compromise as a solution to the slavery question.

The decade of the 1850s, which proved the weakness of the compromise, was marked by a growing division between the North and the South. After the presidential election of 1852, the Whig party, which had been the primary opposition to the Democrats, disappeared as a viable alternative to them. Immigrants from Europe continued to pour into the North, swelling the population of the free states and enlarging northern representation in the United States House of Representatives. Northern states enacted "personal liberty laws," making it illegal for a slave chaser to capture a runaway slave or for the authorities of that state to assist a slave chaser. The abolitionists increased their propaganda against the institution of slavery. In 1852 *Uncle Tom's Cabin,* by Harriet Beecher Stowe, appeared and became a best selling novel. Its impact upon both the North and the South further divided the two sections. The South felt itself on the defensive, and it appeared to be losing to an aggressive, northern anti-slavery movement.

The debate over the extension of slavery into the territories reopened in 1854 when Stephen A. Douglas, Democratic senator from Illinois, introduced the Kansas-Nebraska bill, permitting the people of these territories to decide whether or not they wanted slavery. This policy, commonly known as "popular sovereignty," ended the division between slave and free territory established by the Missouri Compromise of 1820. The debate that resulted from the introduction of this bill crushed all hope that the Compromise of 1850 would settle the territorial question. Furthermore, dissident Democrats, who disagreed with President Franklin Pierce, a supporter of the bill, left the Democratic party and joined with the Whigs (who were seeking an alternative party), and with the free soil advocates to form the Republican party. Kansas became the battleground over which supporters and opponents of slavery fought. Violence became so widespread there that the state became known as "bleeding Kansas." Each side had defenders in both the North and in the South. President Pierce was denied his party's presidential nomination in 1856, when the Democratic party chose James Buchanan, who had not taken part in the Kansas-Nebraska debate.

James Buchanan was elected President in 1856, defeating the first Republican presidential candidate, John C. Fremont. Soon after his inauguration, the United States Supreme Court, in the Dred Scott decision, ruled that Congress lacked the authority to prohibit slavery's expansion into the territories. But Kansas presented serious problems for Buchanan. In 1857 a pro-southern Kansas constitutional convention adopted a constitution permitting slaves in Kansas. Since the constitution was written in the town of Lecompton, Kansas, it has been referred to as the Lecompton constitution. Stephen A. Douglas refused to support this constitution and broke with Buchanan and his southern supporters. Therefore, the southern delegates to the 1860 Democratic Convention refused to support him in his bid for the presidential nomination.

The year 1857 was also noted for its economic depression. While brief, the depression severely damaged the northern economy. The South, whose economy was affected less severely, was led to believe itself stronger and more stable than the North. The nativistic American, or Know Nothing, party arose out of the fear of immigration but proved not to be an effective alternative to the Democratic party. The Republican party was to become the primary opposition to the Democrats. The battles in Kansas and the question of the expansion of slavery gave the Republican party its primary issue.

Anti-slavery activities continued throughout the Buchanan administration and culminated in the attack on Harper's Ferry by John Brown in 1859. While few northerners supported this fanatical attack, many southerners believed that it was part of a northern conspiracy to incite a slave revolt.

In this atmosphere of distrust and dissension, the election of 1860 took place. The Democratic party met in Charleston, South Carolina, and immediately divided on the question of the platform. Stephen A. Douglas's supporters wished to reaffirm the platform of 1856, which had evaded the issue of slavery in the territories. The southern Democrats, meanwhile, insisted that the federal government had to protect slavery in the territories. The Douglas faction won, and the southern delegates walked out of the convention. But since the nomination for the presidency required two-thirds of the votes of the delegates, Douglas failed to receive the nomination. The regular Democratic party reconvened in Baltimore and nominated Douglas. The southern Democrats, meeting in Richmond, nominated John C. Breckinridge of Kentucky.

In Chicago, the Republican convention nominated Abraham Lincoln. Another major political party, the Constitutional Union party, adopted a platform which called upon everyone to stand by the Constitution and the Union; it nominated John Bell of Tennessee.

Following the election of Abraham Lincoln the southern states began to secede from the Union. South Carolina's secession, on December 20, 1860, was soon followed by those of Alabama, Georgia, Louisiana, Mississippi, Florida and Texas. Faced with this situation, President Buchanan took the position that it was up to Congress to decide what measures the federal government should take.

During the period of the secession crisis—between the election of Abraham Lincoln and the firing upon Fort Sumter—Congress met and tried various methods to effect a compromise to dissolve the growing division between North and South. Congress hoped to resolve the situation by appointing committees. The House of Representatives appointed one representative from each state, the so-called Committee of Thirty-Three. The Senate appointed a Committee of Thirteen. All proposals and petitions for compromise were referred to these committees. The most discussed compromise was the plan submitted by John J. Crittenden of Kentucky, who proposed that the United States Constitution be amended to allow slavery in the territories south of a line drawn at latitude 36°30'. North of this line slavery would be prohibited.

In the United States Senate, Senator Daniel Clark of New Hampshire introduced a resolution that

the provisions of the Constitution are ample for the preservation of the Union. . . . it needs to be obeyed rather than amended. . . .[9]

This anti-compromise amendment to the Crittenden compromise was adopted by a vote of 25-23. It was reconsidered on March 2, and defeated. But a vote of 19 to 20 rejected the Crittenden resolutions on that same day.

The Crittenden compromise also failed to receive enough support to obtain passage in the United States House of Representatives.

Another attempt at compromise was the Washington Peace Conference, called by the state of Virginia. It was attended by delegates of most of the states that had not yet seceded. Convening on February 4 in Washington, D.C., they submitted a compromise to Congress that included the same extension of slavery into the territories as the Crittenden plan. But the compromise also proposed compensation to masters whose slaves had run away and included a clause prohibiting Congress from abolishing slavery in the states.

These attempts at compromise received support within the Middle Atlantic states. However, the Republican party, and Abraham Lincoln in particular, opposed any form of compromise that would have extended the institution of slavery. The seceded southern states were unwilling to give up their new-found independence to return to the Union. Those that sought some form of compromise were frustrated. Some then took the position that the South should be permitted to leave the Union peaceably, while others advocated the formation of a central confederacy.

Besides the resolutions and bills that pertained to compromise, the United States House of Representatives voted on nine measures pertaining to the question of secession. Congressman Roger A. Pryor of Virginia, introduced a resolution stating that it would be "impracticable"[10] to use force in order to maintain a state in the Union. On the other hand, Congressman Garnett B. Adrain of New Jersey presented a resolution that declared the Constitution the supreme law of the land. Pryor's resolution failed, but Adrain's passed. Another northerner, Representative Isaac C. Morris, of Illinois, argued in a resolution that

we have seen nothing in the past, nor do we see anything in the present, either in the election of Abraham Lincoln to the Presidency of the United States, or from any other existing cause, to justify its dissolution. . . .[11]

The United States House of Representatives agreed with Morris.

The House of Representatives and Senate passed bills that increased the appropriations for the United States Navy, required the militia of Washington, D.C. to take an oath of allegiance, called upon the militia to execute the laws, and censured the Secretary of the Navy for accepting the resignations of naval officers who had left the service of the United States Navy to join the Confederacy. It also discussed the use of ships as customs houses outside of ports controlled by the seceded states.

These were the resolutions and bills pertaining to the secession crisis that the United States Congress considered. The way in which each of the Middle Atlantic states' representatives voted will be referred to in the following chapters. They are indicative of the thoughts of these representatives on the question of secession, compromise, and the use of force to maintain the Union.

iii

Each of the five Middle Atlantic states could in some ways be considered a border state. All had economic, social and traditional ties with the South. At one time each had a thriving slavery system. Lincoln captured the entire electoral votes of only two of the states, Pennsylvania and New York. As the secession crisis developed, the Democratic party and the people of the big cities urged that the South be permitted to leave in peace or that the Middle Atlantic states form a central confederacy. In some states some sentiment veered toward joining the Confederacy. This secessionist thought divided the Democratic and Republican parties. In some cases, Republicans called for no war with the South. Secession's supporters and opponents used the Middle Atlantic states as a battleground.

2
MARYLAND

i

OF THE FIVE MIDDLE ATLANTIC STATES MARYLAND HAD THE STRONGEST secession movement. Situated below the Mason-Dixon line, the traditional dividing line between the North and the South, it was truly a border state. The state itself can be divided into three sections; the southern counties: Saint Mary's, Charles, Prince George's, Anne Arundel, Calvert, Howard and Montgomery; the Eastern Shore counties: Kent, Queen Anne's, Talbot, Caroline, Dorchester, Somerset and Worcester; and the northern and western counties: Allegany,[1] Washington, Frederick, Carroll, Baltimore, Harford and Cecil, including the city of Baltimore.

Tradition and the tobacco culture aligned the Eastern Shore and the southern counties closely to the South. In 1859 southern Maryland

> raised 94.7 per cent of the tobacco crop of the State, and only 18 per cent of the wheat and 17.5 per cent of the corn.[2]

These areas had few immigrants, resulting in a rather homogeneous population. They believed that they could solve

> their problems through their county and state governments. They firmly believed that those same agencies could also solve the question of slavery. . . . On the question of secession the people of these sections also had definite ideas. They believed that states had rights and powers equal, or perhaps superior to those of the federal government. . . . The idea that the federal government had the right to maintain the Union by military force, they regarded as entirely wrong.[3]

Economically these areas lagged behind the northern and western section of Maryland.

21

The northern and western section of the State resembled the North more closely. Manufacturing was growing in the city of Baltimore and the counties of Baltimore, Howard, Frederick, Washington, and Allegany. According to the United States Census of 1860, the leading manufacturing area of the State was centered in Baltimore City and County. It was followed by the western counties of Frederick and Allegany. This was also an area of small farms with a large German immigrant population. Most of the immigrants settled in Baltimore or migrated into western Maryland. The small farms were worked by free labor, and they produced most of Maryland's corn, wheat and livestock. The German immigrants or descendants of immigrants opposed slavery and states' rights, which appeared to them to be nation-splitting issues similar to what they had left in Germany. The leading agricultural counties, both in the number of improved acres and in the cash value of the farms, according to the United States Census of 1860, were Baltimore, Frederick and Washington. It can be seen, therefore, that the northern and western section of Maryland dominated the State.

Baltimore was a manufacturing and commercial city that although closely linked to the North had southern social ties and traditions. When Fort Sumter was fired upon, it appeared Baltimore would join the Confederacy and take the rest of the State with it. The South offered to make Baltimore a leading commercial city by removing the tariff so that both northern and southern commercial establishments could buy duty-free European goods in Baltimore. However, the commercial classes of Baltimore threw their support to the North when it became obvious there would be a civil war. The city could be blockaded easily by the Northern navy, bringing ruin to their establishments. In addition, the manufacturers of the city did not wish to compete with cheap European goods, which would come into Maryland duty-free. Furthermore, the city of Baltimore was connected to the west by the Baltimore and Ohio Railroad. Grains brought on this railroad were milled and then shipped to other cities in the United States or abroad. With the secession of Maryland, this lucrative business would come to a halt.

One of the great fears of all Marylanders was that the State would become the battleground for opposing armies. During the fall of 1860 and the spring of 1861, a severe economic recession that was sweeping across the North struck the city of Baltimore. Hotels were forced either to shut down or to curtail operations; workers were laid off, and specie was suspended.

Nevertheless, a growing tide of secessionist thought and feeling enveloped the city. Horace Greeley wrote:

. . . Baltimore was a slaveholding city, and the spirit of Slavery was nowhere else more rampant and ferocious. The mercantile and social aristocracy of that city had been sedulously, persistently, plied by the conspirators for disunion with artful suggestions that, in a confederacy composed exclusively of the fifteen Slave States, Baltimore would hold the position that New York enjoys in the Union, being the great ship-building, shipping, importing and commercial emporium, whitening the ocean with her sails, and gemming Maryland with the palaces reared from her ample and ever-expanding profits. That aristocracy had been, for the most part, thoroughly corrupted by these insidious whispers, and so were ready to rush into treason. At the other end of the social scale was the mob—reckless and godless, as mobs are apt to be, especially in slaveholding communities—and ready at all times to do the bidding of the Slave Power. Between these was the great middle class, loyal and peacefully inclined, as this class usually is—outnumbering both the others, but hitherto divided between the old pro-Slavery parties, and having arrived, as yet, at no common understanding with regard to the novel circumstances of the country and the events visibly impending.

The city government was in the hands of the Breckinridge Democracy, who had seized it under a cry of reform; and the leaders of the Democracy were deep in the counsels of treason.[4]

As Greeley pointed out, there was diverse opinion within Baltimore as well as within the state of Maryland. The various areas of the State, with different backgrounds and traditions, of different ethnic composition, and of different economic conditions, responded to the secession crisis in different ways. Southern and eastern Marylanders were more pro-South, and therefore pro-secession; central and western Marylanders were less happy with the South, and therefore resisted secession; the city of Baltimore would supply the battleground for a contest of conflicting elements until the federal troops put an end to any secession movement in Maryland.

Of the five Middle Atlantic states, Maryland had the greatest movement of people between itself and the eleven southern states. Of the total population of the state of Maryland, a little over 1 percent of the emigrants to Maryland from other states came from the Confederacy. Over 14 percent of those who left Maryland went to the eleven southern states.

In 1860 Maryland had 87,189 slaves, a decline from the 1810 high point of 111,502 Negroes in bondage. The total number of slaves had declined each decade with the exception of the 1850 census, when the number was found to have risen by seven-tenths of 1 percent.[5] The percentage of slaves to the total population declined steadily from a 1790 high of 32.2 percent to a low of 12.7 percent in 1860. The total number of slaves declined both absolutely and relatively so that in 1860 there were fewer slaves in Maryland than at any previous time. As early as

1783 the Maryland General Assembly had prohibited the importation of African slaves. In 1831 the Colonization Society of Maryland was formed and the Maryland Legislature supported it for twenty-six years at a cost of $10,000 a year.

Slavery was strongest in the southern Maryland counties, where slaves constituted 40.1 percent of the population; by contrast the Eastern Shore counties' percentage of slaves was 19.3. In the northern and western counties only 4.4 percent of the population were slaves. It is easy to see that the areas which most resembled the South in economic interests had the largest slave populations. While slavery was a dying institution within the state of Maryland, the southern counties remained deeply entrenched in a traditional slave culture. This becomes even more obvious when one observes the election of 1860.

The Democratic party convened in Charleston on April 23, 1860, where the delegates split over the platform. This argument led to a division in the party which resulted in the nomination of two candidates. Maryland supported the Douglas wing of the party on the platform when it voted five to three for the Cincinnati platform. However, when the voting started, Douglas received only two Maryland votes, with five cast for Robert M. T. Hunter. Douglas was finally nominated at a second convention, held in Baltimore; yet during the election campaign, the Maryland Democratic organization supported John C. Breckinridge. When the southern delegates seceded from the Charleston convention and established their own convention, nine of the sixteen Maryland delegates attended.

The Constitutional Union party had significant support in the state of Maryland, and John Bell was the choice of the majority of the delegates from Maryland to the Constitutional Union Convention. The Constitutional Union party, consisting of many old Whigs, was the principal opposition party to the Democrats in Maryland. It avoided the slavery issue and spoke of protecting American industry.

At the Republican party convention in Chicago, Maryland was represented by eleven delegates. Edward Bates of Missouri was the majority choice of the Maryland delegates until the third ballot when they voted nine to two for Abraham Lincoln.

The results of the election are significant for the ensuing secession movement because they show once again the geographic diversity of the State. John C. Breckinridge carried Maryland with a vote of 42,482, a plurality of 722 votes over the second candidate, John Bell, the Constitutional Unionist, who had the support of the Governor of Maryland, Thomas H. Hicks. Stephen A. Douglas of the northern wing of the Democratic party was third with 5,294 votes. Abraham Lincoln ran a poor fourth with only 2,294 votes. No candidate received a majority. Breckinridge received 45.92 percent of the vote, Bell received 45.15 percent, Douglas received 6.45 percent, and Lincoln received only 2.48 percent. Significantly, Lincoln found his greatest strength in the northern and western counties and he made his poorest showing in the southern counties. Outside the city of Baltimore, Lincoln received more votes in Allegany County than in any other. Here he received 12 percent of the vote.

> In the mining districts (Westernport, Frostburg, Lonaconing and Mount Savage) Bell and Douglas ran neck and neck, with 30 percent and 29 percent of the votes respectively. Of the votes Lincoln got a total of 522 votes, 342 of which were from the mining areas. The Cumberland *Civilian & Telegraph,* which had supported the Constitutional Union party, attributed the miners' vote for Lincoln to their interest in the tariff protection promised as part of the Republican platform, saying that it was given "without reference to the Slavery question."[6]

The southern Democrats and their candidate, John C. Breckinridge, carried Maryland owing to their campaign proposal to unite Maryland with the South, and their claim that a vote for Breckinridge would show that Maryland's interests lay with the South. Furthermore, a vote for Breckinridge would repudiate the Republican party and its doctrines. To counter the opposition,

> pleas for the Union were made in behalf of Breckinridge, and his candidacy was dissociated from the South Carolina ultraists.[7]

The southern Democrats appealed to Baltimore's commercial interests by saying that a disruption in the Union would damage trade and that votes for Breckinridge would serve their best interests. The regular Democratic party organization backed Breckinridge. The results show that their appeal to the people of Baltimore paid off because the city,

> where Southern feeling flared up in 1861, gave Breckinridge relatively more votes than did rural Maryland, which placed Bell first, although no candidate had a majority in either city or county.[8]

Breckinridge received 49.6 percent of Baltimore City's vote and 42 percent of the vote of the rest of Maryland. Bell, on the other hand, received 47 percent of the vote throughout the rest of Maryland, and only 44 percent in the city of Baltimore.

While Ollinger Crenshaw separates urban and rural votes and shows that Breckinridge had a following in the city of Baltimore greater than that in the rural Maryland, there is, nevertheless, a better division of the State that shows a different picture. Using the three divisions of southern, northern and western, and Eastern Shore, we see a totally different picture.

Breckinridge had a majority of 50.1 percent of the vote in the southern counties, or those most closely resembling the South. Lincoln received only 21 votes in the entire seven-county area. In the northern and western counties, where Lincoln had his best results, Breckinridge had a plurality of 45.3 percent to Bell's 44.4 percent of the votes. This includes the vote of the city of Baltimore, which gave a plurality to Breckinridge. More interesting was the vote of the Eastern Shore, which gave Bell a plurality of 52.2 percent to Breckinridge's 47.8 percent. Lincoln garnered only 93 votes in this seven-county area. While the Eastern Shore was closely tied to the South, being separated from the rest of Maryland by water, it would feel the disaster of any war to a much greater extent. Governor Hicks was also from this area, and this could account for some of John Bell's strength.

The other leading Bell supporters in the state were Congressmen Henry Winter Davis and John Pendleton Kennedy, both of whom constantly hit upon the theme that a vote for Bell was a vote for the Union. Fifty-four percent of the Marylanders did vote for the Union by opposing Breckinridge, but since this vote was divided among three candidates, Breckinridge was able to carry the State with 45.9 percent of the vote. Therefore, it can be seen that the strongest Breckinridge areas were Baltimore and the southern counties.

With the close of the election of 1860, the southern states began to secede from the Union, leaving the state of Maryland in a quandary about what steps to take. Marylanders first felt the economic effect. A correspondent for the Philadelphia *Inquirer* wrote on November 20, that

> business here continues terribly oppressed. Merchants are doing scarcely anything. The banks are obliged to restrict, and unable to accommodate customers, except limitedly. Stocks are much depressed, large hypothecations being forced to sale at heavy reductions.
> Confidence is generally weakening. . . .
> The value of property, rents, everything, is tending downward. Produce of all kinds has declined. . . .
> Many laborers and mechanics in Baltimore are being discharged, and manufactories are curtailing operations. . . .[9]

He went on to point out that Marylanders hoped that some compromise could be reached to save the Union.

> The growing sentiment with Marylanders is to preserve the Union by adjusting difficulties within the Union, until no other hope is left them but to unite with the consolidated South.[10]

This statement could sum up the feeling of Marylanders not only for the month of November, but for the entire period of the secession crisis.

ii

Three types of secessionists divided the State, each with its own advocates. As the months passed, the group that supported closer ties with the South gained strength, tying itself to Virginia, always saying: "wait for Virginia, if she leaves the Union, so must we." This hope was unfulfilled, for after Virginia left the Union, the federal troops were able to control Maryland. William Wilkins Glenn, editor and owner of the Baltimore *Exchange,* was in close contact with the secession leaders. His diary entry on February 3 read:

> what astonished me most was that there were no leaders in Maryland who were willing to play a prominent part or act independently[.] [T]here was but one opinion—Everyone said, "Wait for Virginia—See what she does."[11]

On April 17 he concluded that

> the Southern men in Maryland assumed a more determined attitude and expressed great indignation at the idea of troops being raised in one state to subjugate another. Then nothing was done—there was no concerted action.[12]

This does not mean that the people of the North realized that the secession movement in Maryland was leaderless. On the contrary, Republican party leaders worried about Maryland's position. Elihu B. Washburne, United States congressman from Illinois, expressed this concern in a letter to Abraham Lincoln written on January 10:

> To my observation things look more threatening to-day than ever. I believe Va. and Maryland are both rotten to the core. We have had one of our friends from N.Y. (the kind I wrote about) in Baltimore, sounding matters there, and he gives most unfavorable reports. *Great danger is to be apprehended from that quarter.* The very worst secessionists and traitors at heart, are *pretended* Union men, and we have found out that one of these very men has been in consultation with Corwin as to how to *protect this city!!*[13]

The majority of Maryland's leaders favored one kind of secession or another. The most difficult figure to understand is the Governor, Thomas H. Hicks. Born in 1798 in Dorchester County, Governor Hicks in many ways represented the views of his native Eastern Shore. After serving in various positions in his County and State, he became a member of the Maryland Constitutional Revision Commission in 1850. When he addressed this body on May 10, 1850, he advocated the principle of secession, saying:

That it shall be the duty of the Legislature whenever a majority of the delegates from the Eastern Shore shall require it, to pass an act authorizing the qualified voters of the Eastern Shore of the state, at the next regular election thereafter, to determine for or against a withdrawal of that part of the State of Maryland, known as the Eastern Shore, from the Western Shore, for the purpose of uniting the same with the State of Delaware; provided such withdrawal and union be peaceable, mutual and in accordance with the authority of the United States.[14]

Originally a Whig, after leaving that party Hicks was nominated for Governor in 1857 by the American or Know Nothing party. He won the gubernatorial race by a mere 8,460 votes after carrying Baltimore with a 9,639 majority.

Claims of wholesale fraud were made, and certainly much illegality in the election occurred, though whether sufficient to have changed the results cannot be estimated satisfactorily.[15]

Nevertheless, Hicks was not the overwhelming choice of the people of Maryland.

In his Inaugural Address in January of 1858, Hicks strongly supported the Union:

Maryland is devoted to the Union and all of the states. . . . [it has] never listened to the suggestions of disunion from the Southern states, and has refused to join with the misguided people of the Northern states in their assaults on slavery.[16]

Therefore, even before the secession crisis of 1860–61, Governor Hicks had vacillated on the question of secession. On one occasion he had upheld the right of a section of the state to secede, and on another he had rejected southern disunion sentiments. The ambiguity in his position becomes more obvious in his statements during the crisis.

Historians have disagreed about the true position of the Governor on the question of secession. Contemporaries saw Governor Hicks as a vacillating man only partially committed to the Union. Horace Greeley, writing in 1865 and referring to Hicks's position on allowing the people to decide the course of the State by their votes in the Congressional elections of 1861, said:

In other words: Maryland might, at any time, relieve herself of all her engagements and obligations to her sister States in the Union by giving a Disunion majority on her vote for Members of Congress! Surely no Secessionist could go further or ask more than that! Yet this was the response of the *only* Governor of a Slave State who had claimed votes for his party in the late Presidential canvass on the ground of its especial and unflinching devotion to "the Union, the Constitution, and the enforcement of the laws."[17]

Henry Wilson, United States Senator from Massachusetts, who wrote in 1877, credited Hicks for keeping Maryland in the Union:

> though a slaveholder, pecuniarily interested in the slave system, and in sympathy with those who were defending it and what they called Southern rights, he was opposed to the policy of secession, distrusted its leaders, and refused"

to call the Legislature into session.[18]

William F. Brand, who wrote the *Life of William Rollinson Whittingham* in 1883, saw Hicks as a person who believed that

> the true policy of Maryland . . . was to be neutral and so to hold a position which would enable her to act as intermediary between the contending parties.[19]

John Nicolay and John Hay, secretaries of President Abraham Lincoln, went even further in 1886 saying:

> It was a piece of exceptional good fortune that the Governor of Maryland was a friend of the Union, though hardly of that unflinching fearlessness needed in revolutionary emergencies. Whatever of hesitancy or vacillation he sometimes gave way to, resulted from a constitutional timidity rather than from a want of patriotism; . . . he was active and energetic in behalf of the Government.[20]

By the turn of the century, Hicks's position was receiving more praise; he was becoming a defender of the Union. George Radcliffe, in his study of *Governor Thomas H. Hicks of Maryland and the Civil War,* stated in 1910 that

> the proclamation of Hicks, taken as a whole, is an exceedingly good presentation of the arguments in favor of a policy of inactivity, and as such received favorable comment throughout the North.[21]

By 1948, when Roy Nichols (*The Disruption of American Democracy*) and William Hesseltine (*Lincoln and the War Governors*) were writing, Hicks had become a Union hero. Nichols said:

> Hicks of Maryland, opposition Governor, had shown himself very able in resisting the pressure of Democratic legislative leaders to call them in session. . . . Hicks refused to act, declaring that Maryland did not want secession. He charged that Democratic conspirators from the lower South were plotting from Washington to drive Maryland against her will [out of the Union].[22]

Hesseltine wrote in the same year:

> Maryland's Governor, Thomas Hicks, had from the first advised the South to be deliberate and calm, and to reflect carefully before it took irrevocable action. When commissioners from the seceding states called upon him, he refused to receive them, and he persistently turned a deaf ear to all who demanded a special session of the legislature.[23]

However, both Nichols and Hesseltine agree that Governor Hicks was receptive to the idea of a central or middle confederacy. The changing interpretations of Governor Hicks indicate the changing interpretation of Maryland's role in the secession crisis. The further removed from the actual period, the more patriotic and heroic the Governor and the State become.

The Governor's statements from November 1860 until after the firing on Fort Sumter must be read with great care to determine his actual position. In the first letter he wrote in November to Congressman Edwin H. Webster of Harford County, dated the ninth, Hicks stated that the State had no available arms to be distributed at the present time, but that since

> . . . we have some delay in consequence of contracts with Georgia and Alabama, ahead of us, and we expect at an early day an additional supply, and of the first received your people shall be furnished. Will they be good men to send out to kill Lincoln and his men? If not, suppose the arms would be better sent South.[24]

George L. P. Radcliffe believed that this letter is

> best regarded as an imprudent attempt at humor between a governor of a state and an intimate friend.[25]

If this is humor, it is not of the sort a Governor should put his name to. If it is serious, then it places the Governor not only with the secessionists but also with the conspirators who would assassinate the President of the United States.

Later in the month the Governor received a letter from five prominent Marylanders, including ex-Governor Thomas G. Pratt, asking him to call a special session of the Legislature. In answer to this letter, Governor Hicks wrote on November 27 that he was

> unable to discover the necessity or the propriety of convening the Legislature of Maryland at this time.[26]

He believed that Lincoln had been elected constitutionally and that the South was

bound in honor to recognize and respect the result, as we would have required the North to do, had either of the other candidates been elected.[27]

Hicks pointed out he was a southerner by birth, a slaveholder and a native of Maryland. Despite this, he saw nothing in the election of Lincoln to justify southern steps toward a separation of the states.[28] He agreed with the authors of the letter that some northern legislatures had passed unconstitutional laws and that Maryland had suffered far more than the states further to the south, but he argued that in his judgment the laws did not reflect the opinion of the North's conservative masses.[29] Expressing the opinion that any extreme measures taken by the southern states would only help fanatics in the North, he urged moderation; and he believed calling the Legislature into session would:

> only have the effect of increasing and reviving the excitement now pervading the Country. It would at once be heralded by the sensitive newspapers and alarmists throughout the country as evidence that Maryland had abandoned all hope of the Union and was preparing to join the traitors to destroy it . . . [it is] my opinion that an immense majority of all parties are decidedly opposed to the assembling of the Legislature at this time. . . .[30]

The Governor eliminated secession neither in theory nor in fact. After pointing out that Maryland was a border slave state, he wrote that:

> there are other border Slave States as much interested in these questions as Maryland can be, which ought to be consulted before we take the initiative in this matter.[31]

Specifically mentioning Virginia as one such state, the Governor felt that it would be

> only wise and proper to await the decision of our nearest Southern Sister, rather than run the risk of clashing with her by hasty action— our people will not fail to act with boldness, when it becomes necessary, because we waited with patience, the true time for action, instead of becoming alarmed before danger had actually arrived, and rushing into peril which prudence may avoid.[32]

Wait for Virginia. If it quit the Union, then Maryland would decide. The word "action" is quite significant here, for it meant that something was to be done; staying in the Union was no action, therefore, action meant secession. Hicks obviously suggested a joint action with the border states, which he later clarified in his statements concerning a central confederacy. Governor Hicks concluded this letter by saying that for the present time

Maryland should wait upon the President and Congress and see if they could settle this dispute. By late November he concluded that Maryland could not act alone independent of the other border slave states. He opposed joining the southern states in a southern confederacy.

On December 6, Hicks wrote to Captain Contee of Prince George's County:

> If the Union must be dissolved let it be done calmly, deliberately and after full reflection on the part of the united South. . . . After allowing a reasonable time for action on the part of the northern states, if they shall neglect or refuse to observe the plain requirements of the constitution, then, in my judgment, we shall be fully warranted in demanding a division of the country.[33]

This in no way changed his earlier views. The letter merely stated more clearly that the time for secession was not the present, but that if conditions did not change, the South, including Maryland, should secede.

On the ninth of that month, he wrote:

> I am now in correspondence with the governors of the border States . . . I do not doubt the people of Maryland are ready to go with the people of those States for weal or woe.[34]

In this letter Hicks made clear that he was pinning his hopes on the border states, not the deep South. He realized that Maryland would be in an exposed position if it should leave the Union, and he wanted the other border states to go out in concert. This position became more open when he later wrote Governor Burton of Delaware.

Governor Hicks still hoped that some compromise could be arrived at before Maryland would have to take action. In a letter to John J. Crittenden, dated December 13, 1861, he urged Crittenden to find some sort of a compromise.

> It is an up-hill work I know, but it can and must be done. . . . Great God! Can it be, that this once great and beautiful Country, this Government the administration of the world—will be broken into fragments? No! it cannot be. Then Sir, what is to be done in our extremity? Patriots pure men, must stand up and beat back the powers of darkness. They must be prudence and perseverance head off these fiends now engaged in the efforts to overthrow our Government.[35]

The month of December was marked by the arrival of two representatives of southern legislatures. The first was A. H. Handy of Mississippi, who on December 18 wrote Governor Hicks that Mississippi

> desires the co-operation of her Sister States of the South. . . . I must

respectfully ask that your Excellency will state to me whether you will convoke the Legislature of your State, for the purpose of counselling [*sic*] with the constituted authorities of the State of Mississippi. . . .[36]

In answer to this letter Hicks met Handy and then wrote him a letter in which he stated the same views he had propounded until that time. After saying that Maryland was a southern state of people of a conservative turn of mind who, at present, were inclined not to join any secession movement until all attempts at compromise had been exhausted, Hicks held out the offer that at a later date Maryland might join a secession movement in the event there was no compromise. He concluded by saying,

until the effort is found to be in vain I cannot consent, by any precipitate or revolutionary action, to aid in the dismemberment of this Union.

When I shall see clearly that there is no hope of such adjustment, and am convinced that the power of the Federal Government is to be perverted to the destruction instead of being used for the protection of our rights—then and not till then, can I consent so to exercise any power with which I am invested, as to afford even the opportunity for such a proceeding.

What ever [*sic*] powers I may have I shall use only after full consultation, and in fraternal concert with the other Border States, since we, and they, in the event of the dismemberment of the Union will suffer more than all others combined.

I am now in correspondence with the Governors of those States, and I await with solicitude for the indications of the course to be pursued by them, when this is made known to me I shall be ready to take such steps as our duty and interest shall demand, and I do not doubt the people of Maryland are ready to go with those states for weal or woe. I fully agree with all that you have said as to the necessity for protection to the rights of the South, and my sympathies are entirely with the gallant people of Mississippi who stand ready to resist any infringement of these rights. But I earnestly hope they will act with prudence as well as with courage. Let us show moderation as well as firmness, and be unwilling to resort to extreme measures until necessity shall leave us no choice.[37]

A week later, Jabez L. M. Curry arrived from Alabama hoping to convince Maryland to join the new Confederacy. Curry did not see Governor Hicks, but on January 8 the Governor wrote him that if Maryland joined a southern confederacy its geographic position placed its slaves in a position to escape to a foreign nation. If war broke out, the border states, especially Maryland, would be the battlefield. For these reasons Maryland must step slowly in any advance towards secession. He concluded by saying that the people of Maryland were devoted to the Union and that they would never agree to disunion of the states for any cause. They may be compelled to submit to Disunion—to the dismemberment of this Government, when, in fact (not in anticipation or from fear) this Union shall become actually the instrument of destruction to their rights and peace and safety. But until that time arrives they demand their rights, under the Constitution in the Union. . . .[38]

While this statement is more pro-Union than some of the statements that he had previously issued, it nevertheless leaves the door to secession open when the other states secede and compromise fails.

Jabez L. M. Curry returned to Alabama and reported to the Governor of that state, that

from conversation with prominent citizens, and from other sources, I am firmly of the opinion that Maryland will not long hesitate to make common cause with her sister States which have resolutely and wisely determined not to submit to Abolition domination.[39]

Hicks certainly did not give him this opinion.

With the advent of the new year, Governor Hicks took the position that a central confederacy, made up of the border states, would solve the problems that were facing Maryland. On January 2, he advocated this idea first to three members of a Union meeting (J. L. Adkins, Thomas P. Williams and Finch Tilgham), who were taking a series of resolutions to the Governor. They reported that he

preferred a central confederacy confined to the border slave holding states [and that he was firm in] his determination not to convene the Legislature. . . .[40]

On the same day, Hicks wrote to Governor William Burton of Delaware, expressing the same idea that the best place for the border slave states was in a separate nation, a central confederacy. While this is the only letter in existence of those written by Governor Hicks to various governors in December, his conversation with Ambrose R. Wright in February confirms that this was the purpose of all the letters. To Governor Burton he said:

Do you not think our honor and safety and interests will be best preserved for the present as we are, and if no compromise can be affected by Congress or otherwise to restore our distressed Country to her former fraternal relations, that we could then form ourselves into a Central Government as the last alternative? Delaware, Virginia, Kentucky, Missouri, Tennessee, and I believe North Carolina and Georgia will unite with Maryland, if this last dreadful alternative is forced upon us, which may God forbid! . . . We of the border States cannot allow our interests to be compromised by the extremists of the South, whose interests, social and pecuniary, differ so widely from ours. Above and beyond all I do believe that by a firm, wise and prudent course, we of the border States may at last secure a restoration of the Government to its former design and effect; at all events, let us try it.[41]

Hicks still hoped that the Union would be saved by compromise, but he was not optimistic about this possibility. He was a slaveholder and wished to unite with slaveholding states, and his proclamation to the people of Maryland dated January 3 left no doubt of this:

I have never lived, and should be sorry to be obliged to live, in a state where slavery does not exist, and I never will do so if I can avoid it.[42]

This precluded his joining the North against the South.

However, the Governor feared the extremists of the South as much as those of the North. His solution was to get the other border states to form a central confederacy. In this way a neutral group of buffer states would prevent the two sides from fighting, and Maryland would not become a battleground. At the same time, the common interests of these states would be served.

To prevent the State from joining the South, the Governor refused to call the Legislature into special session. Many persons in the North interpreted this to mean that he was holding the State in the Union. If this were true, he had the ulterior motive of holding it there until he could convince other border (slave) states to join a central confederacy.

In reply to a letter calling for a special session of the Legislature, and sent to the Governor by eleven Maryland state senators, the Governor answered by referring them to his address to the people of the State. On January 6, the Governor stated that he believed that those who advocated calling a special session of the Legislature, were advocating the immediate secession of Maryland from the Union and that they had prepared the necessary resolutions. This he felt would bring on a civil war, which could only be detrimental to the state of Maryland.[43]

Three days later Samuel F. DuPont wrote to his wife, Sophie, that he had spoken to Governor Hicks who expressed the opinion that the people of Maryland were

still union conservatives and that there were conspiracies to drive Maryland out of the Union and into the Southern Confederacy.[44]

Hicks expressed the fear that Governor Wise of Virginia would attempt to take Washington, which was created solely from land that Maryland had given to the federal government. DuPont left the meeting convinced that Hicks was a Union man. Yet, another interpretation can be made. Hicks feared that events would move too fast for his central confederacy. If Governor Wise took Washington, he would also take former Maryland soil. This would also mean civil war, a disastrous event that Hicks was desperately attempting to avoid.

The position of Maryland created a great deal of anxiety within Republican circles. Simon Cameron wrote to Abraham Lincoln on January 3 saying that

> the Secretary of State called on me this morning to say that Gov[ernor] Hicks will remain firm.[45]

A friend of Lincoln's, Josiah M. Lucas, wrote to the Governor on January 11 that he had

> just received a letter suggested by him [Lincoln] in which I am author-ized to say that your recommendation will weigh Tons for any appoint-ments in Maryland, with the prayer that you will stand firm.[46]

It appears that Lincoln was not beyond offering the Governor the patronage of federal positions in the State if he kept Maryland in the Union. This, of course, would undermine the small Republican party, but then, he was more concerned about holding the State in the Union. Hicks appears never to have answered this letter, and no further reference to it can be found. It nevertheless shows the Republican leader's anxiety about the Governor's behavior.

Governor Andrew Curtin of the neighboring state of Pennsylvania displayed his anxiety more pointedly. He wrote on January 15:

> I have just returned from the ceremony of my inauguration, and, as the first act of my official career, I write to express to you my profound admiration of the patriotic resolutions you have displayed in assisting to maintain the Union. . . .[47]

Governor Curtin then stated that he was sending a delegation of three leading Pennsylvanians to convene with the Governor. This was his way of determining the true position of the Governor of Maryland. Hicks replied to Curtin's letter by saying that he was a slave owner and that

> my feelings and sympathies are naturally with the South; but, above and beyond all these, I am for the Union. . . .[48]

The ambivalence of Hicks's position once again appears in this reply.

In letters to John J. Crittenden during the month of January, Hicks stated that he was opposed to coercion. In a letter dated January 29, he expressed the idea that Congress should arrive at some compromise but that this was up to the northern members. If they

[do] otherwise let them go to Hell and take the country with them.[49]

This once again shows that Hicks was not an unconditional Union man and that he was not optimistic about the reunification of the country. He believed that such reunification was up to the North, and that if it did not materialize, Maryland would have to leave the Union. At the same time, he disliked the course that South Carolina had taken.

On January 26, Governor Hicks replied to Governor William H. Gist of South Carolina, acknowledging the receipt of the secession resolutions passed by the South Carolina Legislature. Hicks centered his argument against immediate secession on the question of runaway slaves, stating that Marylanders suffered more from northern conspiracies and assaults than the slaveholders of the deep South. He pointed out that the people of Maryland

do not see the remedy for such outrages in a measure, which, if it were possible, could only secure the continuance of them under shelter of a *foreign* asylum upon her borders.[50]

This was an interesting position for a man advocating that Maryland join a border slave state confederacy. But, during the first few months of 1861, he expanded his central confederacy to include the Middle Atlantic states.

Probably the most interesting letter written by Governor Hicks in January was his letter of the 25th to General Scott asking for the federal government to supply Maryland with arms. Hicks specifically asked whether the general government could supply him with

2000 minnie Rifles . . . to meet an emergency if it shall arise.[51]

General Scott refused. If Hicks opposed coercing the South, as he had stated to Crittenden, why did he want rifles?

Throughout the months of February and March, Governor Hicks supported an independent position for himself and for Maryland. When Ambrose R. Wright, Georgia's commissioner to Maryland, proposed that Maryland join the Southern Confederacy, Hicks replied that secession was revolution. To the Georgia commissioner, Governor Hicks reaffirmed his position that he hoped for the creation of a central confederacy. Wright, in his report to the Governor of Georgia, stated that he found Hicks:

not only opposed to the secession of Maryland from the Federal Union, but that if she should withdraw from the Union he advised and would urge her to confederate with the Middle States in the formation of a central confederacy. He also informed me that he had already, in his official character, entered into a correspondence with the Governors of those States, including New York, Pennsylvania, New Jersey, Delaware, Virginia, Missouri, and Ohio, with a view, in the event of an ultimate disruption of the Federal Union, to the establishment of such central confederacy.[52]

While Hicks accepted the right of revolution, he felt that it was the last step to be taken and that existing conditions certainly did not justify such a step. Once again, he took a conservative position when he was dealing with the southern states.

During the first two months of the year 1861 two meetings on the question of secession were held in Baltimore. A two-day pro-Union meeting was held on January 10–11 at the Maryland Institute. Several speakers there urged that Maryland stay in the Union. One was Reverdy Johnson, a former United States Senator and Attorney General, who had been the defense counsel for Dred Scott. The Convention adopted a series of resolutions that expressed their "devotion to the Union," supported the Crittenden compromise, and called upon the Governor to let the people vote for or against the calling of a convention to decide the question of secession.

The State Conference Convention, composed of men who wanted some form of secession, met on February 18, at the Universalist Church. The Convention was a last desperate attempt to have Maryland secede from the Union. Since the Governor was not going to call the Legislature into session, the secessionists organized this convention hoping to promote support for the secession of Maryland.

> They declared their fidelity to the existing Union of the States, and their unwillingness to take any step involving a consideration of their severance from it, until its disruption, by the failure of all measures of compromise and conciliation should force the people of Maryland to select that fragment of the wreck which was fittest and worthiest to be trusted with their fortunes.[53]

The State Conference Convention adjourned to meet again in March when the members selected a delegation to go to Virginia and recommend a border state convention. Virginia however did not act on this suggestion. Ambrose R. Wright, the representative from the state of Georgia to Maryland, attended the convention and affirmed Maryland's dependence on Virginia.

> I found the members of that convention, comprising, as it did, a number of the best men and highest talent of the State, while they thought the cotton States had acted with undue haste and precipitancy, almost unani-

mous for resistance to Black Republican rule, and determined to co-operate with the seceding States in the event that Virginia should determine to withdraw from the Federal Government.[54]

At its February meeting the Convention resolved to act with Virginia and expressed opposition to coercion of the southern states by the federal government. Once again the Maryland secessionists put their trust in the state of Virginia, as they were unwilling to act alone and be separated from the states that had already joined the Southern Confederacy. They supported the idea of a central confederacy and failed because they were unable to obtain Virginia's support.

Hicks wrote to President Lincoln on March 11 urging that the President appoint John J. Crittenden to the United States Supreme Court:

> the appointment of Mr. C. [Crittenden] will do much to disarm them, on that occasion.[55]

That is, to disarm those individuals who proposed that Maryland join the Southern Confederacy. He appealed to Secretary of State William Seward on March 28, saying that

> everything depends upon proper appointments to leading places in border states.[56]

He stated that the Lincoln administration does not

> understand as I do the condition of things here, and in the border states.[57]

He implied that he should be the one to make the decisions for the state of Maryland. Hicks said he was

> a union man and supporter of your Administration as far as it may be wise and proper, and, thus far I have no fault with it. . . .[58]

Once again his position seemed contradictory. But considering all his statements, he was saying, "Let me take care of Maryland, I know best what to do for her." He stated this position in a letter to General Scott when, on March 18, he once again asked for 2,000 rifles:

> I write to know if arms can be furnished for some 2,000 men if it should become necessary to put down rebellion in this State. I am strongly inclined to believe that a spirit of insubordination is increasing, and that any unfortunate movement on the part of the Virginia convention, now in session, may cause an outbreak in Maryland. . . . It would not, perhaps, in the event of an outbreak be prudent to send any of your force now in Washington, and it is important that we have arms for those we can rely upon in the State.[59]

The letter makes his independent position absolutely clear. "Let me handle the situation; do not send in the United States Army," is the plea implicit in this letter.

Before the firing on Fort Sumter by the Southern Confederacy, Governor Hicks wanted Maryland to join with the other border slave states in a central confederacy. He did not, however, want Maryland to join with the southern states, whose institutions he felt would only harm the state. When Virginia appeared to be ready to leave the Union, he, unlike other Marylanders, wanted Maryland to maintain an independent position, and use his authority and the United States arms supplied to his followers to control the elements who wanted to join Maryland with the South. At the same time, he opposed the use of force as a weapon to keep Maryland or any other state in the Union. When Fort Sumter was fired upon, this plan became unworkable.

What has confused many people is that Hicks did not advocate joining the South; therefore, he seemed to want to keep Maryland in the Union. This is incorrect. Hicks was a secessionist: he advocated letting the South go in peace, and he favored a central confederacy. He wanted to keep Maryland out of the Southern Confederacy, but he did not necessarily want to stay with the North. His hoped-for central confederacy could only be attained if he prevented the Legislature from meeting and he controlled the agitators who proposed linking Maryland with the South.

iii

In Congress, Maryland was represented in the Senate by one senator from Baltimore, Anthony Kennedy, and one senator from the Eastern Shore, James A. Pearce. Kennedy, brother of John Pendleton Kennedy, was a native of Baltimore who moved to Virginia where he became a member of the House of Delegates and a magistrate on the bench of the Jefferson County Court for ten years. When he returned to Baltimore in 1851, he was elected to the Maryland House of Delegates. In 1857 he was elected as a Unionist to the United States Senate. While he delivered no speeches dealing with secession, he voted on all the major resolutions and bills. He supported compromise, including the Crittenden compromise. At the same time, he voted against an anti-southern resolution introduced by Senator Clark, which directed all the energies of the federal authority toward maintaining the government as it existed. He nevertheless voted for the naval appropriation bill which enlarged that service, a bill many southern or pro-southern senators voted against. On the basis of his voting record, it is difficult to categorize him as secessionist or nonsecessionist.

Senator James Alfred Pearce was born in Virginia, attended the College of New Jersey; after one year of law practice in Maryland he left for Louisiana to become a planter. He returned to Maryland in 1828 and practiced law in Chestertown. In the 1830s he was elected to the United States House of Representatives and in 1843 he was sent to the United States Senate, where he remained until his death in 1862. He was elected as a Whig the first three times and as a Democrat in 1861. Out of seven major resolutions or bills dealing with secession, he cast only three votes. He opposed the Clark resolution and voted twice against naval appropriation bills.

On February 5, Pearce addressed the United States Senate and said that he opposed a war against the seceding states.

> I have no idea that this Union can be maintained or restored by force. Nor do I believe in the value of a Union which can only be kept together by dint of a military force.[60]

While many sources held that he was not a secessionist, including the Philadelphia *Inquirer,* he nevertheless felt that force would not bring the prodigal back into the fold.[61] He wanted the South to go in peace.

Maryland was represented by six Representatives: one from the Eastern Shore, James A. Stewart; two from southern Maryland, Edwin H. Webster and George W. Hughes; one from western Maryland, Jacob M. Kunkel; and two from Baltimore, James M. Harris and Henry Winter Davis. All six were Democrats.

James A. Stewart, born in Maryland, became a lawyer, and engaged in ship and house building before he was elected to Congress in 1854. He served in Congress until 1861, after having declined to run for reelection in 1860. He was a strong believer in states' rights and in peaceful settlement of the dispute between the states. On December 13, he introduced a resolution to be submitted to the Committee of Thirty-Three that:

> if any measures can be adopted to preserve in their purity the constitutional rights of all the States within the Union; and if, in their [Committee of Thirty-Three] judgment, this be impracticable, then further to inquire as to the most reasonable and just mode by which their rights may be secured in a state of separation. . . .[62]

In another speech delivered to the House of Representatives on March 2 Stewart pointed out that the states were sovereign and the people held primary allegiance to them, having delegated only certain powers to the general government. He went on to point out that the Declaration of Independence established the right of the people to change their form of government when they felt the necessity. After making it clear that he considered himself a southerner and that the people of the state of Maryland wanted a peaceful settlement of the pending dispute, he said,

> if it cannot be settled satisfactorily, and the North and South must part, I think I am not mistaken in my estimate of the public opinion of our people when I assert that I believe, with great and unparalleled unanimity, they will cast their destiny with their southern brethren.
> . . . If no full and final settlement takes place, her destiny is with the South; her interests, her inclinations, her institutions, her habits, and her peace, will all prompt to that course. Nor do I believe she will ever be much impressed with the idea that her policy is to be in a central confederacy, where she would be between the upper and lower millstone, compelled to fortify herself all round. . . .[63]

Stewart supported the southern arguments for leaving the Union when he said

> a candid world, including all the good, sound, and true men of the North, as well as the South, will pronounce that there were full, ample, complete, and unanswerable moral reasons on the part of the South in dissolving all paper connection—for it was nothing more—with such a set of Constitutional-despoilers, who had got upon the inside track, and which all the conservative and gallant men of the North had not the power to eject.[64]

He proposed a convention of all the border states to settle the dispute. He opposed coercion of the South, and believed that northerners would not fight their southern brethren.

While Congressman Stewart obviously did not advocate the secession of Maryland openly, he supported southern secession, both as an abstract right and as a necessity. His pessimism about the settlement of the problems with the North suggests that he was indirectly advocating the secession of Maryland. He had a poor voting record, voting on only seven out of twelve resolutions or bills directly affecting the secession crisis. While he supported compromise and the Committee of Thirty-Three, both his voting record and his speeches show a pro-southern bias. He was a secessionist who advocated that the South should be permitted to go in peace, if not one who advocated Maryland's joining the Southern Confederacy.

Edwin H. Webster was born in Maryland, admitted to the bar to practice law in Bel Air, where he was elected to Congress in 1858 and served until 1865. He took an ambiguous position on the question of secession, in that he considered himself a southerner; but he nevertheless joined the Union army in 1862. Webster refused to support the Morris resolution. He declared that it was too broad when it stated that in no conceivable state of circumstances should the Union be dissolved.[65]

He also voted against the Adrain resolution that stated that

it is the duty of our Government, as of all Governments, to see that its laws are respected and its citizens protected.[66]

He voted in the negative because the House of Representatives had just voted against a pro-southern resolution that he felt made the Adrain resolution look like a sword instead of an olive branch.[67]

In a speech delivered on February 18, he stated that he was "not a friend of secession" and

that the policy of the seceding States, in attempting, at this time, to exercise it, has been precipitate, unwise, and selfish.[68]

At the same time he opposed coercion, as it was certain to result in a civil war. He supported compromise with the seceded states. But if they failed to return,

then, too, you [the federal government] can take such course as may seem best, wisest, and most patriotic, to preserve the dignity of the flag and the unity of the country.[69]

Webster's voting record was evenly divided between pro-southern and pro-northern votes. Webster was not a secessionist, but a man who wanted to adopt a go-slow policy; he would have given the states all the time they needed to return, but if they did not rejoin the Union he felt it would be up to Congress to force them to do so. He supported a unified country, not a let-them-go-in-peace policy.

Born in Elmira, New York, George W. Hughes attended the United States Military Academy, served in the Mexican War and finally settled in Maryland. Elected to Congress in 1858, he served only one term. He was southern both in conviction and action. In a letter "To My Constituents" dated December 17, 1860, he called upon the Governor to convene the Legislature and urged that a convention be called to decide the fate of Maryland. He went on to state that

it is yet possible, nay, probable, that if by forbearance and moderation a civil war at the outset can be avoided, a new, powerful and homogeneous confederacy may be formed by the gravitation towards Maryland, as a common nucleus, (with Washington as its capital), of numerous States, under the impelling force of a mutual interest and common policy. . . .[70]

While he did not say what states would join in the new confederacy, he did say that,

come what may, I go with "Old Maryland," but I must be permitted
to say, in all frankness and candor, that my feelings, sympathies, and
the dictates of my judgment are with the South.[71]

On February 5, Hughes addressed the House of Representatives, and
after stating that he supported the Crittenden compromise, he took the
position that a state had the right to withdraw from the Union and that
the federal government had no right to force it to remain.

I have always believed, and still believe, that a united South is per-
fectly able to assert and to defend its rights in or outside the Union;
and, for one, would have preferred that the contest should have been
waged within the Union; but that was a matter I could not control.
Unfortunately, there is no united South, and attempts are making to
drive us still further asunder. Let me warn the border slave States
against the cunningly-contrived scheme for separating us from the "cotton States," for we are essentially one people, with a common interest,
"bone of their bone, and flesh of their flesh." It is a common device of
the enemy "to divide and conquer." This effort to divide us is a delusion
and a snare.[72]

This speech implies that while Hughes once supported the idea that
Maryland could form a central confederacy, he was not supporting a union
of Maryland with the South. His voting record was consistently pro-
southern and in favor of compromise. Without a doubt, Hughes was a
secessionist who, while staying with Maryland, hoped that it would join
the South.

The fourth Maryland congressman was Jacob M. Kunkel, who was
born in Frederick, Maryland, and practiced law there. He was elected
in 1856 and reelected in 1858, as a Democrat. He stated that he would
have voted for the Pryor resolution if he had not been paired. The Pryor
resolution read:

that any attempt to preserve the Union between the States of this
Confederacy by force would be impracticable, and destructive of republican liberty.[73]

He cast his votes consistently with the South and for compromise. He
delivered no major speeches on the floor of the House of Representatives.
However, Samuel S. Cox said that Hughes and Kunkel "seemed to be
most sympathetic with the South."[74]

Baltimore was represented by two congressmen, both of whom supported
the Union and voted with the North. James M. Harris was born in
Baltimore and practiced law there. First elected to Congress as an American in 1854, he served until 1861, not being a candidate in 1860. In a

speech to the House of Representatives on January 29, 1861, he stated that he opposed secession and felt that it lacked foundation in constitutional doctrine; furthermore, that the only way a state could leave the Union was by revolution. He felt that the secession movement gained daily with the northern representatives' failure to arrive at a compromise that would settle the dispute and end the secession movement. The Crittenden compromise, which Harris supported, was such a compromise. He felt that the secession movement in Maryland was supported only by a few people; however, if Virginia seceded Maryland might follow.

> . . . I cannot say that, when Virginia has taken her position, Maryland may not feel herself also pressed, by the various considerations that will influence her, to join hands with that illustrious sovereignty.[75]

His voting record was consistently pro-northern. Harris opposed secession but feared Maryland's possible secession if no compromise was achieved or if Virginia seceded.

Baltimore's second congressman, Henry Winter Davis, was born in Annapolis, practiced law in Alexandria, Virginia, and moved to Baltimore in 1850. He was elected to the United States House of Representatives in 1855 as an American and served until 1861, with no success in achieving reelection in 1860. He had supported William Pennington, a Republican, for the Speakership in 1860 and was censured for this by the Maryland House of Delegates. During the presidential election of 1860, he was one of John Bell's leading Maryland advocates. Moreover, Davis had earlier secured the gubernatorial nomination of Thomas H. Hicks.[76]

Davis opposed secession, both as a constitutional abstraction and as a practical reality. He felt that it was unconstitutional and that Maryland would be the battlefield in the event of a war. In a speech to the House of Representatives on February 7, he supported coercion of the seceded states:

> I say that the Constitution of the United States, and the laws made in pursuance thereof, must be enforced; and they who stand across the path of that enforcement must either destroy the power of the United States or it will destroy them. . . . But the laws of the United States provide their own method of enforcement; and when they are enforced, those who resist must take the consequences.
> . . . In this manner, without anything like war upon States, without any attempt to do damage to any citizens, excepting those who may have arrayed themselves in arms against the United States, the Government can vindicate its authority and maintain its power. This is not war. The Constitution calls it enforcing the laws. It is no more war than arresting a criminal is war. It is supporting the civil power by the

military arm, against unlawful combinations too powerful to be otherwise dealt with.[77]

Henry Winter Davis was the strongest supporter of the Union among the Maryland congressmen and he cast all his votes either for compromise or for the Union.

Maryland had three secessionist congressmen, all with districts located outside the city of Baltimore. It is interesting to find a secessionist congressman from western Maryland, a pro-Union area. The fact that Webster, from southern Maryland, was also a Unionist, shows that individual choice played a large role in determining whether a person became a secessionist. None of the congressmen left the Union to go South after the war began.

iv

An ex-congressman, John Pendleton Kennedy, played a major role in determining Maryland's fate. He had served as President Fillmore's Secretary of Navy and had voted for John Bell in the presidential election of 1860. Kennedy was the leading advocate of a middle or central confederacy. According to his Journal, he completed his pamphlet *The Border States* on December 15; however, it is dated December 17, before the secession of South Carolina.

In this pamphlet, Kennedy put forth a scheme to unite the border states. First, he proposed that they meet in an informal conference with one or two representatives from each of the states to determine joint action. He felt that the border states had personal grievances which had to be considered separately and not as an adjunct of the Gulf states of the lower South. The conference would consider the grievances of the border states; and if the North refused to accept them,

the Border States and their allies of the South who may be disposed to act with them, will be forced to consider the Union impracticable, and to organize a separate Confederacy of the Border States, with the association of such of the Southern and Free States as may be willing to accede to the proposed conditions.[78]

Once this conference proposed a separate confederacy, the governors of the states, through their legislatures, would submit the plan to the residents of their states for approval. A general conference would then be called to establish a government.

Kennedy felt that such a plan would prevent federal coercion of the states already seceded. To him it was the duty of the border states, that pending the whole course of this proceeding, the Border States and those concurring with them shall engage to prevent, by all the means in their power, any attempt on the part of the Federal Government or of any State or States to coerce the seceding States by armed force into submission.[79]

Kennedy expressed the idea that in this way the border states could preserve the peace and act as the

natural and appropriate medium through which the settlement of all differences is eventually to be obtained.[80]

Once this confederacy was constituted, Kennedy continued, the "whole body of the Middle and Western States"[81] would constitute such a formidable body that the states of the lower South would be forced to pause and reflect upon their actions. Kennedy pointed out that the border states could not join with the states of the deep South because the border states opposed the reopening of the slave trade, free trade and its commercial policies, and the policy of expansion by conquest.

A certain inconsistency runs throughout Kennedy's argument. On the one hand, he said that:

Here are all the elements necessary to the organization of the polity of a first-class power. In extent of territory, in resources, in population, it may take rank among the master States. . . .[82]

Then, on the other hand, he wrote:

Supposing a disintegration of the Union. . . . The Border States, in that event, would form, in self-defense, a Confederacy of their own, which would serve as a center of reinforcement for the reconstruction of the Union.[83]

He did not seem to realize that the creation of a central confederacy would create a buffer zone between the northern and southern nations, thus preventing the North from forcing the South to stay in the Union. This would effectively destroy the Union.

Kennedy conceived of the central confederacy as a magnet that would attract the other states of the Union and ultimately effect its re-creation.

A beneficent power of gravitation would work with irresistible energy in bringing back the dislocated fragments.[84]

He listed the various states which would join his confederacy, beginning with the Middle Atlantic, and progressing to the mid-western and western and, finally, the southern. He omitted New England. Many persons who proposed a central confederacy advocated leaving New England out of the reconstructed Union. They felt that New England had created the situation that led to the secession crisis. Kennedy does not specifically mention boycotting New England from the restored Union, but he nevertheless failed to include that group of states in his new nation.

On Christmas day, Kennedy wrote Governor Besiah Magoffin of Kentucky, urging him to call a conference of border states to initiate his plan. He informed the Governor that the object of his pamphlet:

> was to suggest some considerations to the Border States which might induce them to adopt a course of concerted action, both with a view to the adjustment of the difficulties between North and South, and to their own defence and security in the unhappy event of a separation.[85]

In concluding, he said,

> my friend, Gov. Hicks of this state, I am very sure, will be most happy to cooperate with you.[86]

Kennedy's statement appears to be accurate. During this period, Governor Hicks was writing to various border states' governors urging them to form a central confederacy. Whether or not the two men were working cooperatively is impossible to determine, for nothing to this effect appears in their correspondence.

In a letter dated December 26, 1860, Kennedy commented that while he agreed with Governor Hicks's position,

> the only difficulty his view presents is in the cooperation of New York and Pennsylvania in the preliminary movement. They will eventually join us. . . .[87]

Hicks's position was centered more to the South while Kennedy wanted to include all the Middle Atlantic states. Nevertheless, both men had the same idea in mind—to unite the border states in a central confederacy. Kennedy wrote on December 27:

> Our destiny is with the Middle States, on both sides of Mason Dixon's Line.[88]

In a letter to Hicks, dated January 17, Kennedy urged him to assemble the Maryland State Senate to select two or three people to attend a convention of the border states. At the same time Kennedy told the Governor that he supported Hicks's position on the question of secession.

One of the primary reasons that Kennedy wanted to include the states north of the Mason and Dixon line was that he was afraid Maryland would provide the battlefield for any war between the North and South. Undoubtedly the North would defend or try to recapture its capital, which meant that there would be fighting in Maryland. Also, such a formidable body as the central confederacy would have the

> powers and influence to negotiate as the representatives of the slave interest, with the free States. . . .[89]

Many people supported Kennedy in his efforts to form a central confederacy, among them Benjamin C. Howard, who was a delegate to the Washington Peace Conference. Howard expressed the hope that Pennsylvania would join Maryland to prevent Maryland's being the northern border of such a confederacy. He also said that the country would be sliced into separate confederacies.

Bishop William R. Whittingham of the Protestant Episcopal Church wrote Kennedy that he agreed with his proposals, stating that

> the present "strength" is, assuredly "to sit still," and whether as an honored member of the old Union strengthened and reinvigorated by the storm now shaking it; or as a prominent constituent in a great Central Confederation, strongest and noblest of all the disintegrated elements of the old Union.[90]

Two Bostonians, George S. Hillard and Robert Winthrop, defined the border states to include Pennsylvania and New Jersey as well as the slave states. Kennedy's uncle, Philip Kennedy, writing from Martinsburg, Virginia, also defined border states as beginning with New Jersey.

As the crisis continued, John P. Kennedy's position went through a metamorphosis. In January he expressed the opinion that the seizure of the forts by the South was a "sad blunder."[91] The result would swell Union sentiment.

> It is treason, and an indignity to the Sovereignty of the United States. That incident alone has changed the temper of the whole North. It has done very much the same thing here. The hauling down of our glorious Stars and Stripes—a stout feat—has awakened a volume of ardor in favor of the Union which might otherwise have slept. . . .[92]

By February 10 Kennedy was advocating that the South be left alone; that they be permitted to form their confederacy, and that they be allowed to go in peace. He blamed secession on the Knights of the Golden Circle and their conspiracy. He now rationalized the writing of his pamphlet as a warning to the border states that secession was a scheme of the Knights of the Golden Circle, a secret society of persons who throughout the 1850s had advocated secession. However, he maintained that coercion

would be a blunder and that the best way to reunite the country would be
to permit the South their experiment, which he predicted would fail in
five years and the South would rejoin the Union.[93]

By March 15 Kennedy was writing that Lincoln meant nothing but
peace and that he would not attempt to coerce the South to return the
forts. He saw a growing Union sentiment within the border states:

> they are every day growing more convinced that their duty is to preserve
> the Union and to fortify themselves within it. . . . [Maryland] is as
> true to the Union today, as she was to the cause of the colonies in 1776.
> Three fourths of our people are against secession *in any event*—nine
> tenths against it in the present state of the question. . . .[94]

By April Kennedy had once again changed his mind: he saw the secession
movement expanding. Advocating that the South be permitted to go in
peace, he said:

> I still hope that Mr. Lincoln will recognize the importance of this mode
> of treatment and adopt it. But, in the meantime, we, of the Border
> States, are drifting southward, and it may soon be too late to arrest
> that movement.[95]

He felt that discontent would spread in the South if it was left alone; then
a Union sentiment would grow, and the federal government would coerce
the South, with the support of the conservative men from both the North
and the South. But,

> a war needlessly provoked by the administration—a single blow struck,
> would instantly break down all this conservatism, and drive the whole
> of the Border States into a separation.[96]

On April 14 he wrote in his Journal that the expedition to Fort Sumter

> strengthens the secession men and may end in driving us all out of the
> Union. I learn, however, that our union majority in this state is still
> staunch. . . .[97]

By the time of the firing upon Fort Sumter, Kennedy had wandered a
long way from his position of December, when he had written his pamphlet.
By April he was no longer writing about a central confederacy but urging
the Administration to let the South go in peace. He saw that the South
had blundered by seizing the forts and that the North was now united in
attempts to regain them. He still opposed Maryland's joining the Southern
Confederacy, but this meant that it would have to remain in the Union.
Although he opposed a war at this time, he appeared to favor forcing the

South to rejoin the Union when there was a stronger southern Unionist sentiment.

The firing upon Fort Sumter forced Kennedy, like many others, to make a decision; he chose the Union. He now accused the Confederate States of using force, and he urged that Maryland stay in the Union to oppose southern coercion. Kennedy felt that he had been abandoned by the southern states that joined the Confederacy, especially by Virginia. In May he wrote that Virginia,

> should at least, consult the other Border States . . . and shape her course in conformity with their common views.[98]

A feeling of being omitted from the decision-making process and being consulted only as a last resort became evident when Kennedy wrote:

> It is only now, when a severe experience has demonstrated the necessity of friends able both to pay and to fight, that these States [border states] are approached with flattering appeals to take a stand in the very front of war and bear the brunt of its worst assaults.[99]

This was too much for him. He now argued that the best position for the state of Maryland was in the Union. Since his central confederacy had failed, he was unwilling to make Maryland the battleground for the war.

While John P. Kennedy advocated the establishment of a central confederacy, William Collins wrote a series of pamphlets expressing the impossibility of Maryland's defending itself outside of the Union. An admitted Unionist who stood for the Union even above that of the state of Maryland, Collins's first pamphlet, *An Address to the People of Maryland,* was dated December 20. He pointed out that Maryland was defenseless against the North; that its northern border was "purely artificial,"[100] and once Cumberland was captured, the coal fields that supplied many Marylanders would be in enemy hands. He stated further that the Chesapeake Bay could be blockaded easily to seal the city of Baltimore. Collins pointed out that the North would not let its capital be captured or surrounded by an enemy without a fight. He opposed joining the Southern Confederacy because Maryland's slaves would flee, and without the Fugitive Slave Law there would be no way to recover them. The state of Maryland would pay taxes higher than any other state in such a Southern Confederacy without receiving the benefits. Philosophically, Collins opposed the right of secession or the sovereignty of a state. That peaceful secession would never occur; that Maryland would suffer the most and benefit the least was the thesis of his pamphlet. He wrote two other similar pamphlets.

Collins expressed the ideas of those who opposed secession in any of its forms. His pamphlet comprehensively presents the arguments and the fears that occurred to every Marylander who thought about the idea of secession. It was obvious to many that the state of Maryland could not sustain itself if separation meant war. This is why those who advocated secession, such as John P. Kennedy, predicted that either Pennsylvania would join Maryland or that the separation would be peaceful. Collins plays the role of the antagonist who presents the ideas of those opposed to secession. These were the questions that the secessionists had to answer if they were to hold a believable position.

v

The Virginia Legislature, hoping to find a compromise for the secession crisis, urged the states to send representatives to Washington to hold a Peace Conference. Since the Legislature of Maryland was not in session, Governor Hicks appointed seven men to represent the State. These men voted for every provision of the compromise when it was presented in its final form. Only two presented their ideas on secession during the debates. Reverdy Johnson of Baltimore did not believe in the right of secession, but felt that the right of revolution existed and introduced a resolution on February 27, which stated:

> the Union being formed by the assent of the people of the respective States, and being compatible only with freedom, and the republican institutions guaranteed to each, cannot and ought not to be maintained by force, we deprecate any effort by the Federal Government to coerce in any form the said States to reunion or submission, as tending to irreparable breach, and leading to incalculable ills; and we earnestly invoke the abstinence from all counsels or measures of compulsion toward them.[101]

This resolution would have tied the federal government's hands and prevented it from enforcing the laws. It was not voted on by the Convention. Johnson, on the one hand, advocated the right of revolution and, on the other, refused the federal government the right of self-defense.

The second delegate who mentioned secession was Benjamin C. Howard of Catonsville, who had expressed the hope that there would be a central confederacy. He supported the compromise as a way of urging the seceding states to return to the Union. However, like Johnson, he denied the constitutional right of secession but affirmed the right of revolution. He was not certain that the compromise would keep Maryland in the Union, but he was sure that:

If Virginia secedes our State will go with her, hand in hand, with

Providence as our guide. This is not intended as a threat. God forbid! It is a truth which we cannot and ought not to conceal.[102]

He did not deprecate this movement towards secession. In fact, he stated it with the certainty of a person who expected it.

Since only two of the seven members of the delegation expressed themselves on the matter of secession and since they all voted for compromise, one cannot describe the delegation as secessionist. The Governor had appointed the members to represent the State. They appear to have done so, expressing hope for a compromise and, at the same time, predicting secession.

vi

The secession movement was strongest in the Eastern Shore and southern counties. Dr. Samuel A. Harrison of Talbot County, an Eastern Shore county, summed up the feeling of the Eastern Shore people. He said that the majority of the Union men felt that while they opposed "the principle of secession" they also

> think that force should not be employed to enforce obedience to the laws upon the ground that the general government has no such right, others think that force should not be employed as inexpedient.[103]

In southern Maryland many people expressed the opinion that Maryland would go with the South if war broke out. Henry W. Thomas and W. Sirus wrote to John J. Crittenden urging that some compromise be arrived at by March 4, or

> Maryland may withdraw from the Union before the above mentioned day. . . .[104]

A statement made before the Committee of the United States House of Representatives investigating attempts to seize Washington, D.C., confirmed the possibility of Maryland's secession. James Hicks, Jr. of Montgomery County stated that he was a lieutenant in a volunteer company.

> . . . if it should become necessary, we would go with the South; that if a war should break out between the two portions of our nation, the north and the south, we should certainly side with the south.[105]

At the same time, the Naval Academy at Annapolis was riddled with secessionists. W. Rogers Hopkins expressed the opinion that

> as to treason I know of but five loyal officers out of some 40 officers &

other gentlemen employed here . . . Blue Cockades have been plenty here among the Midshipmen. . . .[106]

In the western and northern counties the majority opposed secession; however, a significant minority opposed coercion. Maryland historian, J. Thomas Scharf, who served in the Confederate Navy, concurred with this viewpoint when he said

> the majority of the people of that section [western Maryland] were pronounced and decided in their support of the Union after hostilities had actually commenced, there was a very large and respectable element which sympathized with the South, and which deprecated the coercion of the Southern States.[107]

In Harford County, H. D. Fernandis, among others, wrote that the people of Maryland would never recognize the right of secession, but at the same time neither would they ever permit coercion of the southern states. He concluded by agreeing with the Constitutional Union party which according to him stated in February that:

> if it be found we cannot live together in harmony under the Constitution our fathers framed, let us as brethren agree to part in peace. . . .[108]

However in a letter written in January to Governor Hicks, B. A. Garlinger said that two-thirds of the people of Washington County supported the Governor's decision not to convene the Legislature.[109]

The city of Baltimore, which would show secessionist sympathies when the war broke out, contained many extremely vocal secessionists. John Thompson Mason, the Collector of Customs at the port of Baltimore, expressed such sentiments in a meeting held in Annapolis in February 1861. Mason

> began a violent harangue, in which he denounced the unionists and declared himself in favor of prompt secession of the State. . . .[110]

Many members of Baltimore's wealthier and more educated classes were secessionists, a fact confirmed by John M. Tormey in a statement to the Committee of the United States House of Representatives which was investigating attempts to seize Washington, D.C. He claimed that as chief clerk of the Circuit Court of Baltimore City, he could, from his position, observe that when,

> members of the bar come in there, . . . I hear them say that if Virginia secedes, of course Maryland would also. . . .[111]

Abraham Lincoln received letters from Marylanders expressing the fear of secession. Captain Hazzard of the United States Army, wrote Lincoln that

> . . . nearly all the wealthy and influential citizens [of Baltimore] are disunionists. . . .[112]

Lincoln received further confirmation of this climate of fear in May, when he received a letter signed, "Tellula." It stated that there were two types of persons making up the Baltimore secessionists: the first, the old traditional families, the Eastern Shore aristocracy, who have social sympathies with the South; the second, the commercial class of Baltimore, who hope to get rich by trading with the South.[113]

Lincoln himself heard of the Baltimore sympathies when the train he was supposed to have taken through Baltimore was attacked. A crowd of "not less than 10,000 people"[114] met the train when it arrived in Calvert Station;

> the most terrific cheers ever heard were sent up, three for the Southern Confederacy, three for "gallant Jeff Davis" and three groans for "the Rail Splitter."[115]

While these sentiments represented the feelings of a large part of the people of Baltimore, no one can say how many. However, Unionist sentiment existed in the city. On January 10, 5,000 Baltimore citizens signed a petition approving Governor Hicks's refusal to call the Legislature.

Levi K. Brown, a leading Maryland Democrat writing to President Buchanan in November, stated that

> the general feeling however amongst our leading men is for neutrality at present.[116]

The Democratic State Executive Committee had decided to withhold any expression of opinion until the views of the leading Democrats could be ascertained. According to Brown,

> Senator Pearce is opposed to secession at present . . . Others are divided. . . .[117]

The following month Brown wrote that a meeting was held at which time

> the Electors, members of Congress and some twenty representative men of our state were present.[118]

They decided that the state Legislature should be convened and that a convention of border states held; that this convention should

> submit to the northern states and the Gulf states such terms as would maintain the Union. When all shall have failed, if they must fail, then Maryland to join the retiring states south.[119]

By February, Brown, having lost any former optimism, said,

> the pervading sentiment of the democracy of the state including the Reformers, and many Bell and Douglas men making a majority of 15,000 is just what I represented to you in the first interview after the election. It has been unexpressed because I have by entreaties kept its representative organ my state committee from action. But I must confess my fear that the subject has passed my control. . . .[120]

According to Brown, by February the Democratic party was committed to secession, but it was unable to use its majority because the Governor would not call the Legislature into session. These sentiments expressed to President Buchanan confirmed the view that the secession movement in Maryland was growing throughout the crisis and that it was strongest in the Democratic party.

It is difficult to determine the exact role that the churches played during the secession crisis in Maryland. The Methodists of Maryland were pro-Unionist.

> The lawyers and politicians of Baltimore were for secession, wrote a correspondent to the Cincinnati *Commercial,* but the Methodists and mechanics of the city were "almost to a man for the Union."[121]

As was the Bishop of the Protestant Episcopal Church, Bishop William R. Whittingham, who, while supporting John P. Kennedy's central confederacy,

> viewed secession as a defiance of an ordinance of God, and by its very nature it was tantamount to sin.[122]

He did not represent the viewpoint of his constituents, for even he

> estimated that two-thirds of the laity and one-fifth of the clergy were in disagreement with him.[123]

The upper classes and the aristocracy who worshipped in the Episcopal Church appeared to be the secessionists. The lower classes were pro-Union and anti-secession.

Four of Maryland's former governors—Enoch L. Lowe, Thomas G. Pratt, Philip F. Thomas, Francis Thomas—expressed sympathy with the South, and one, Lowe, joined the Confederacy. Governor Lowe, a native of Frederick,

> openly advocated that Maryland should secede and join the Confederacy.[124]

During the Civil War he went South and spent most of his time in Georgia. To the Committee of the United States House of Representatives on February 1, he predicted that Maryland would follow the lead of Virginia. Governor Thomas G. Pratt,

> gave to the confederate forces his moral support throughout the contest and the services of his son.[125]

The same can be said for Governor Philip F. Thomas, whose sympathies lay with the South and whose son joined the Confederate Army. Governor Pratt was arrested in 1861 and held for several weeks. The Annapolis *Gazette* reported that Governor Francis Thomas raised a regiment of 3,000 soldiers to fight for the South.[126] Lowe, Pratt and the two Thomases had all been governors during the 1840s and 1850s and it is obvious that the history of Maryland might have been different if any one of them had been governor in 1860–61.

Maryland supplied many men to the Southern Confederacy. Three are particularly important because of the high positions they held in it. Franklin Buchanan, who was a captain in the United States Navy, resigned on April 22 and offered his services to the state of Maryland, so sure was he that the State would secede. Two months later he wrote Senator James A. Pearce about the reasons for his actions.

> I resigned in good faith to my native state, Maryland, fully under the impression she was out of the Union, and I could not raise my arm against her, for some days, all throughout the state nearly, believed her virtually withdrawn from the Union, during that unfortunate affair of April last . . . such was the light in which every person I met, viewed it . . . the change to Union was as sudden as from Secession to Union. . . .[127]

Buchanan explained that he had opposed secession but that

> my feelings are all in favor of the South and I cannot war against her. . . .[128]

When he found that Maryland was going to remain in the Union, he offered to recall his resignation, but the Navy Department refused his request. He still held that it is

folly for the North to suppose she can subjugate the South.[129]

But he concluded that he, along with many other Maryland officers, had too hastily withdrawn from the Navy and Army. Nevertheless, he would never enforce the laws against the South. Buchanan joined the Confederate Navy and rose to the rank of Admiral.

Another Marylander who was to become a famous Confederate Naval officer was Raphael Semmes, later to be the commander of the *Alabama*. On January 26, he wrote to Howell Cobb, that

if invited by the Confederacy of the Cotton States I will accept service in its navy and abandon my present position. The chances are that Maryland (my native state) and all the other border slave states will speedily follow you, but whether they do or not I will cast my destiny with yours if you will permit me.[130]

He continued to say that he felt that no slave state could remain in the Union and fight the other slave states. A few days later he wrote that he hoped that a civil war could be averted.[131] Yet he believed the Union was broken beyond repair.

Another Marylander of distinction who fled to the South was Robert Ould. He had been the United States District Attorney and was a friend of President James Buchanan. He became the Confederate agent of exchange for prisoners of war.

vii

A review of the newspapers of the State shows that the secession movement was quite extensive. The press sampling represents the diversity of opinion throughout the entire State. In 1860 the United States Census Bureau listed 49 weekly newspapers in Maryland. Of these, 28, or 57.1 percent of the newspapers in existence in 1860, will be referred to in the following pages and their positions on secession will be perceived. Of these 28 newspapers, 3 are located on the Eastern Shore, 3 in the southern counties, 12 in the northern and western counties, and 10 in the city of Baltimore.

One of the three Eastern Shore newspapers, the Easton *Star,* supported John C. Breckinridge in the election of 1860. After the firing upon Fort Sumter, it opposed coercing the South and called upon the federal government to recognize the Southern Confederacy. Its rival, the Easton *Gazette,* had endorsed John Bell and, during the secession crisis, pointed out that there could be no peaceful separation, that compromise was the only alternative to war. Once war broke out the newspaper supported the federal government. The third newspaper was the Cambridge *Herald,* which had supported no candidate and had no editorial column, making it impossible to determine its views on the question of secession.

In southern Maryland the papers were divided; two were for Breckinridge, and one for Bell. The pro-Breckinridge newspapers included Upper Marlborough's *The Planter's Advocate,* which wanted Maryland to join the Confederacy. It opposed the idea of a central confederacy of the border states. After Fort Sumter, it referred to the movement of the Union Army across Maryland as "the invasion of our soil by Northern troops. . . ."[132] The *Montgomery County Sentinel,* which had also supported Breckinridge, urged that the Governor call a special session of the Legislature. In January it took the position that "in the event of a dissolution of this Confederacy, . . ."[133] the state of Maryland should join the Southern Confederacy. After the firing upon Fort Sumter, it called upon the federal government to permit the South to go in peace. Both of the pro-Breckinridge newspapers, therefore, advocated Maryland's joining the Southern Confederacy.

The third newspaper was the Annapolis *Gazette,* which had endorsed John Bell in the election of 1860 and would take various positions during the crisis. According to George L. P. Radcliffe, a biographer of Governor Hicks,

> the Annapolis *Gazette* was generally believed to be the organ of Hicks, though the latter denied that any paper could claim its utterances to be possessed of any official sanction from him. Still Hicks at times used this paper as his mouthpiece. . . .[134]

At first this newspaper urged Maryland to take a neutral position, believing that there would be several confederacies, not just two. The journal wanted Maryland to declare its independence once the Union was broken.

> The only hope of preserving our property and our rights, is by making Maryland a government separate and distinct from all others.[135]

Two months later, in February, the Annapolis *Gazette* advocated that Maryland join the border states and form a central confederacy. The following month, when this seemed impossible, the *Gazette* took the position that the North was not the enemy of the state of Maryland and that it should stay in the Union. By April, before Fort Sumter was fired upon, the *Gazette* argued that

we are for the Union, "for better or for worse," for weal or for woe—
and to *that* complexion must it come at "last."[136]

The *Gazette* took a position similar to that of Governor Hicks when it
advocated a central confederacy; but when it supported the Union, it
drifted away from the Governor who was still advocating an independent
position for the state of Maryland.

In western Maryland there were no pro-Breckinridge newspapers, but
two newspapers supported Stephen A. Douglas. The Cumberland *Democratic Alleganian* opposed coercion of the southern states and favored a
policy by the federal government that would have permitted the southern
states to secede. The Frederick *Maryland Union,* on the other hand, took
as its motto "OUR FEDERAL UNION—IT MUST BE PRESERVED."[137]

The four newspapers that had endorsed John Bell called upon the federal government to enforce the laws and urged Maryland to stay in the
Union. These newspapers were the Cumberland *Civilian & Telegraph,*
the Middletown *Valley Register,* the Frederick *Examiner,* and the Hagerstown *Herald of Freedom and Torch Light.* This again points out that
the Union strength was located in the western section of Maryland.

In northern Maryland four newspapers had supported John Bell. Two
of the pro-Bell newspapers supported the Union: the Elkton *Cecil Whig*
and the Bel Air *National American.* The Towsontown *Baltimore County
American* urged that Maryland unite with Virginia and the other border
states and form a central confederacy. The fourth newspaper, the Westminister *American Sentinel,* appears to have stood by the Union; but since
only a few issues of this newspaper exist, nothing can be said conclusively.

The two other northern Maryland newspapers that had been either
noncommittal or not in existence for the period of the election of 1860,
were secessionist. The Bel Air *Southern Aegis* accused the North of aggression and stated that the Constitution

must be upheld. Failing in this, with one hand grasping the Constitution
and the other holding a declaration of independence, let us proclaim
our freedom and renounce all allegiance to the North.[138]

The Towsontown *Baltimore County Advocate,* after the South attacked
Fort Sumter, wanted the United States government to recognize the South-
ern Confederacy. Once again, the only supporters of the Union were the
Bell newspapers.

The largest single concentration of newspapers whose issues are in
existence today are those from the city of Baltimore. Of the ten newspapers only two supported political candidates. The Baltimore *Daily*

Exchange endorsed John C. Breckinridge. It stated that while it did not recognize the constitutional right of secession, it opposed the use of force to retain a state in the Union. A. S. Chambers, a reporter for the *Exchange,* wrote that the paper

> turned its face to the South, and its editorial rooms were soon recognized by the numerous body of Southern sympathizers in Maryland, as the headquarters for reliable information of Southern politics, plans, and performances.[139]

However, Chambers was careful to point out that the activities in this office were strictly verbal.

> I never knew of that office being anything worse—so far as antagonism to the Washington Government was concerned—than a depository of "contraband" news. There certainly was never any hint of any sort of conspiracy or purpose to aid the Confederacy in any way, though "blockade runners" were always welcomed. . . .[140]

The Baltimore *American and Commercial Advertiser* had supported John Bell. After the secession of South Carolina this newspaper urged that the State be permitted to go in peace. As other states left the Union, it took the position that no force should be used to bring them back. When it became obvious that the South was going to form a separate nation, the *American* argued that the border states should form a central confederacy which would include Pennsylvania. It also advocated that the southern states be permitted to leave the Union. The *American* hoped that a war could be prevented:

> If one conclusion is profoundly settled in the public mind of Maryland, it is that no possible profit can accrue to either side from an appeal to arms.[141]

There were four Baltimore newspapers that endorsed no candidate in the election of 1860. Among these were: the Baltimore *Family Journal,* a literary newspaper; and the Baltimore *Price Current,* a business newspaper. Neither of these discussed political issues. The Baltimore *Evening Patriot* was a pro-Union paper that had criticized President Buchanan's failure to act. The largest of the noncommittal newspapers was the Baltimore *Sun.* It opposed the North's use of force to maintain the Union and felt that the southern withdrawal from the Union was successful. After the firing upon Fort Sumter, it urged that the Confederate States be recognized. John B. Jones, writing after the war, stated that when he visited the publisher A. S. Abell on April 9, 1861. The publisher of the Baltimore *Sun,* [was] an old acquaintance. Somewhat contrary to my expectations, knowing him to be a native of the North, I found him an ardent secessionist. So enthusiastic was he in the cause, that he denounced both Maryland and Virginia for their hesitancy in following the example of the Cotton States. . . .[142]

There are four other Baltimore newspapers for which only a few issues are in existence, too few to determine whether they supported any candidate in the election of 1860. Of these papers, three supported peaceable secession: the *Baltimore Republican, The True Union,* and the *Methodist Protestant,* a religious newspaper. The fourth, The Baltimore *Clipper,* was a Union newspaper.

Six of the ten Baltimore newspapers supported some form of secession. It was only the newspapers located in the western part of the State that were opposed to secession. The other sections were relatively evenly divided between pro-Union and pro-secession newspapers. There are not enough newspapers from the Eastern Shore to provide an accurate picture of the area's feelings. None of Maryland's newspapers supported Abraham Lincoln in the election of 1860. The Unionist strength was found among the papers that had endorsed Bell; seven of the eleven were opposed to secession. The pro-Douglas newspapers were evenly divided. The secessionist newspapers supported either Breckinridge or no candidate in the election of 1860. Whether one divides these newspapers geographically or politically, secessionist sentiment was about evenly balanced by Union sentiment.

viii

Once the Confederate States of America fired upon Fort Sumter, President Lincoln called upon the states to furnish troops to defend Washington, D.C. This placed Maryland, particularly Baltimore, in an awkward position. Even though many rejected the idea of seeing federal troops pass across Maryland to take up positions against the South, they had no legitimate way of calling a convention in which Maryland could decide on the question of secession. The city of Baltimore witnessed expressions of sympathy for the Confederacy, including the raising of Confederate flags and the formation of military companies that were to fight with the South. A States-Rights Convention held on April 18 passed resolutions that called upon the people to oppose any invasion. This obviously meant the northern troops that were on their way to Washington, D.C.

These conditions existed in Baltimore when the Sixth Massachusetts Regiment, while marching through the city, was attacked by a mob on April 19. Four soldiers were killed and probably twice that many citizens. Many on both sides were wounded. The mayor and the police chief tried to escort the soldiers through the town, but the citizens of Baltimore nevertheless attacked the Regiment. A mass meeting was called for 4:00 P.M., April 19, in Monument Square.

> At the appointed time a huge gathering assembled: the speakers, for the greater part, delivered strong anti-coercion speeches; instead of the national banner, a flag was displayed bearing the arms of Maryland . . . the occasion was a great secession meeting.[143]

Mayor Brown later wrote about the speech he delivered:

> In my speech I insisted on the maintenance of peace and order in the city. I denied that the right of a State to secede from the Union was granted by the Constitution. . . . I deprecated war on the seceding States, and strongly expressed the opinion that the South could not be conquered. I approved of Governor Hicks' determination to send no troops from Maryland to invade the South.[144]

Governor Hicks spoke next.

> I coincide in the sentiment of your worthy mayor. After three conferences we have agreed, and I bow in submission to the people. I am a Marylander; I love my State and I love the Union, but I will suffer my right arm to be torn from my body before I will raise it to strike a sister State.[145]

Therefore, both men were expressing themselves in favor of permitting the South to secede. The use of force to preserve the Union was contrary to their wishes and they were, in effect, trying to make Maryland neutral in the struggle.

Governor Hicks later denied that he had said anything that would encourage the South. But A. S. Chambers, who was on the speaker's stand, disagreed. Chambers commented that

> . . . I looked into the faces of more people than I have ever before seen and I have never since seen so many together in mass meeting. . . .

Governor Hicks was introduced by Mayor Brown who

> I think, . . . in the course of the introduction took occasion to declare himself a Unionist. At this announcement the most venomous and long-continued public hissing occurred. . . . Charles Marshal, afterward the Military Secretary of Gen. Robert E. Lee, begged the crowd to hear Governor Hicks; but although Col. Marshal's Southern sympathies were well known, the hissing continued; but Col. Marshal was persistent, and finally the venom of the crowd seemed to have spent itself. . . .

Governor Hicks rose to speak

white as a sheet and trembling like an aspen leaf, while his teeth audibly rattled, made a few remarks. . . .

Chambers disagreed with Hicks's subsequent denial that his comments encouraged the South.

I never could exactly agree with the Governor as to his version of what he did say, as I stood close to and directly behind him and was listening to him so closely that I heard his teeth chatter in the face of that wild mob. . . .[146]

In the presence of such a mob it is understandable that Hicks might not have remembered what he had said or that he may have made comments that were favorable to the mob.

On the same day Mayor Brown sent a message to President Lincoln, which was carried by three leading citizens of Baltimore. It said in part:

Under these circumstances it is my solemn duty to inform you that it is not possible for more soldiers to pass through Baltimore unless they fight their way at every step.[147]

Late that night news arrived that more troops were assembling in Pennsylvania and intended to pass through Maryland. Mayor Brown and the Board of Police met and concluded that

it was necessary to burn or disable the bridges of both railroads so far as was required to prevent the ingress of troops. This was accordingly done at once, some of the police and a detachment of the Maryland Guard being sent out to do the work.[148]

According to the Mayor, Governor Hicks was informed of this

and urged to give his consent, for we desired that he should share with us the responsibility of taking this grave step. This consent he distinctly gave in my presence and in the presence of several others. . . .[149]

Hicks later denied that he had given his consent to burn the bridges. Three men who were present at the time, former Governor E. Louis Lowe; Marshal Kane of the Baltimore police; and the mayor's brother, John C. Brown, all later stated that Governor Hicks had given his consent.

While these events properly belong to the Civil War era and therefore outside the scope of this study, the attitudes of these men during this period of stress show much of their secessionist thinking. Mayor George W. Brown had been elected as a reform candidate opposing the American party; however, in the election of 1860, he supported John Bell. Mayor Brown issued a proclamation on April 18, in which he supported the position that Maryland troops should not be sent from their state to fight in another. He stated that

> we may rest secure in the confidence that the storm of civil war which now threatens the country will at least pass over our beloved State and leave it unharmed; but if they shall be disregarded, a fearful and fratricidal strife may at once burst forth in our midst.[150]

After the war, Brown wrote that Lincoln's proclamation calling for troops was met

> in Maryland with mingled feelings in which astonishment, dismay and disapprobation were predominant. On all sides it was agreed that the result must be war, or a dissolution of the Union, and I may safely say that a large majority of our people then preferred the latter.[151]

In other words, Marylanders preferred to permit the South to leave the Union and as a state, take a neutral position.

The Baltimore City Council voted a half million dollars for the defense of the city; guns were collected and troops were raised. Some historians have tried to see this as an attempt to drive Baltimore into the Confederacy. Finding that this is indefensible, others present the viewpoint that Brown was a Unionist. He was neither. He was a neutralist and his position sanctioned secession. He clearly stated that the

> prevention of war was the object of the city authorities. . . .[152]

He further wrote,

> I thought that the seceding States should have been allowed to depart in peace, as General Scott advised, and I believe that afterwards the necessities of the situation and their own interest would induce them to return. . . .[153]

He even used the words "armed neutrality"[154] when referring to the city of Baltimore during this period of crisis. The federal government considered the Mayor a threat, and, on September 17, he was arrested and held for about two months.

The other major figure was Governor Hicks. His position, similar to that which he had taken before the firing upon Fort Sumter, was one of neutrality. On April 18, he set forth his position in a proclamation assuring

> the people that no troops will be sent from Maryland, unless it may be for the defence of the national capital.[155]

Hicks felt that this federal territory really belonged to Maryland since it was given to the federal government by Maryland, and he refused to allow any other state or nation to take it away from Maryland. He wanted "to preserve the people of Maryland from civil war," so that

> the people of the state will in a short time have the opportunity afforded them, in a special election for Members of Congress of the United States, to express their devotion to the Union, or their desire to see it broken up.[156]

Hicks made it clear that he was not totally committed to one nation, that it was up to the people of Maryland to decide whether they wanted the nation divided. His position depended on keeping Union troops out of the State until that election.

General Benjamin F. Butler was stationed off Annapolis, ready to land troops. Hicks wrote him on April 20 that he should not land Union troops on Maryland soil. The same day he wrote General Kimmell that the United States had sent a mustering officer to Frederick to enlist volunteers and that this officer "has no power to raise men"[157] within Maryland. He also wrote to Simon Cameron, the Secretary of War, that the

> rebellious elements had control. . . . They had arms, and the principal part of the organised [sic] Militia forces and we were powerless under the circumstances.[158]

Using this excuse, he declined

> . . . (for the present) acting upon the requisition made upon Maryland for four regiments.[159]

He could have urged that the federal government put down the rebellion, or he could have tried to remove the guns from "the rebellious elements," but he did neither.

On April 22 he wrote both to General Scott and William H. Seward, the Secretary of State, urging that no more troops be sent through Maryland either by way of Annapolis or Pennsylvania. He went so far as to urge that the British Ambassador, Lord Lyons,

> be requested to mediate between contending parties of our country to prevent the effusion of blood.[160]

On this same day, General Butler in his reply to Hicks's letter carefully pointed out that the troops under his command were

> *not Northern troops; they are a part of the whole militia of the United States, obeying the call of the President.*[161]

This subtle reply to the Governor shows clearly that Butler thought Hicks did not consider Maryland to be part of the Union.

A day later, using the excuse that General Butler had taken possession of the Annapolis and Elk Ridge Railroad, the Governor refused to call the state Legislature into session at Annapolis. Hicks later called the Legislature into session in Frederick, but only after some change of mind. His original intention was to convene the Legislature in Baltimore. A copy of his original draft shows that Baltimore, a city then in the hands of the secessionist mobs, was to be the place where the Legislature was to meet.[162] Why he should have changed his mind and picked the Unionist stronghold of Frederick is unexplainable. Whether it was the fear of the mobs or political considerations or other reasons cannot be conclusively stated.

General Butler, not one to take attacks lightly, replied to the Governor: The reason he had taken possession of the railroad was to prevent it from being destroyed, as State authorities would not protect it. Butler offered to vacate Annapolis if the State authorities would protect the railroad. The next day Butler wrote again to Governor Hicks urging him to countersign an order to Governor Curtin of Pennsylvania authorizing him to occupy the Pikesville Arsenal, which had been seized by the state of Maryland. Hicks refused to countersign such a statement, claiming that he was not in communication with the other parts of the State. But in a message to the special session of the Maryland Legislature, on April 25, he admitted he had ordered the seizure of this federal arsenal at Pikesville to prevent a mob from capturing it.

Governor Hicks's position on the fate of the state of Maryland was presented in his message to the special session of the Legislature.

> I honestly and most earnestly entertain the conviction that the only safety of Maryland lies in preserving a neutral position between our brethren of the North and of the South. . . . Entertaining these views, I cannot counsel Maryland to take sides against the General Government, until it shall commit outrages upon us which would justify us in resisting its authority. As a consequence, I can give no other counsel than that we shall array ourselves for Union and Peace, and thus preserve our soil from being polluted with the blood of brethren.[163]

Governor Hicks walked a thin line between joining the South, which he had consistently opposed, and supporting the Union. He did not want the state of Maryland to become the battleground for such a conflict. Therefore, he chose what he believed to be the middle ground—neutrality. But such a neutral position would, in effect, cut the national capital off from the North; it would divide the Union; it would permit secession; indeed it would recognize the right of secession. A similar position taken by

Mayor Brown had led him to jail. But the Governor, under pressure from the federal government, became more pro-Union. Lincoln, who would not have wanted to arrest a high official, had met his first intransigent governor. He would meet more before the war was over.

ix

While Mayor Brown and Governor Hicks were the leading figures during this period, they had widespread support among the populace. Alexander Randall of Annapolis, a strong Union man, stated:

> every man was rushing around thro' the Streets [of Baltimore] to resist the passage of more troops to Washington. . . . the civil authority, even Police, with all their powers appeared utterly incapable of restraining the armed & excited people. . . .[164]

What Randall did not know was that the Baltimore police were supporting the armed mobs. Charles Howard, a member of the Police Board, wrote to Colonel Isaac R. Trimble, who later joined the Confederate Army, on April 22, that

> the Board of Police fully appreciate and acknowledge the zeal and promptitude with which the Citizens of Baltimore have manifested their desposition to organize themselves for the defence of the City. . . . And it is hoped that such organizations will be continued, and made as general and as perfect as practicable.[165]

Howard was later arrested by the federal government, along with other members of the Baltimore Police Board.

A delegation of thirty-five men from the Young Men's Christian Association went to Washington and told the President

> that his duty as a Christian statesman was to "recognize the independence of the Southern States."[166]

There can be no accurate estimate of how many people supported or opposed the Lincoln administration. J. N. Trimble, writing to Charles I. duPont on May 11, gave the opinion that

> the interest and will of three fourths of Md., are Southern but it is no time now to disclose her feelings or her purposes.[167]

All over the state of Maryland secessionist activities continued, even after the firing upon Fort Sumter.

A few months later General John A. Dix urged the federal government to break up the military companies in the Eastern Shore counties of Caroline, Queen Anne, and Carroll, which he considered secessionist.

The western county, Allegany, was probably the strongest Union county. Military companies from this county were offering their services either to Pennsylvania or the United States government. After the news of the Baltimore riots,

> a military company was formed in Lonaconing and its services offered to the Secretary of War at Washington.[168]

During April a Home Guard was organized in Frederick. General John A. Steiner, secretary of the Guard, wrote that

> the object of the formation of the Guard was to protect the property of the citizens of Frederick, and to prevent the secession of the State of Maryland from the Union, or rather to aid the United States in keeping Maryland in the Union.[169]

He also felt that the Guard kept the state Legislature from taking a more active position toward secession.

But even in Frederick there was secessionist activity. Steiner wrote:

> In retaliation the Rebels of Frederick applied the incendiary torch to the old Court House, and burned the same to the ground, doing this so that the Guard would be deprived of their regular rendezvous. . . .[170]

Bradley T. Johnson, who later became a General in the Confederate Army, raised a company of seventy men from Frederick for the Confederate Army.

Another significant sign of the extent of the Maryland secession movement was the Confederacy's reaction to the events in Maryland. Jefferson Davis, on April 22, telegraphed Governor Letcher of Virginia to "sustain Baltimore if practicable."[171] J. J. Hooper, private secretary in the Confederate War Department, wrote a Captain J. Lyle Clarks of Baltimore that the Confederacy would welcome any Maryland troops.

Virginia not only urged Marylanders to join the Confederacy but also sent arms into the state. The extracts of the proceedings of the Advisory Council of the state of Virginia include the notation that:

> Major General Kenton Harper, in command at Harper's Ferry, is hereby ordered to deliver to General [George H.] Steuart, at Baltimore, one thousand of the arms recently taken at Harper's Ferry.[172]

General Steuart, who was with the First Light Division, Maryland Volunteers, in Baltimore replied that he had received 351 muskets and carbines from General Harper. He continued that the road from Annapolis Junction to Baltimore is uninjured, and I am very anxious, with the co-operation of General Harper, to occupy a strong position at or near the Relay House, so as to guard and keep open for our own accommodation the railroad communication from Baltimore to the West, and at the same time cutting it off from Washington.[173]

Marshal Kane of the Baltimore police was also involved with Virginia, for on his way to destroy the railroad bridges he sent a telegram:

Send expresses over the mountains and valleys of Maryland and Virginia for the riflemen to come without delay.[174]

The Board of Police of Baltimore received arms from the state of Virginia during April 1861. T. Parkin Scott, a member of the Maryland House of Delegates from Baltimore County, sent a letter to the Board of Police on May 2, requesting payment for the shipment of these muskets.

On the 22d of April 1861, I obtained through Governor Letcher an order from the adjutant general of Virginia on the ordnance officer at Staunton for 5,000 flint-lock muskets as a loan for the use of the Maryland troops, and with said order I proceeded to Staunton and there obtained 2,000 stand in part of said order and employed G. R. Mason to carry them in wagons to Winchester, and on the 26th of April I had them forwarded thence to Baltimore consigned to William T. Walters and they were here delivered to your board.[175]

Marshal Kane also sent Francis J. Thomas, Adjutant General of Maryland Volunteer Forces, to Norfolk to obtain artillery. Thomas succeeded in procuring forty-nine guns and having them sent to Baltimore.[176] Later, he was commissioned Colonel in the Virginia militia. Besides showing the close connection of Maryland and Virginia, these activities also pointed out that Virginia saw the likelihood of Maryland's seceding from the Union. Virginia would probably have contributed less arms if it did not believe that Maryland was able to secede.

The Legislature convened in a special session in Frederick on April 26, one week after the Baltimore riot, and the Lincoln administration feared the lawmakers would vote for secession. General Winfield Scott issued special instructions to General Benjamin F. Butler giving the commanding general the authority to act if the Legislature attempted "to arm their people against the United States. . . ." Butler was even given the authority to authorize "bombardment of their cities" if it was necessary to prevent this legislative action.[177]

On three occasions the members of the Legislature passed resolutions that called for neutrality, or the recognition of the Confederacy, or the right of the people to decide which section they wished to join. But they also agreed that the Legislature had no authority to pass an ordinance of secession. The southern, Eastern Shore and the Baltimore City legislators led the fight for these resolutions. So dangerous did the Lincoln administration consider these legislators that in September, Simon Cameron, the Secretary of War, ordered the arrest of many of them. As with many others in the state of Maryland, they were willing to go just so far; they were not willing to vote for a state convention that would decide the question of Maryland's secession.

Ten seats in the Maryland House of Delegates had been declared vacant because of election-day violence. The special election to fill these seats took place five days after the Baltimore riots, and the Unionists did not even put up a slate of candidates. By June, when Abraham Lincoln called for a special session of Congress, not only did the Unionists put up a slate of candidates for the Congressional election, but they were successful. Only Congressman Henry May of Baltimore refused to take the unconditional Union oath. The secession bubble had burst. By then any fear of secession had vanished—Maryland would stay in the Union.

x

Why did the secession movement fail in Maryland? First, it lacked a vehicle for expressing itself. Governor Hicks refused to call the Legislature into special session, and without the Legislature no state convention could be called to decide on the question of secession. When the Legislature was finally called into special session, the Union Army was moving across Maryland and it was too late. Hicks delayed calling the Legislature because he wanted Maryland to unite with the border states or to remain neutral, but the effect of his delay was to result in Maryland's staying in the Union. Not a Unionist, he was ready to see Maryland secede, but only on his terms. He lost and so did the secession movement.

The force of the federal government and the fact that large numbers of federal troops poured across the state made it impossible for Maryland's secession sympathizers to unite and repel the troops, even though the authorities in Baltimore did seize the city. By the middle of May, General Benjamin Butler was able to march into Baltimore and occupy the city. He later seized the arms stored by the Confederate supporters and made a series of arrests.

Mrs. Benjamin G. Harris, who kept a diary of the events, first records that on April 21,

the last news from Baltimore is terrible, that the fight has commenced, several of the citizens killed—what can Lincoln mean by allowing such inhuman butchery to go on—everyday brings some new terror. . . .

A week later,

> brother fighting against brother Washington & Annapolis filled with
> Northern troops, & yet they are not satisfied, "the cry is still, they
> come. . . ."

But by the middle of May,

> Maryland has succumbed to Lincoln, and degraded herself.[178]

She is able to record the hopes of April that were crushed by the Union
Army in May. She is typical of the people of Maryland who supported
the southern cause. Robert A. Pryor, as a Confederate officer writing in
May in Virginia, summed up the situation:

> Maryland overwhelmed and reaction there against us.[179]

A third factor was the secessionists' lack of adequate leadership. They
were divided among the various forms of secession. Most Maryland
secessionists were unwilling to act without Virginia. But when Virginia
acted it was too late for Maryland. William W. Glenn attended a secret
meeting of pro-southern leaders in Baltimore on April 17 and wrote that
all they did was talk. Glenn, in his diary, concluded,

> there was not only no leader of a Southern party in Baltimore at that
> time but there was no newspaper to advocate the cause.[180]

While many Baltimore newspapers supported the southern cause, none was
willing to rally the secessionists and lead Maryland out of the Union.

If these were the institutional factors that led to the failure of the
secession movement in Maryland, there were also intellectual reasons why
there was no action on the part of the secessionists. Foremost was the fear
that Maryland would become the battleground for the war between the
two sections. Many Marylanders believed that the State was defenseless,
and could not stop an invasion of the northern army. The movement to
permit the South to secede in peace had been based on this same argument.
The Marylanders who had supported peaceable secession hoped to avoid
a war. To let the South go in peace would have prevented a war. But if
Maryland was now to join the South or form a separate nation, the State
would be the battleground for a war with the North, which would have
defeated the ends that they had long sought.

One of the outstanding historians of the state of Maryland, J. Thomas
Scharf, wrote that there

was one point upon which we believe the people of this State were almost unanimous, and that was against the idea of coercing the Southern States by the physical power of the Federal government or the northern people.[181]

While Scharf, being a Confederate himself, is probably exaggerating the number of people who opposed coercion, it is nevertheless fair to say that a majority of the people did. As a result they were unwilling to ally themselves with the South and make Maryland the battleground for such a war. The strong opposition to coercion worked both ways; before the firing upon Fort Sumter it was to the advantage of the South, and after the firing it was to the advantage of the North.

If Maryland had joined the South and had a war ensued, the economy of Maryland would have been ruined. While the South argued that it would be of great economic advantage for the state of Maryland to secede and join the Confederacy, the results of the riots in Baltimore showed that the opposite was more likely. The South argued that the tariff restrictions would be eliminated and that Baltimore would become the trading center for the Confederacy. However, once the riots began in Baltimore, no trains entered the city and ships left the harbor. A severe economic recession fell upon the city, and it touched almost everyone. At the same time, the price of coal and wheat rose. It was a simple lesson that if Maryland went with the South her trade would cease because her railroads to the North would be cut off and the Chesapeake Bay could easily be closed by the Union Navy. In addition, Maryland's slaves could escape to the North, and there would be no way of recovering them. Obviously, therefore, Maryland's economic interests lay with the North.

The total effect created a vacuum in which the Union Army and the authority of the federal government balanced the scales in their favor. The result was that Maryland stayed in the Union, while many Marylanders joined the Confederate cause, and others remained in Maryland hoping for the success of the Confederate States.

Geographically, the secession movement was located in the Eastern Shore and the southern counties; secessionists controlled the municipal authorities of Baltimore and many of the citizens of that city supported the movement, which was widespread throughout the rest of Maryland. No area of the State lacked for advocates of secession. The sections of Maryland that were traditionally most southern in outlook and the areas of greatest slave concentration carried the greatest secessionist opinion. But even the western section of the State had its secessionists. Maryland was a secessionist stronghold.

3
DELAWARE

i

THE SMALL STATE OF DELAWARE PLAYED A MINOR ROLE DURING THE
secession crisis. Primarily agricultural, its agriculture was five times
greater than its manufacturing. While a railroad connected Delaware to
Philadelphia and the North, the Delaware and Chesapeake Canal made
trade between Philadelphia and Baltimore possible. Much of Delaware's
production traveled to northern cities, and its leading manufacturer,
E. I. DuPont de Nemours & Company, sided with the North during the
secession crisis.

Of Delaware's three counties, the northernmost, New Castle, manufactured eight times as much as the other two counties combined. Its
value in real estate was twice that of the other counties, and while the
most southern county, Sussex, had more farms, New Castle's farms exceeded them in value by two and one-half times. Therefore, New Castle
County dominated the State's economy. The three major industries of
New Castle County were the cotton, flour and gun powder mills. Wilmington's carriage builders sold the bulk of their vehicles to southern
customers.

While economics connected Delaware with the North, its sentiment
traditionally wed it to the South. The southern counties, Kent and Sussex,
were especially southern oriented. Primarily agricultural areas with little
manufacturing, they were

> settled for the most part, . . . by persons of Maryland and Virginia
> ancestry. . . .[1]

while New Castle County became more diversified because of its European
immigrants.

74

Delaware had a small population movement into and out of the State. Of the people who left Delaware, 3.7 percent settled in the eleven states that would make up the Confederacy. Of the people who moved into the State, 1.4 percent migrated from these states. Of Delaware's total population, .2 percent came from the eleven southern states.

Sussex County, the most southern, always had the largest slave population—usually about twice the combined total of the other two counties. This trend continued until 1860, when 74.5 percent of Delaware's slaves lived in Sussex County. New Castle County had only 11.3 percent of Delaware's slaves in 1860. There were only 1,798 slaves in Delaware in 1860.

> Although 587 persons were listed as slaveowners, only eight owned over fifteen slaves.[2]

Slavery had never been strong in the state of Delaware. In 1790 the State had its largest slave population, totaling 8,887. From then on slavery decreased every decade except during the second decade of the nineteenth century when it rose by about eight percent. The Delaware Constitution of 1776 prohibited importation of any more slaves, and laws soon enacted forbade the sale of slaves that would result in their leaving the State. The first "Black Code," not enacted until 1831, was a result of slave uprisings in Virginia. Its acts restricted free Negroes as well as slaves. A bill to free all slave children born after 1860 was introduced in the Delaware Legislature in 1847 but failed to pass when the Speaker of the Senate broke a tie and voted against it. The bill had already passed the Delaware House of Representatives.

The number of foreign immigrants in New Castle County influenced the decline of slavery, as well as the secession movement. Of a total of 9,160 foreign-born in Delaware, 8,570 were in New Castle County, and more than half were Irish. The free Negro population centered largely in New Castle and Kent Counties. The slave population amounted to only 1.6 percent of the total population. Only 72.6 percent of the Delaware population were whites born in the United States. This free labor supply of immigrants and free Negroes competed with slavery. The numbers of immigrants and free Negro men meant that the southern traditions of Delaware faced serious inroads that were only partially economic.

In Delaware the election of 1860 was marked by as many, if not more, factions within the Delaware political parties as in the national parties. The Democratic party split not only between the Breckinridge and Douglas factions, but also between James A. Bayard of New Castle County (elected to the United States Senate in 1851 with the support of the State's federal officeholders) and Willard Saulsbury (elected to the United States Senate in 1859 with the support of the lower counties). Both men endorsed Breckinridge after the Democratic Conventions. William G. Whiteley, Delaware's sole member to the United States House of Representatives, was a Democrat. But he supported the protective tariff because he believed that it was necessary for Wilmington's industry. The Douglas faction in New Castle County, led by Samuel Townsend, was unable to secure delegates to the Democratic Convention in Charleston. Townsend was a leader of the Democratic party in New Castle and a railroad promoter; James A. Bayard and William Whiteley represented that County at the National Convention.

At the Charleston convention, Delaware cast two votes for and one against the Cincinnati Platform. When the southern states started to withdraw, both Bayard and Whiteley withdrew and joined the "seceders" convention. The balance of the Delaware delegation remained, casting only two votes for Robert M. T. Hunter. Bayard became the permanent chairman of the "seceders" convention in Charleston, and Whiteley became a vice-president. On the third day of this rump convention, Bayard asked permission to withdraw as permanent chairman and his request was granted. When he returned to Delaware, the New Castle Democratic party reelected him to the regular Democratic Convention which was to meet in Baltimore and subsequently this convention seated him along with Whiteley. However at the Baltimore convention, Delaware voted for no candidate. Bayard was called to Washington; and was therefore, absent for the voting. He would have voted for Breckinridge.[3]

Opposition to the Democratic party centered around the People's party, led by George P. Fisher of Dover. It had been formed in 1858 to replace the Whig party, which had broken up after the 1852 election. Republicans, generally considered abolitionists, had little support in the State except on the tariff issue. The weak and disorganized Constitutional Union party pinned its hopes on capturing the People's party state convention in June. When it failed, "it was too late to form an effective machine."[4] The People's party held its convention in Dover in April and refused to send delegates to any national convention. The result was a statewide rather than a national party. But the People's party had informal representation at both the Republican and Constitutional Union national conventions. They refused to endorse either Abraham Lincoln or John Bell for the presidency, instead leaving the decision to individual members. They did unite, however, on a congressional candidate, George P. Fisher, a supporter of Bell.

At both the Republican and Constitutional Union national conventions Delaware was represented, but took no active part. The Delaware Constitutional Union party convention supported Bell, George P. Fisher for Congress and its own candidates for the Legislature.

While George P. Fisher supported John Bell, he was in contact with Thurlow Weed of New York and received campaign money from the New York Republican party. Fisher wrote to Weed on November 19, stating,

> I should like to see you very much and thank you in person for the interest you have taken in my election.[5]

Furthermore, a supporter of Fisher and the People's party wrote to Weed after the election pointing out that "the needful aided us greatly."[6] This was an obvious reference to the New York Republican party's financial aid to the People's party of Delaware. The People's party was, therefore, an ally of the Republican party.

The election results are revealing. While Breckinridge carried all three counties, the People's party's candidates for the Legislature carried New Castle and half of the legislators from Sussex County. The division in Sussex County was brought about by the People's party's ability to make a deal with the Democrats who opposed Willard Saulsbury. George P. Fisher, the People's party and Constitutional Union party candidate for Congress, won his election, while remaining silent on the slavery issue. If the anti-Breckinridge parties had united they might have been able to defeat Breckinridge. Douglas ran a poor fourth in all three counties. Lincoln ran second in New Castle and Kent, but third in the statewide vote by 22 votes. Breckinridge received only 45.74 percent of the vote; Bell, 24.09 percent; Lincoln, 23.79 percent, and Douglas, 6.38 percent.[7] The Democrats together had a majority of the vote, but then so did Breckinridge's opposition. Breckinridge received 48 percent of Delaware's rural vote and only 33 percent of the vote in Wilmington.

> The rural votes were far more pronounced in support of him than was the city of Wilmington. Lincoln was second to Breckinridge in the city but last in rural areas. . . .[8]

Lincoln received 23 percent of the rural votes and 28 percent of the Wilmington vote. Douglas ran fourth in both categories.[9]

ii

Northern Delaware's factories suffered as a result of the growing recession that followed the election of Lincoln; nevertheless this area remained primarily pro-Union. In December the Mayor of Wilmington addressed a Union meeting, urging the South to wait upon northern concessions as well as a compromise to settle the dispute. However, a hundred-gun salute in the city of Wilmington greeted South Carolina's secession.[10]

Robert Milligan of Wilmington, wrote Samuel F. DuPont in April saying that he needed 1,000 ball cartridges for muskets,

> as we expect to have trouble here whenever Virginia and Maryland secede. There has been a Secession Convention here on Friday and Saturday last, and Jas. A. Bayard, and Harry Courrelly have gone South together. They have 170 men, drilled by a Philadelphian twice a week, and all the best arms in the State, also two good Brass field pieces. Thos. F. Bayard is the 1st Lieutenant. We have some 40 of the old pattern U.S. Muskets altered to percussion locks, but lack ammunition of any kind. I have no doubt myself, that before this month expires we shall have to try our strength at crossed Bayonets, with these Breckinridge Traitors.[11]

Dr. A. H. Grimshaw, postmaster of Wilmington, was an ardent Republican. He wrote on April 13 that:

> Our Governor is a Secessionist, most of our Breckinridge men are the same. All the arms are in the hands of these men, who have formed companies and are drilling under a paid officer from Philad.[elphia]
> In New Castle five miles from Fort Delaware (nearly opposite), Ogle, late Sheriff, has a company and cannon. The Union men have not a single gun. . . . We have no arms, we can get no arms. I enrolled sixty odd men & drilled them for some time, but having no arms I disbanded the company.[12]

The federal government turned a deaf ear to all requests for arms; nevertheless, armed companies of soldiers had formed, and they were drilling in northern Delaware. Since these companies represented both southern and northern advocates, it appeared that a civil war might erupt in Delaware.

In southern Delaware the same thing was happening. In January, former Governor William H. Ross asked Thomas Bayard to send him arms,

> where they would be placed "in the right kind of hands," presumably Democratic. A week later two wagons of equipment were moved from Georgetown to Seaford for the use of a "secessionist company" near Ross' home.[13]

George W. Hazzard, a Captain in the United States Army, wrote to Abraham Lincoln in December, mentioning the existence of these armed groups but felt that an army detachment of 500 men could keep the area in the Union.[14] When Fort Sumter was fired upon, the Georgetown *Messenger* wrote that some of the inhabitants of Seaford "fired several guns in honor of their country's disgrace."[15]

The fear that Delaware would become the battleground of a civil war not only between the North and the South but also among its own citizens was prevalent. The Smyrna *Times* noted

> that one firm in Wilmington had sold 1,500 pistols and that militia companies, all of which were said to be sympathetic with secession, had been formed in Milford, Wilmington, Odessa, Dover, and Newark.[16]

Congressman Whiteley wrote to James A. Bayard, pointing out that the strengthening of Fort Delaware might have arisen "from the formation of our military companies."[17] The fact that Congressman Whiteley wrote to James A. Bayard referring to armed companies existing in the State as "ours" meant that they had some part in the formation of these organizations. But what is even more surprising is that the congressman would question arming a military post of the United States as being in opposition to such military companies. It seems obvious that both Whiteley and Bayard were cooperating with military companies that were going to oppose the federal government. Thomas Bayard, James's son, was a noted leader of one of these companies.

New Jersey's interest in Fort Delaware soon after the firing upon Fort Sumter further indicates that New Jersey doubted the course that Delaware might take. There is no questioning the fact that the entire state of Delaware was an armed camp and that many individuals were ready to join the Southern Confederacy. But, as in Maryland, it would depend upon the actions of the Governor and the state Legislature.

iii

The Governor of Delaware, like the Governor of Maryland, played an important role in this crisis. Governor William Burton was a Democrat from Georgetown, elected in 1858 to a four-year term. On January 1, 1861, the Governor delivered an annual message that concerned itself almost entirely with the causes of the conflict between the North and the South. After mentioning that South Carolina had seceded from the Union, he stated that

> five, and probably seven, if not more, of the Southern States will decide upon similar action during the present winter.[18]

After expressing his sorrow over this occurrence, and his hope that secession would end, he pointed out that true as the people of Delaware have been to the Union and the Constitution, which is the letter and the spirit of its existence, and clinging as they still do to their faith in the "immense value of the national union, to their collective and individual happiness," they cannot but feel conscious that the people and the Government of some of the States have either forgotten, or wilfully violate their constitutional obligations and fraternal duties toward each and every of the co-equal sovereignties that compose the United States.[19]

The reason for the secession of South Carolina, according to the Governor was

the war which an anti-slavery, fanatical sentiment has waged upon more than two thousand millions of property—a war waged for so long a time from the pulpits, from the political rostrum, by the press and in the schools—all teaching the sentiment that slavery is a crime and a sin, until it has become the received opinion of a very large portion of one section of our country.[20]

He accused the anti-slavery advocates of being aggressive and disunionist. Defending the South he said, it

. . . has just cause of complaint against the North. . . .

Governor Burton urged the North to repeal these laws and stop obstructing the enforcement of the Fugitive Slave Law. He also hoped that the South would meet the North in a spirit of compromise.[21]

The Governor included in his message a communication from the Governors of South Carolina and Louisiana and stated that the Honorable Henry Dickinson, Commissioner from Mississippi, wished to address the Legislature. Governor Burton concluded his message by recommending that a state convention be called so that the people of the state of Delaware could decide what course of action to follow.

The Governor's sentiments lay with the South and the pro-slavery element. He felt that anti-slavery advocates of the North had created the crisis and that they were the disunionists. The South was acting only in defense of its institutions. He believed that Delaware should stay in the Union as long as it could, and that secession was a decision that should be made by the people of Delaware meeting in a special convention.

Governor Hicks of Maryland wrote to Burton suggesting that the border states form a central confederacy. To this suggestion of secession Burton replied that

it is impossible for Delaware to exist as an independent Sovereignty.

He avoided answering directly. Using the reasoning that Delaware was a divided state, Burton said:

most all of our trade is with the North,

and that

a majority of our citizens, if not in all three of our Counties, at least in the two lower ones, sympathize with the South.[22]

Governor Burton once again expressed the opinion that a state convention would be called to determine Delaware's future once the Union was broken. Referring to the idea of a central confederacy, Burton wrote that

it has never been discussed to any extent in our State, and I know not the feelings of our citizens in relation thereto.[23]

Governor Burton remained silent during the rest of this period of crisis and the Legislature did not take up his suggestion for a convention. Only after the firing upon Fort Sumter did the Governor issue an additional statement. Ten days after the attack on Fort Sumter he published a proclamation to the people of Delaware and wrote a letter to Simon Cameron, Secretary of War. Cameron had requested one regiment of Delaware militia. Burton replied that the

laws of this State confer upon the Executive no authority whatever enabling him to comply with your requisition, there being no organized militia in the State nor any law authorizing such organization.[24]

He further pointed out the existence of volunteer companies but stated that it was up to each company to do what it pleased. The Proclamation concluded with the statement that,

they will, however, have the option of offering their services to the General Government, for the defence of its Capitol and the support of the Constitution and Laws of the Country. . . .[25]

Governor Burton opposed the invasion of the South or "coercion." His sympathies lay with the South and he was unwilling to help the federal government suppress the Confederacy. Although he looked toward a neutral Delaware, he did not reach this position through support of a central confederacy.

Horace Greeley pointed this out when he wrote that,

neither the Governor nor the great body of his political adherents rendered any aid or encouragement whatever to the Government down to the close of his official life, which happily terminated with the year 1862.[26]

iv

Three southern states sent representatives to the state of Delaware to determine whether it would secede or at least support the South. The first of these was David Clopton of Alabama. On January 1, in a carefully worded letter to Governor Burton, Clopton suggested that Delaware might consider secession. A bond of friendship existed between the slaveholding states, he said, and

> the withdrawal of all the slaveholding States [*sic*] and the organization of a Southern confederacy would possess a moral, political, and physical power which no government would dare to oppose.[27]

He concluded that it was up to the people of Delaware to make the decision and he requested that the two states "advise and consult together."[28] Clopton reported to Governor Andrew B. Moore of Alabama that "the sympathy of many of the citizens of Delaware" was with the South, although the Legislature was not a true voice of that sentiment since its members were not elected during this period of crisis. He felt that

> the people of Delaware are averse to a dissolution of the Union and favor a convention of the Southern States, perhaps of all the States, to adjust and compromise . . . . yet, in the event of dissolution, however accomplished, a large majority of the people of Delaware will defend the South.[29]

Clopton also stated that he thought that there would be a state convention to decide the fate of Delaware.

The second representative of the South to visit Delaware was Judge Henry Dickinson of Mississippi. He spoke to a joint session of the Legislature and reported to his Governor that

> The Governor, officers of State, and six-sevenths of the people of Delaware are cordially with Mississippi in the Southern cause. The present Legislature opposed to immediate secession. The people will demand a convention and Delaware will co-operate with Mississippi.[30]

Both Houses of the Delaware Legislature listened to Judge Henry Dickinson, Commissioner from Mississippi, who urged that Delaware join the Southern Confederacy. After hearing this gentleman, State Representative John A. Moore introduced into the House a resolution that having extended to Hon.[orable] H. Dickinson, Commissioner from the State of Mississippi, the courtesy due to him as the Representative of a Sovereign State of the Confederacy, as well as to the State he represents, we deem it proper and due to ourselves, and to the people of Delaware, to express our unqualified disapproval of the remedy for the existing difficulties, suggested by the resolutions of the Legislature of Mississippi.[31]

This resolution passed unanimously in the Delaware House of Representatives but by only a five to three vote in the Senate: One senator from Kent and two from Sussex voted against it. All three senators who opposed the resolution were slaveholders.

D. C. Campbell of Georgia was the third Commissioner from the South to visit Delaware. On February 12 he wrote to Governor Burton that while Delaware does not have

as deep an interest in the institution of slavery as the other border slave-holding States . . . .

it had certain advantages in seceding.

Those Southern border States, therefore, who are far advanced in manufacturing and mechanical skill have now tendered to them the entire South for a market and that without rival.[32]

He pointed out that a Southern Confederacy would have free trade, and the ports of Delaware would benefit from the commerce.

After meeting the Governor and prominent citizens of the State, Campbell reported to the Georgia Convention that

a large majority of the people were aggrieved at the aggressions of the Northern upon the Southern States. . . .

He said, adding

that their sympathies and interests were with the latter, and that on the withdrawal of Virginia and Maryland from the United States, Delaware would unquestionably follow them and write her destinies with the Confederate States of the South.

He felt that the Legislature did not represent a true voice of the majority of the people. Campbell concluded that Delaware

will not consent to unite her destinies with a Northern confederacy. . . .[33]

All of these southern representatives were optimistic in their belief that Delaware would join the South. They expressed the opinion that the

Delaware Legislature did not represent the views of the majority of Delawareans and that a state convention would be called. They were convinced either by the Governor or the secessionists that there would be a state convention. Obviously they were convinced by people with a southern bias that the State would secede. They found a large pro-southern segment of the Delaware community. While this may or may not have been a majority of the people of the State, sufficient secessionist sentiment nevertheless existed to convince these gentlemen that it was supported by a majority of Delawareans.

Edward Ridgely, Delaware's Secretary of State, wrote to Mrs. Charles I. duPont in late April 1861 that he was opposed to

> any policy that might tend, either directly or indirectly, to coerce the seceded States. I believe that such a step would forever destroy the possibility of a re-union. . . .[34]

He went on to deny the right of secession but felt that there was a right of revolution. This is another example of a member of the government of Delaware who endorsed peaceful secession.

On February 15 the Delaware House of Representatives adopted a strongly worded Unionist set of resolutions in answer to the request of the state of Georgia that Delaware join the Southern Confederacy. These resolutions allowed a state no right of secession. While they recognized the right of revolution, they expressed the opinion that no conditions existed to justify such an act. Alexander Johnson, State Senator from Kent County, wrote Thomas F. Bayard that

> the Joint Resolutions introduced in the Senate following the address of the Georgian was adopted; but not without strenuous opposition by the party of the three brothers, [the Saulsburys] . . . . the same power introduced and passed in the House yesterday other resolutions as a substitute, which when sent here will I think be turned to good account. . . .[35]

Bayard and his supporters did not wish to have the Delaware Legislature deny the right of secession.

A second set of resolutions rejecting Georgia's invitation to join the Southern Confederacy were passed in the Delaware Senate on February 26. They were an amended version of those passed in the House. In fact, only the preamble remained of the House version. The resolutions called for a convention of all the states to adopt amendments to settle the slavery controversy. They did not reject the right of secession as the House version had. Three senators from New Castle and one from Sussex County opposed the resolutions.

Senator John Green of Kent County introduced a series of resolutions that required the Governor of Delaware to write the governors of the border and Middle Atlantic states inviting them to send delegates to a convention in Philadelphia held for the purpose of creating a central confederacy. In the preamble, he stated that he hoped that this

> convention of delegates from such States would adopt a Constitution and form a Union which would not only command the respect of the world, but ultimately, if not at an early day, induce all the other members of the confederacy, North and South, to unite with us therein and be perpetual.[36]

The resolutions, defeated on March 8, were never introduced into the Delaware House of Representatives.

The Crittenden amendments received strong support from the Delaware Legislature. The preamble to a set of resolutions approving of them read:

> in our opinion, [they will] remove the cause that produces the danger of dissolution of the Union. . . .[37]

On January 16, the Delaware House of Representatives adopted a series of resolutions approving the Crittenden amendments, opposed only by one representative from Wilmington and one from Sussex. The next day these resolutions passed the Senate with one negative vote from New Castle County.

Opposition to the Unionist resolutions or to resolutions that opposed the South usually came from the representatives of the two southern counties. Never sufficient to defeat a pro-Union resolution, it was strong enough to threaten the passage of the anti-Mississippi resolution in the Senate. The letter of Alexander Johnson indicates that local Delaware political disputes played a prominent role in the votes of the Legislature.

As one of the northernmost slaveholding states with an economy tied to the North, the state of Delaware found itself in a difficult position. It could secede only if the states of Maryland and Virginia did so first, and then only with the assurance that there would be no war. If Delaware had seceded without waiting for Maryland and Virginia, it would have been geographically separated from the rest of the seceded states and face the danger of being easily overrun by the federal government. A strong feeling of peace permeated the thinking of the Legislature when it rejected offers to join the South and when it supported the Washington Peace Conference and the Crittenden amendments.

v

While the Delaware Legislature was taking a position unfavorable to secession, Delaware's representatives in the United States Congress took a favorable one. Delaware had one member in the House of Representatives and, of course, two United States Senators. Congressman William G. Whiteley served until March of 1861, not having been a candidate for reelection in 1860. Born in Newark, Delaware, he was graduated from Princeton College, and he practiced law in Wilmington. He had been elected to the House of Representatives as a Democrat in 1856 and 1858.

Congressman Whiteley served on the Committee of Thirty-Three and signed a minority report of that Committee. This minority report was signed by five congressmen, all from either southern or border states. Whiteley and these congressmen advocated peaceful secession. They believed that

> . . . the doctrine of the indissolubility of the general government has no foundation in the public law of the world. . . .[38]

Also

> . . . that no power was conferred upon the general government, by the Constitution . . . .[39]

to keep a state in the Union. They became specific when they stated that

> you cannot coerce fifteen sovereign States. . . . That a separation, which has become inevitable, shall be bloodless.[40]

Whiteley signed a statement advocating the secession of all slaveholding states, including Delaware. Specifically, it proposed that there should be no war, but peaceful separation.

Succinctly, they stated their position:

> Whether any State has or has not the right to secede under the Constitution, it is a fact that four States have already seceded; and that in a few short months—perhaps weeks—all of the other slaveholding States will have in like manner seceded, with the purpose of maintaining their new position, by force of arms, if no adjustment is made of the differences between them and the nonslaveholding States.[41]

After expressing support for the Crittenden compromise amendments, they used the rest of the minority report to establish procedures for the peaceful separation of the Union into two sections. With little hope for a reconciliation, they strongly advocated a peaceful separation of the Union, or peaceable secession.

After the firing upon Fort Sumter, William G. Whiteley held to his previous position. On June 27 at a mass meeting in Dover he stated:

> In God's name let them go unmolested. . . . Would Delaware give money or men to hold States as conquered Provinces? . . . Could the South be subjected? Never![42]

Congressman Whiteley's voting record showed a consistency in voting for compromise with the South.

George P. Fisher succeeded William G. Whiteley in the United States House of Representatives. He was elected in 1860 as the People's party candidate. Born in Milford, in Sussex County, he had served as Secretary of State of Delaware and, later, as private secretary to President Millard Fillmore. His views on secession were not made public during the crisis.

Willard Saulsbury was elected to the United States Senate in 1858. He was born in Kent County and practiced law in Georgetown, Sussex County. As a Democrat he represented the viewpoint of southern Delaware in that party. He delivered his most famous speech during the crisis on December 5, stating

> that my State having been the first to adopt the Constitution, will be the last to do any act or countenance any act calculated to lead to the separation of the States of this glorious Union.[43]

He pointed out that

> when that Union shall be destroyed by the madness and folly of other, (if, unfortunately, it shall be so destroyed,) it will be time enough then for Delaware and her Representatives to say what will be her course.[44]

Most historians have taken this as a statement advocating the preservation of the Union; however, he was actually saying that Delaware would wait for the other states and then decide whether to secede. Saulsbury advocated the adoption of the Crittenden amendments and predicted that

> if those propositions are rejected by this Senate, peace will have fled the land. . . .[45]

A letter he sent to a meeting held in Wilmington in December clearly presented Willard Saulsbury's true position:

> Delaware should not enter into any confederacy in which either S[outh] C[arolina] or New England States are parties, unless all the states shall have again be reunited, into one confederacy . . . let Delaware preserve her separate and independent position until the conservative central states—slaveholding and nonslaveholding—shall unite in a new republic

whatever may be the fate of the extremes, let the great centre be composed and secure.[46]

His advocacy of a central confederacy removes all the ambiguity from his previous statements. He stood for keeping Delaware in the Union until secession was a fact. Then he wanted Delaware to join the other border states in a central confederacy. Thus he opposed coercion of the Southern Confederacy, but at the same time he did not want to join it. His voting record in the Senate was consistent—he voted with the South. However, he did not vote on the issue of compromise.

The other United States Senator from Delaware, James A. Bayard, had been elected to the Senate in 1851 as a Democrat. He was born in Wilmington where he practiced law. Bayard was a leader in the Democratic party in Delaware, especially in northern Delaware. For some time a feud between him and the Saulsburys had existed within the Democratic party.

James A. Bayard supported the secession of the state of Delaware and felt it should join the South. He was neither open nor candid about his views, which he, for the most part, confined to the letters he wrote his son, Thomas F. Bayard. As early as December 4, 1860, he wrote:

I have no hope left for the Union, and all we can do now is to separate peaceably if possible.[47]

He realized the weakness of his state and due

to our feebleness politically we ought . . . to wait the progress of events which we can neither control or retard in the slightest degree.[48]

In a letter to James Riddle of Wilmington, he stated his opposition to coercion.

Also opposing the idea of a central confederacy, Senator Bayard said:

I think Saulsbury's declaration as to both South Carolina and New England silly and arrogant, and it will tell against him, as it will offend both the Republicans and find no favor with the Democrats. His great Central Republic is stuff and the least practicable of all divisions which can take place in the country. . . .[49]

Bayard urged the state Legislature to call a convention of the people of Delaware to act in this period of crisis. This was to be the ploy through which the State could leave the Union. Delaware, he felt, was tied to Maryland, and he was afraid of the Governor of Maryland because he

is thwarting the sentiment of a majority of her people and placing her in a false position.[50]

"We must go with Maryland," he said,

and Maryland must go with Virginia and as to Virginia there is no doubt all this will be apparent within a month. . . .[51]

Although Bayard supported the Crittenden amendments he felt that they were too late. During the early months of 1861 he wrote about introducing a series of resolutions, but after consultation with the southern leaders kept postponing their introduction.

I have postponed my speech for a few days (and the Resolution I intend to offer), at the request of the Commissioners from the new Republic. . . .[52]

Clearly, he was working with the Southern Confederacy.

For three days in March (20–22) Bayard delivered a lengthy speech saying that he would introduce a series of resolutions which would include:

Resolved by the Senate of the United States, That the President, with the advice and consent of the Senate, has full power and authority to accept the declaration of the seceding States, that they constitute hereafter an alien people, and to negotiate and conclude a treaty with "the confederate States of America," acknowledging their independence as a separate nation. . . .[53]

He never introduced this resolution. Bayard stated that the right of secession was a right of revolution. He used the terminology of the Declaration of Independence, *i.e.,* that the people of a state had the ultimate sovereignty. Bayard opposed the use of force to maintain the Union. His answer was that the right of secession, while revolutionary, was nevertheless a right of the states. The President and Senate should recognize it and thus avoid war.

According to Judah Benjamin, a leader in the Southern Confederacy, both James Bayard and he had read one of the more famous books of the period, John B. Jones's *Story of Disunion.*[54] This book predicted warfare in the border states, especially in New Jersey. It may have been one of the factors that Bayard considered when he described war in such fearful terms.

James A. Bayard did not think in terms of Delaware's acting alone, but always in terms of Virginia's secession, followed by Maryland's and then Delaware's. Even after the firing upon Fort Sumter, he continued to hope that Maryland and Delaware would secede.

We must, of course, wait the action of Virginia for unless she and Maryland go South, we are tied hand and foot—it would therefore be better to await the action of these States before calling our Legislature as it can be readily assembled. . . .[55]

This meant, of course, that when Maryland failed to secede, Delaware remained with the North.

At the same time Bayard hoped that the Governor of Delaware would ignore Lincoln's call for troops. Just prior to the firing upon Fort Sumter and immediately after, Bayard traveled in the South. His letters urged that Delaware not tie itself to the North but go with the South. On his return to the North he was mobbed in Philadelphia. Later, in a letter explaining his actions, he continued to urge peaceful separation. His voting record in the Senate was with the South.

Thomas F. Bayard, son of James A. Bayard, voiced sentiments similar to his father's. He had joined a military company in January 1861 and, during the crisis, wrote his father regularly.

Those who attended the Washington Peace Conference made up another group of prominent Delawareans who considered the question of secession.

As soon as Virginia's Legislature issued a call for a Peace Conference, the Delaware Legislature appointed five persons as representatives. The five delegates were: David M. Bates, Wilmington; William Carson, Bridgeville; John W. Houston, Milford; Henry Ridgeley, Dover; and George B. Rodney, New Castle. Only one of Delaware's delegates spoke to the Conference, John W. Houston of Milford, Sussex County. He pointed out to the assembled group that slavery as an institution in Delaware was disappearing and that

> it is not unlikely that she may soon favor the abolition of slavery within her limits. Her progress has been in that direction. When the present Constitution was adopted, Delaware had fifteen thousand slaves. Now she has not more than eighteen hundred.[56]

In its report to the Legislature, the five commissioners said that after having first supported the Crittenden amendments and finding that they would not be accepted, they agreed to the majority propositions. They felt that "the preservation of the Union"[57] was vital to the State. Delaware took a relatively inactive role in the Peace Convention.

vi

The duPont family was of immense importance in the State. Papers exist for four duPonts of the period, showing all of them to be supporters of the Union. Henry A. duPont was a cadet at the United States Military Academy at West Point. He felt that the South had definite grievances and that the North was being unfair to the South. Having advocated a peace policy until the firing upon Fort Sumter, he wrote Captain Samuel F. DuPont that

the outrages on the Union members of the Virginia convention and the anarchy which now reigns in Maryland have completely disgusted me, and have changed in toto my views on the questions of the day in which I now entirely concur with you. . . .[58]

His father, General Henry duPont, had voted for John Bell in the election of 1860 and supported the Union. He refused to sell powder to the South after they fired on Fort Sumter.[59] Evelina Bidermann, daughter of Eleuthere Irenee duPont, wrote to Henry A. duPont:

the Union party are very strong here but they are not so cunning as the others. . . .[60]

Her letters show the existence of an active secessionist group within northern Delaware, which she feared. She referred to Thomas Bayard as a secessionist as well as to a hotel keeper by the name of Almond. Both men were reputed to be raising regiments: Bayard in Wilmington, and Almond in New Castle.

Samuel F. DuPont, an ardent Unionist, wrote on February 4, 1861:

I stick by the flag and the National government as Congress have one, whether my state does or not and well they know it.[61]

In January he had written to Henry Winter Davis, a leader of the Unionists in Maryland, that he supported the Crittenden amendments and urged Davis to push the Republicans for their adoption. He also pointed out, two months later, that he opposed not only slavery but also the abolitionists. He was fearful that

if the Governor of Maryland gives way I would not be surprised that Delaware would play the fool too. . . .[62]

But by March Samuel F. DuPont felt that

there is no alternative left but to acknowledge and recognize the Southern confederacy and establish barrier custom houses.[63]

He admitted in a letter to William Whetten that with the recognition of the Southern Confederacy the border states would also secede. DuPont blamed the Breckinridge Democrats, who "are almost to a man rank Secessionists."[64] But by the middle of April, before the firing upon Fort

Sumter, Samuel F. DuPont wrote that he hoped war would begin, then

> that will stop the shilly shallying, unite the North if it be not so already. . . .[65]

E. I. DuPont de Nemours & Company, makers of gunpowder, suffered from seizures by the southern states and the Confederate government. The DuPont Company, as the family, remained true to the Union and refused to send powder and fuse to the southern states.[66]

vii

The secession movement found not only private support throughout the State but also support from the press. In 1860 Delaware had only ten weekly newspapers, according to the United States Census of that year. Copies of five survive. Four supported secession. The *Delaware Gazette* of Wilmington was a Democratic newspaper advocating the peaceful secession of the southern states. On March 23, 1861, the newspaper supported Senator Bayard's position, urging recognition of the Southern Confederacy as the best method of preserving the peace. After the firing upon Fort Sumter, the newspaper supported the Union.

The Smyrna *Times* was the second secessionist newspaper. In 1860, it supported no presidential candidate and advocated that the South go in peace.

> The seceding states might be persuaded but not forced either to yield the fort [Sumter] or return it to the Union. . . . War would not bring the South back into the Union but destroy both sections.[67]

The Dover *Delawarean* supported Breckinridge in the election of 1860. It was edited by Eli and Gove Saulsbury, brothers of Willard. On January 12, it stated that:

> the people of Delaware is [*sic*] almost unanimously in opposition to secession, yet the idea of coercion meets with but little favor. . . . it will be better for the welfare of the country that the general government shall not interfere with the action of the seceding States, but give them an opportunity to try their experiment outside the protection of the Union.[68]

The editors suggested that the Union might be reunited after a short period of time.

The following month the *Delawarean* went even farther in its support of the South, openly threatening the Lincoln administration if it attempted coercion:

Against such a policy we protest. As an American citizen we protest against the inauguration of a policy which is to result in the dread calamities attendant upon internecine strife. War, under any circumstances, is to be regretted; but fraternal strife is the sadest, [sic] most abhorrent form of war. Better let the cotton States secede, better let the public property now in their possession remain there, than involve this country in endless conflict. If, however, the administration of Mr. Lincoln should be shaped by the councils of madness, and civil war should result, then we apprehend that he and his advisers will have cause to tremble for themselves. He that draweth the sword sometimes perishes by the sword, and Mr. Lincoln might possibly find that truth verified in his own end. Let him beware. "Caesar had his Brutus."[69]

The *Delaware Republican* had supported Lincoln in the election of 1860 and believed that the best method of redress for the South lay within the Union. This newspaper advocated that:

Our State has nothing to gain, but much to lose, as indeed has every State, by secession. In the Union there is safety—out of it, war.[70]

Using the economic argument it expressed the idea that:

In establishing a Southern Confederacy we can have no guaranty of peace, slaves would escape by hundreds, and land would depreciate to one half, if not three fourths its present value, without estimating the cost of life and treason.[71]

The *Delaware Republican,* accused of supporting a war against the South to bring it back into the Union, denied the charge by asserting that it merely supported the government.

We do not advocate a crusade against the revolting States, we do not desire that war be made on them, but we do wish the revenues may be collected quietly, the postal service may be discontinued, if interfered with, hoping and believing that the people will, on reflection, become convinced that their true interest is in the Union, and the reaction in public feeling will drive from power and place the men who have brought the present troubles on our country. We have at no time advocated war or bloodshed, on the contrary we deprecate it, but we have merely desired to see the forts of the country put in a position that they will forbid rather than from sheer weakness of the garrison invite an attack.[72]

Such a position, if adopted by the federal government, would have permitted the South to remain independent. Therefore, even the *Delaware Republican,* which supported the Lincoln administration, would permit a form of peaceful secession.

The Georgetown *Messenger* was the only true Unionist newspaper in Delaware. It stated that

> it would be far better that every secessionist was hung, than this Government should be overthrown and its free institutions destroyed.[73]

No issues of this newspaper exist for the election of 1860.

Since so few newspapers of this period have survived, it is difficult to make any generalization except that the secession movement among the newspapers was common throughout the State and not limited to the southern part.

viii

With the firing upon Fort Sumter by the Confederate Army, most Delawareans were forced to make a decision on the question of supporting the Union. Those who would join the South went South or prepared to leave. Exact totals are impossible to estimate. Not all of those who remained, however, were loyal supporters of the war against the South.

On April 16, soon after the firing upon Fort Sumter, there was a Union meeting in Wilmington, where a series of resolutions were passed condemning any attempt to take Delaware out of the Union. The *Delaware Gazette,* which had previously advocated peaceful secession, now supported the war. A week later, Secretary of War Simon Cameron, taking no chances, provided the Mayor of Wilmington with arms for the defense of the city.

> I have furnished four hundred muskets to the mayor of Wilmington, eighty of which have been used to arm DuPont's workmen, embodied for the defense of the mills, and the residue appropriated to the organized volunteers of the city, whose loyalty is vouched for by the mayor.[74]

The Unionists raised a regiment and sent it to Washington. This was a volunteer unit, which Governor Burton had said could do as they pleased. They were not an official military unit of the State.

Southern Delaware was the strongest area of secession. There were numerous reports of pro-southern demonstrations on the part of individuals and groups. Alexander B. Cooper, later Speaker of the Delaware Senate, gave one example:

> Most of the leading boys and young men of the town were democrats [*sic*] and in full sympathy with the south, whose sovereign rights were being destroyed and taken away from it. . . . Perhaps two of the strongest and most out-spoken, "Jeff Davis," democrats as the republicans of the town called us: were William L. Lord, late[r] Governor

and Chief Justice of Oregon, and Napoleon B. Knight. They were then both students at Law in the office of George P. Fisher in Dover. . . .[75]

On June 27, 1861, at a Dover mass meeting attended by 1,500 to 1,600 people from all over the State, resolutions were passed that

advocated allowing the seceding States to peacefully withdraw from the Union, if it be necessary to do so to avoid war.[76]

The meeting called upon the federal government to end the war and recognize the independence of the Confederate States. This reaffirmed the strength of the secession movement in southern Delaware. Although this meeting occurred two months after the firing upon Fort Sumter, the secession movement was still strong. It was a time when the idea of peaceful secession was at its lowest ebb in the North.

Thomas F. Bayard expressed the view that:

the discontented States should be allowed to withdraw rather than run the awful risk of such a war.[77]

He opposed the war but like his father, James A. Bayard, remained in the North during the war.

The fear of war haunted the entire border region—a ubiquitous fear that specific towns would be the sites of devastation not only from organized armies but also by undisciplined guerrilla bands. The *Delawarean,* soon after the firing upon Fort Sumter, urged that the towns of Delaware establish vigilance committees. The press felt that it would be up to the local communities to defend themselves.

Hence it may not be amiss for the inhabitants of every village in the State to form associations for the protection of themselves against such lawless bands of marauders as may deem this an opportunity for lawlessness and plunder. We hope our State may not be visited by any such bands. But it certainly can do no harm for our citizens to be prepared to protect their homes and firesides from any descent of freebooters or marauders.[78]

The Smyrna *Times* spelled out the division and uncertainty within the state of Delaware after the firing upon Fort Sumter:

The secession feeling is produced by Southern pride—not from any interest or advantage that can be derived from it. We have always been classed with the South from the fact that slavery is one of our institutions. Hence this Southern sympathy. The proclamation of President Lincoln for raising seventy thousand volunteers to go to Washington, greatly increased the secession feeling throughout the State. Previous to that time they were very few in number.

. . . . A considerable portion of the State is thoroughly Northern in its convictions. They would prefer to be annexed to Pennsylvania, rather than become a member of the Southern Confederacy, and such has been suggested, we believe, by some of the Wilmington papers. . . .

On the other hand, almost the entire interest of Delaware is with the North. Nearly every article of merchandise is from the North. All the trade, both of imports and exports, is carried on with Northern cities. . . .

The people, therefore, incline to the Union still—that is, a majority of them. This matter of interest is acknowledged and felt by all. From all parts of the State we hear expressions of devotion to the Union.[79]

Since the secession movement was widespread throughout the State, it is difficult to give geographic distinction to the secession movement in Delaware. However, the southern two counties were generally more secessionist especially in the Legislature where the southern counties' representatives supported pro-southern resolutions. But secessionist military groups were training in the northern and southern sections of the State.

ix

On the whole, Democratic party leaders favored one form of secession or another. Senator Bayard and his son, along with the Saulsburys of southern Delaware, advocated secession, but they disagreed on the method of achieving it. Substantial Breckinridge support within the State in the election of 1860, while not a majority, showed powerful backing for secession among the rank-and-file Democrats. The fact that Congressman Whiteley signed the Minority Report of the Committee of Thirty-Three, with the southern Representatives, revealed his strong southern ties. These ties were also evident in the desires of people of Delaware not to war with the South. Governor Burton tried to keep his state neutral, but the force of events prevented neutrality. Even after the firing upon Fort Sumter, however, a strong peace movement prevailed in Delaware.

Why then did the secession movement fail? One major reason was fear that the State would become a battlefield in any war between the North and the South. The secessionists of Delaware opposed any attempt by the federal government to coerce the South. Some hoped that, with the creation of two nations, Delaware would eventually secede and join the South; others preferred a central confederacy, and still others simply wanted to prevent war by permitting the southern states to leave the Union in peace. However, as in Maryland, once the war began, military realities became the prime factor in the failure of the secession movement. Many people felt that once war began and Delaware tried to remain neutral or to join the South, it would be invaded by the Union Army. Slaveholders feared that their slaves would flee, and that they would never be able to retrieve them. Merchants and businessmen did not want to sacrifice their northern business. Delaware wished no more than Maryland to become the northern-most state in a southern confederacy.

Strong economic and cultural ties with the North that offset traditional southern ties were a second factor in the failure of the secession movement.

As in Maryland, Delaware had not managed to stimulate any organized effort toward secession—secessionist sentiment was widespread but amorphous. The secessionists were unable to decide whether they preferred to join the South or to form a central confederacy or to remain neutral. The Legislature refused to take the steps necessary for secession. It called no convention that would have permitted the people to decide whether they wanted to leave the Union. Governor William Burton, while supporting the South, was ineffective as a leader. He failed to make any statement for or against secession after his Annual Address in January. He urged, however, that a convention be called to decide whether the State should remain in the Union but he was unable to obtain legislative approval. With no vehicle to withdraw legally, the secessionists had to depend upon the use of military companies. But such military force as they could muster could not achieve their aim because it was insufficient in the face of the Union Army.

The secessionists hoped that Virginia and Maryland would secede from the Union so that they could either lead Delaware into the Southern Con-federacy or form a central confederacy. When Virginia waited until after the firing upon Fort Sumter, it became impossible for Maryland to secede or to remain neutral. Delaware was then left in the position of having either to act alone or to remain in the Union. If Delaware had seceded, she would have been cut off from the South as well as the neutral states of Kentucky and Missouri. Delaware had simply waited on events, which favored the Unionists. Moreover, when Virginia seceded so late, it made it impossible to set up machinery for secession, such as elections and conventions.

The Union Army waited until it was ready and then moved into Dela-ware and crushed the secessionist militia units. In some ways the fact that the United States government accepted the volunteer units instead of requiring Governor Burton to produce military units showed Abraham Lincoln's willingness to compromise for the moment. But when the time came, he effectively forced the state of Delaware to support the Union cause against the wishes of many of its residents.

4
NEW JERSEY

i

NEW JERSEY SHOULD BE CONSIDERED A BORDER STATE DURING THE secession crisis. Geographically, southern New Jersey is located across the Delaware River from Delaware. Cape May is on approximately the same latitude as Washington, D.C.—more than 60 miles south of the Mason-Dixon line. New Jersey had numerous economic ties with the South. Newark, one of the leading industrial cities of the nation, was practically a

> Southern workshop. For about two-thirds of a century the shoemakers of Newark shod the South, its planters and its plantation hands, to a large extent. For generations the bulk of the carriage, saddlery, harness and clothing manufactured in Newark found a ready and profitable market south of Mason Dixon's line.[1]

Two of Newark's leading manufacturers, William Wright and Nehemiah Perry, were also leading Democratic politicians. Wright manufactured harness and saddlery, which "attained a commanding position in the southern trade."[2]

During the presidential campaign of 1860, Henry W. Hilliard of Alabama said that "Newark was well known and respected in Alabama."[3] The other leading cities of New Jersey also carried on a profitable trade with the South.

The resort towns along the New Jersey coast, especially Cape May, were centers of recreation for people from the South. Many southern families sent their sons to the College of New Jersey.

Over the years, the people within New Jersey had developd many family ties with the South, and several leading Confederates were born

98

in New Jersey. Among them were Henry Ellet, who was offered but declined the position of Postmaster General of the Confederacy; Samuel Cooper, Adjutant and Inspector General of the Confederate Army; and two other generals were born in New Jersey. The exact number of Jerseymen who joined the Confederacy is impossible to determine.

The census statistics of 1860 indicate that 6,068 Southern-born New Jersey inhabitants had moved to New Jersey. This was about one percent of the State's total population. Even more significant was the movement of Jerseymen to the South. Of the 16 southern states, New Jersey supplied more inhabitants in seven than any of the three major midwestern states (Illinois, Indiana, and Ohio). Though these midwestern states contributed a larger percentage of their populations to the border and southern states, New Jersey spread its emigrants throughout the entire South. There was, indeed, a definite north–south movement between New Jersey and the South.

These economic and social ties clearly mark New Jersey as a border state. Its attitude towards slavery and its political position during the secession crisis confirm this status. There were only eighteen slaves in New Jersey in 1860, but they were not freed until the passage of the Thirteenth Amendment. Slavery was defended within the State, and slaves had considerably swelled the agricultural labor force during the late eighteenth and early nineteenth centuries. Slaves were introduced into New Jersey as early as 1630, and

it is said that ten years later nearly all the inhabitants of northern New Jersey owned slaves.[4]

During the reign of Queen Anne (1702–1714), a special system of trials and punishments was established for slaves. In 1790, New Jersey had a total of 11,423 slaves. By 1800 the total number of slaves had risen to 12,422, an 8.74 percent increase over 1790. New Jersey's slave total from that point onward decreased steadily.

The Quakers, who were numerous in south Jersey, denied the right of membership to slaveholders in 1776. An Abolitionist Society was formed in New Jersey in 1786 and by 1804 had succeeded in passing a law requiring gradual abolition.[5] In 1818 it became a misdemeanor to take a slave out of the State provided that his residence was changed by such an act. In 1846 an act was passed providing that all slave children born after this time would

become and be an apprentice, bound to service to his or her present owner, and his or her executors or administrators, which service shall continue until such person is discharged therefrom. . . .[6]

This act seems to rescind the act of 1804 since it does not give the child the right to demand freedom on his twenty-first or twenty-fifth birthday. The institution of slavery was glossed over with the name of "apprenticeship," and since the United States Census did not count apprentices, there is no way of knowing how many people were in this condition of servitude.

The Colonization Society was strong in New Jersey.

> New Jersey men were among the original sponsors of this effort. The branch of the society in this State included among its membership individuals outstanding in position and prestige.[7]

The slaves were located in the northern part of the State, especially in the rural areas. By 1850 New Jersey still possessed 236 slaves: 75 in Monmouth County, 41 in Bergen County, 31 in Passaic County, 31 in Somerset County, 19 in Morris County, 11 in Middlesex County; 9 in Hunterdon County, 6 in Mercer County, 6 in Essex County, 3 in Hudson County, 2 in Warren County, and 1 each in Atlantic and Sussex Counties. The counties possessing the largest number of slaves were the same counties that had continued to possess the largest number of slaves since 1790. By 1860 half the slaves were living in Somerset County. The tendency for slaves to be concentrated in the northern part of the State was not new. In 1811 it was observed

> that in the whole southern part of the state (Burlington then reaching to the ocean), there were only 319 [slaves], being only about one-seventh of the number in the county of Bergen alone, and about one-thirty-fourth part of the whole slave population.[8]

This was undoubtedly due to the large anti-slavery Quaker population in the southern part of the State.

Slavery had its defenders within New Jersey. One leading advocate of the institution was Samuel Blanchard How, who in 1856, while living in New Brunswick, wrote a pamphlet entitled "Slaveholding Not Sinful." It was an address to the General Synod of the Reformed Protestant Dutch Church of North America.

E. B. Bryan of Charleston, South Carolina, writing in DeBow's *Industrial Resources* of 1853, stated that New Jersey agriculture had not been improved to the extent that it should,

> evincing either a want of enterprise on the part of proprietors, or a fault in the system of labor; the latter cause is, perhaps that which may most reasonably be assigned, for no one can doubt the energy and enterprise of the people of New Jersey. This is a good instance of the unprofitableness and misapplication of slave labor in the northern states.[9]

Both How and Bryan were for increasing the number of slaves in the State.

New Jersey's Democratic congressmen supported pro-slavery measures during the 1850s.[10] Camden's James Scovel, leader of the Douglas Democrat faction of the party, pointed out that

> New Jersey became pro-slavery in sentiment, or, at least, the dominant party was for slavery rather than for the Union.
> It sent Senators to Congress who defended the institution. It sent members to the lower House who worshipped at the shrine of Jefferson Davis—then as now, the leading spirit of Southern Aggression.[11]

This pro-slavery attitude would only become too obvious in the election of 1860.

ii

The Republican party in New Jersey in 1860 was still named the "Opposition party." At the Chicago convention the New Jersey delegation played a leading role in the nomination of Abraham Lincoln.

The Democratic party met in convention in Charleston, South Carolina, and split on the issue of the extension of slavery into the territories. Two of New Jersey's seven votes were cast in favor of the southern position on the question of the extension of slavery; the rest of the delegation supported popular sovereignty. Robert Toombs of Georgia, who later became Secretary of State in the Confederacy and a General in the Confederate Army, wrote to Alexander H. Stephens, who later became Vice President of the Confederacy, on May 7, 1860:

> Pennsylvania was really for the platform of the So[uthern] States. So was New Jersey, but [William] Wright violated his instructions. I am sick of the very contemplation of such a lot of rogues as those Northern delegates proved themselves to be, and I now see that the contest is to be transferred to the South, which is the greatest calamity that could befall us.[12]

This letter shows the extent of the feeling on the part of at least one leading southern politician that the South had expected to receive support from the Middle Atlantic states.

No New Jersey delegate attended the convention held by the seceders from the Democratic Convention. Moreover, when this convention moved to Richmond, no one from New Jersey was present. At the Baltimore convention of the Democratic party New Jersey had a full delegation, but only two votes were cast for Douglas. The rest of the delegates did not vote.

The Constitutional Union party, at their national convention, nominated John Bell. Since the New Jersey Constitutional Union party knew that they were weak, they were eager to join a fusion ticket of the parties opposed to Lincoln. Only in late October was a successful fusion set of electors completed and placed on the ballot. However, the Douglas Democrats failed to fulfill their promise to join such a ticket and refused to withdraw their own set of electors.

The Republicans were able to elect four of their seven electors, receiving about 58,300 votes. The fusion ticket elected three electors with over 62,000 votes. These electors had run on both the Douglas and fusion slate. The other four fusion electors, forced to run against both the Republicans and the Douglas electors, therefore lost. The election results gave three electoral votes to Douglas and four to Lincoln. If the Douglas Democrats had withdrawn their set of electors, obviously all the fusion electors would have been elected by 3,400 votes to 6,900 votes, and Lincoln would have received no electoral votes from New Jersey.

Since the Breckinridge electors did not run separately, it is impossible to determine the strength of the Breckinridge supporters. But the difference between the fusion and the Douglas vote reveals the numerous Breckinridge and Bell supporters within the State.

The election also proved that in New Jersey more people opposed than supported Lincoln. Lincoln was able to carry only Atlantic, Burlington, Cape May, Cumberland, Gloucester, Mercer, Morris, Ocean, Passaic, and Salem Counties. With the exception of Morris and Passaic Counties, all of the counties are located in either the central or southern part of the State. New Jersey voters favored a protective tariff, and the Republican party platform had a strong tariff plank. But the Republican party made its best showing outside the cities. It failed to win a majority of either the urban or rural areas. In Jersey City and Hoboken, Lincoln received only 42 percent of the vote; in Newark, he received 46 percent, and in rural New Jersey he received 49 percent of the vote.[13] Clearly, the support for the Republican party lay elsewhere than in the protective tariff. The traditional anti-slavery support in southern New Jersey seemed to play a more important role in the election than the protective tariff.

In the congressional races the Democratic party won three of the five seats. The Republican party sustained its greatest loss in the congressional district that included Newark and Jersey City. There, William Pennington, the Speaker of the United States House of Representatives, was defeated by Nehemiah Perry, who had business connections with the South. The Republicans claimed election fraud and said that employers had threatened their workers with dismissal if a Republican won, but these

charges were never substantiated. The two Republican congressmen
elected were from the southern part of New Jersey.

The elections to the New Jersey Legislature, which centered on local
issues, were a different matter. The Republicans elected 28 assemblymen
while the Democrats elected 26. The six other assemblymen were members
of the Know Nothing or American party. In the New Jersey Senate race
both the Republicans and Democrats elected four senators. This gave the
Republicans the advantage of twelve senators to the Democrats' nine.

iii

Soon after South Carolina seceded from the Union there was an attempt
to join New Jersey to the proposed Confederate States of America. A
letter appeared in the Newark *Evening Journal,* signed by the letters
"X.Y.Z." The same letter appeared later in the New Brunswick *Times.*
Since these newspapers favored the secession of the state, this letter was a
"trial balloon" to test the sentiments of the people of New Jersey. The
author stated that there were but three possibilities for New Jersey,

> one to join a Northern Confederacy; another to join the Southern
> States; the third, to stand alone as an independent State.[14]

In the author's opinion, the latter two would be the only choices possible.
He remarked that

> New Jersey men would doubtless settle this matter in a few hours
> peaceably, by a delegate convention, and afterward by a direct vote
> of the people.[15]

After discussing the disadvantages of joining a Northern Confederacy,
"X.Y.Z." stated the economic arguments for joining the Southern Confederacy. He said that New Jersey would become the manufacturing
center for the South. Perth Amboy, which had once been a leading port,
by this time had fallen into disuse. He argued that it

> would be the rival of Philadelphia and the equal of any port in the
> Southern States in commercial business.[16]

He did not think New Jersey would ever possess large numbers of slaves
again, but that it would "be a barrier to the system of negro stealing,"[17]
which he felt was being practiced by some elements of the northern population. He also pointed out that grain produced in New Jersey could be

sold in a southern confederacy. He concluded that there should be a peaceable dissolution of the Union. The people of New Jersey will

> at the ballot-box decide that we will form no union with the Northern fanatics at the expense of our sense of moral right, and at the cost of our dearly earned position of happiness and prosperity.[18]

The author "X.Y.Z." put forth economic reasons for New Jersey's joining the Confederate States and presented the idea that New Jersey, as a border state, had a brighter future with the South. An article in the New York *Tribune* confirmed his point of view about Perth Amboy. It stated that the

> town of Perth Amboy is infested by a knot of Secessionists, who, not content with talking treason, have at length begun to outrage loyal citizens.[19]

While the "X.Y.Z." article was the only one to express the hope that New Jersey would join the Confederacy, certain men supported this position. One was former Governor Rodman M. Price. He vacillated between joining the South and creating a central confederacy, hoping that the states of New York and Pennsylvania would also secede and join New Jersey to form this central confederacy. These states, according to Price, would eventually join the southern states.

On January 26, 1861, Rodman Price, in writing that he could not accept the invitation to address a mass meeting at the Cooper Institute in New York City, stated that he supported the compromise efforts of Senators Crittenden and Bigler. Price felt that the

> Union is broken, our noble government is rent asunder that I have very little hope that absolute permanent and eternal dissolution can be prevented. . . .[20]

He therefore addressed himself to the question of which section the people of New York and New Jersey should join. "The abolitionists of the east," he said,

> have been aggressive . . . . the South [is] acting defensively. . . . May I assure them that the National Men of New York will if they have to march go East, rather than South, to hunt down the inciters of revolution and ready to be as unanimously give what is due [*sic*]. The people of New York City like those of New Jersey, have never recognized any section of their country, have never distinguished locality among American Citizens, they have only known "their country, their whole Country. . . ."[21]

In the spring of 1861, Price wrote L. W. Burnett of Newark that he believed that the Union was permanently dissolved and that all the slave states would join the Confederacy. He made his position clear when he wrote:

> What position for New Jersey will best accord with her interests, honor, and the patriotic instincts of her people? *I say emphatically she would go with the South* from every wise, prudential, and patriotic reason.[22]

He also wrote Burnett that New York and Pennsylvania would join the South. His letter appeared in the Trenton *Daily True American* on April 9, 1861. If the South seceded, he reasoned, the commerce and manufacturing of New Jersey would be ruined. Eventually this would lead to the ruin of the agricultural segment of the population. To join the South, however, would continue the State's prosperity.

Price advocated that no immediate steps be taken, but that if the Union were dissolved—which he felt probable—New Jersey must be free to decide. He even considered the possibility that New Jersey might take an independent position as a separate nation. Price's sympathies lay with the South, and he hoped that New Jersey and the other Middle Atlantic states would join the Southern Confederacy. But before New Jersey acted he wanted the Union broken. By any definition of the word, Price was a secessionist, but one who was afraid to act too openly.

The Newark *Daily Advertiser,* on April 10, 1861, quoted the New York correspondent of the Philadelphia *Inquirer* as follows:

> The letter recently written by ex-Governor Price is a straw which shows how the tide is setting among the Democratic politicians of his stamp. General E. R. V. Wright, of Bergen, is likewise as busy as a bee. He has undertaken to get up a mass meeting, in Jersey City, next week, not only to endorse "the South," but to declare that in case the Border States swing off with Jeff Davis's Confederacy, New Jersey will follow their example. . . .

Edwin Ruthven Vincent Wright, the unsuccessful candidate for Governor on the Democratic ticket in 1859, had supported President James Buchanan's policy in Kansas. Whether or not Wright was a secessionist is questionable because on April 15, 1861, soon after the firing on Fort Sumter, he wrote the Trenton *Daily True American.*

> I am not a secessionist, but on the contrary am for the constitution, justice to every State, and as firm and loyal as any living man in my attachment to the federal Union.

However, the tide of events was swinging toward the Union. Wright had taken five days to reply to the Philadelphia *Inquirer* article. It appears that he was now trying to join the winning side.

iv

The Democratic party in New Jersey contained men like Rodman Price and William C. Alexander who believed the South had the right to secede. But most of its members favored a position that would permit the South to leave in peace. Joel Parker, who was to become the Governor of New Jersey during the latter part of the war, was an

opponent of coercion of the South until the War came when he supported the Government.[23]

Men who later became leading "Copperheads," like James W. Wall, who was elected to Congress during the Civil War, favored peaceable secession. C. Chauncey Burr, another "Copperhead," also wanted the federal government to permit the southern states to leave the Union.

So widespread was this feeling within the Democratic party that Charles Perrin Smith, a leader of the "Opposition party" and Clerk of the New Jersey Supreme Court, wrote in his diary:

In New Jersey it was declared that no troops should be raised, or, if raised, they would not be permitted to leave the State. They insisted that New Jersey's interest required that she should link her fortunes with the South; and the full force and discipline of the Democratic party was brought to bear in that direction. An Ex-Democratic Governor, advocated this course in a formally published letter, and many other prominent men were scarcely less bold in their utterances. . . .[24]

Governor Olden was elected and became "the War Governor of New Jersey." Had he failed, there can be but little doubt that New Jersey would have been forced temporarily, at least, to have "cast her lot with the South in the great Rebellion which soon followed."[25]

The Democratic party did not collectively express itself on the question of secession. The party met in convention in Trenton on December 11, 1860, to present its viewpoint. The convention represented all factions of the Democratic party. It passed a series of resolutions in favor of compromise, blaming the North for creating a situation that led the South to secede from the Union. But, these resolutions mentioned neither secession nor coercion.

v

Three major groups existed within the Republican party in New Jersey. The first supported Abraham Lincoln's position that there should be no compromise with the South, but they were relatively few. The second group consisted of the leaders of the Republican party, Governor Charles S. Olden and William L. Dayton, who ran for Vice President of the United States with John C. Fremont in 1856. They favored a policy of compromise with the South. Dayton, in writing to John P. Kennedy of Maryland, referred to his pamphlet, *The Border States*. Dayton wrote Kennedy that while he did not endorse his views, Kennedy had presented his case very well. Dayton felt that once the Union was divided it could never be reunited. In his letter to Kennedy, Dayton strongly favored compromise with the South.

A third group of Republicans opposed the use of force to retain the South in the Union. Joseph P. Bradley, who was later to become a Justice on the United States Supreme Court, argued that

> if the border slave States do join the Southern confederacy, coercion is out of the question. We are then a broken and divided empire. Our glory and our greatness are extinct.[26]

The Republican party was as divided on the question of the use of force as it was on the question of compromise. The extent to which the Republicans supported the position taken by Bradley is difficult to ascertain; however, some Republican newspapers called upon the federal government to let the South go in peace.

Governor Charles S. Olden had been elected in 1859 on the Opposition party ticket. Olden was a Quaker and a conservative Republican. He had voted for Millard Fillmore of the American or Know Nothing party in the presidential election of 1856 and had supported neither the Republican nor the Democratic tickets. When elected he promised to enforce the fugitive slave law. He opposed the extension of slavery into the territories, and favored a policy of compromise with the South.

In his annual address of 1861, Olden stated that, as far as secession was concerned:

> We do not consent to such a proposition, nor for a moment recognize the right—the principle of which, if carried out, would lead to anarchy.[27]

At the same time he urged the repeal of the personal liberty laws and pleaded for a peaceable settlement of the question of secession:

The people of the State, beyond all question, stand as a unit in favor of the Union, and are prepared to defend it, and to make all reasonable and proper concessions to insure its perpetuity. . . .

Unwilling to abandon the cause, and clinging to the hope that the Committees of Congress appointed for that purpose will agree on measures of compromise, we anxiously await the result. If it should appear that their views cannot be harmonized, then I earnestly recommend that (unless some more approved plan is proposed,) without delay adopt a resolution inviting all the states to appoint delegates, in such manner as can be most speedily and satisfactorily done, who shall meet and endeavor to agree upon terms by which our Union may be saved. We cannot believe it possible that such a convention would fail to agree on terms acceptable to a majority in all sections of the country, and these terms could then be presented to Congress as the united wish of the people of the States.[28]

While Governor Olden cannot be considered a secessionist, he failed to advocate the use of force to hold the states in the Union. He wanted some type of compromise. He failed to propose an alternative if this were not possible. Of all the Republican governors, he appears to have taken the most conciliatory position towards the South. Yet when the Union was attacked at Fort Sumter, he became its staunch defender.

The Republicans controlled the New Jersey Senate, whereas the Democrats had a majority in the Assembly. On January 24, a "Joint Resolutions in relation to the Union of the States," passed the Senate by a vote of 11–6. All the Democrats voted for it while six Republicans voted against it. The Assembly approved it the following day by a vote of 31–11. The bill was signed on January 29, 1861. These resolutions took the position that while the nation was a single unit and should be defended, there should also be some type of compromise with the South. They approved the Crittenden amendments and urged the New Jersey congressional representatives to support them. They called for a convention to propose compromise amendments to the United States Constitution. The resolutions advocated the repeal of all personal liberty laws and appointed nine men to meet with the other states in a Peace Conference to be held in Washington. One resolution summed up the spirit of the resolutions:

That however undoubted may be the right of the General Government to maintain its authority and enforce its laws over all parts of the country, it is equally certain that forbearance and compromise are indispensable at this crisis to the perpetuity of the Union; and that it is the dictate of reason, wisdom, and patriotism, peacefully to adjust whatever differences exist between the different sections of our country.[29]

The Republican party both within and without the State officially opposed compromise with the South. Yet these resolutions passed the New

Jersey Legislature and were signed by a Republican governor. This can be explained by the fact that in the Assembly 24 Republicans did not vote. If they had cast negative votes, they would have defeated the resolutions. The Republicans attempted to rationalize their position and accused the Democrats of passing resolutions that did not represent the sentiments of the people of New Jersey. The people of New Jersey were earnest in their desire for peace, even if it meant compromise and the extension of slavery. Governor Olden had expressed the same sentiments in his Annual Address and was therefore, willing to sign the resolutions.

This was the only major set of resolutions passed by the New Jersey Legislature during the secession crisis that concerned itself directly with the question of secession or coercion. Other measures bearing on this issue were passed in early May soon after Fort Sumter. A resolution was introduced into the New Jersey Assembly that authorized monies

for the purposes of war, to repel invasion and suppress insurrection. . . .[30]

This resolution, advocating the defense of the State against invasion and suppression of rebellion, was approved by the Assembly, but seven assemblymen voted against it. The Senate also approved it, but four senators opposed its passage. These assemblymen and senators who voted against this resolution were mainly from areas which had had a large slave population, and had not supported Lincoln. Clearly, these legislators were opposed to a war with the South. Other measures introduced in both houses of the Legislature would have raised taxes rather than bonds and reduced the number of rifles available to the militia. The same legislators who had opposed the appropriations for the war voted against tax-exempt bonds. All of these measures were aimed at making the war more expensive for the individual or reducing the fighting capacity of the New Jersey militia.

Those legislators who took this anti-war stand hoped that by making the war unpalatable the citizens of New Jersey would permit the South to go in peace. The Legislature had supported compromise with the South, and some legislators never relinquished this hope, even after the war began. The most ambitious attempt at compromise was the Washington Peace Conference.

The Conference began on February 4, 1861, where New Jersey was represented by an influential group of delegates, including its Governor.

Of all the Northern states, New Jersey probably welcomed Virginia's invitation most enthusiastically. The conservative Republican Governor, Charles S. Olden, promised that the Garden State would make all reasonable and proper concessions to save the Union, ...[31]

New Jersey favored compromise and placed much hope in this Conference.

One of the delegates from New Jersey, Commodore Robert F. Stockton, who had served in the United States Senate from 1851–53 and was active in the American Party, was

> strongly anti-coercion, and was an admirer of the culture and institutions of the South. . . .[32]

On February 19, he said,

> Do you talk here about regiments for invasion, for coercion—you, gentlemen of the North? You know better; I know better. For every regiment raised there for coercion, there will be another raised for resistance to coercion. If no other State will raise them, remember New Jersey.[33]

This is a harsh statement as it declares war on the government if it should attempt to force the states to stay in the Union. He went on to call for a peaceful settlement of the dispute:

> I have shown that if peace be not secured, the uprising of the South would be a revolution, and cannot be treated as mere insurrection. The bravado, therefore, of offering armies to the Government, can only have the effect, at this crisis, of preventing a peaceful adjustment. Against all such demonstrations we must fix our faces like flint. Peace we must have. The Union can only be preserved by peace.[34]

The following day Frederick T. Frelinghuysen, a Republican who was to become Attorney General of the State during the war and later a United States Senator, called for compromise:

> You, gentlemen of the South, have asked that the arrangement may be extended to territory hereafter to be acquired. New Jersey has voted in this Convention against interference with slavery in the territory, present or future, and she is the only Northern State that has cast her vote in favor of your demand.[35]

The rest of the New Jersey delegation did not speak at the Convention. But New Jersey voted for every provision presented in the compromise. The radicals of the North now looked for some excuse and someone to blame for their defeat at the Washington Peace Conference.

> Vindictive partisans looked about for someone to blame. "The great mistake," Goodrich [Governor John Z. Goodrich, of Massachusetts] wailed, "is in Gov. Curtin and Gov. Dennison sending so many conservatives."[36]

It is interesting that Governor Goodrich blamed the Republican Governors of Pennsylvania and Ohio and not New Jersey's Republican Governor or its delegation.

vi

The New Jersey delegation to the United States Congress, like its delegation to the Peace Conference, failed to say much during this period of crisis. Democratic Senator John R. Thomson served on the special committee of five senators who considered the Crittenden compromise. He voted with Senators John J. Crittenden and William Bigler to accept the Peace Conference compromise. In presenting the resolutions adopted by the New Jersey Legislature approving the Crittenden compromise, he said,

> if the right of coercion was as clear as a sunbeam in the Constitution, in our present circumstances it be worse than madness to enforce it. But it is not clear and undisputed.[37]

Thomson then went on to say that states should be permitted to leave in peace.

> Let us win our erring sisters back to our embraces by kindness, by justice, by good feeling, and by good deeds; but to attempt to force them by arms, and by blows and bloodshed, is as wicked as it is impossible. If we cannot preserve them in the Union without force, in the name of our common ancestors, in the name of humanity, in the name of liberty, which would be crushed out in the attempt, in the name of high Heaven, let them go in peace. Time and returning reason in the North and in the South may reunite us in a stronger bond than has ever yet bound us together. And if this should never happen, we may still hope by leagues and treaties, offensive and defensive, to compel the respect of the world, and insure a degree of prosperity, if not as great as under our present Union, still such as is enjoyed by no other nation under Heaven.[38]

While Senator Thomson supported the idea that the southern states should be permitted to go in peace, his votes in the Senate were not pro-southern. He supported every attempt at compromise but voted for the naval appropriation bills.

Republican Senator John C. Ten Eyck opposed the Crittenden amendments and other attempts at compromise. He delivered no major address during this period and voted primarily with the North. He supported the Republican position and was willing to see a war with the South, which he considered self-defense.

New Jersey was represented by five congressmen. Jetur R. Riggs, a Democrat, split his vote on the major issues, voting four times with the

South and five with the North. He also supported every attempt at compromise.

Garnett B. Adrain was an anti-Lecompton Democrat who broke with his party on the issue of secession. He supported compromise measures with the South and the doctrine of popular sovereignty, and he wanted the personal liberty laws repealed. Congressman Adrain was the most active congressman from New Jersey. On December 17, he introduced a series of resolutions that upheld the Constitution as the supreme law of the land and called upon the states to repeal any statutes in violation thereof. On January 7, he introduced a controversial resolution which praised Major Anderson for his withdrawal from Fort Moultrie to Fort Sumter and supported the President in all constitutional measures to enforce the laws and preserve the Union.

In a speech before the House of Representatives delivered on January 15, 1861, Congressman Adrain not only spoke out against joining the South, but also against peaceable secession.

> It is secession—peaceable secession, as it is called—but in fact, rebellion. Now this idea of a State going out of the Union just when she pleases, . . . and without any cause at all, is so contrary to all just notions of the character of our form of government, that it cannot and must not be tolerated. . . . This whole theory of a peaceable secession is utterly fallacious, and was never dreamed of by the men who formed the Federal Constitution and established our form of government.[39]

He defined coercion from a Republican point of view.

> If by coercion is meant a declaration of war against her, then I am not for that; but if it means the faithful execution of the laws of the Federal Government, then I am for their execution.[40]

Adrain wanted the laws to be enforced, he said,

> the laws of the land must be sustained and enforced. . . . The faithful observance of the Constitution and execution of the laws is no war. It is no just cause for a war, although a war might result from it. . . .
> The faithful execution of the laws is not only necessary for the protection of the rights and property of the Government; but for the very existence of the Government itself.[41]

Adrain took the standard position of the Republican party that the enforcement of the laws even if it meant war was not coercion.

There were three Republican congressmen. William Pennington was the Speaker of the House of Representatives, and while he did not vote on the questions presented to the House of Representatives he nevertheless supported the compromise put forth by the Committee of Thirty-Three.

John L. N. Stratton served on the Committee of Thirty-Three and signed the majority report of that Committee. On the major votes taken during this crisis Stratton voted with the North. John T. Nixon, the third Republican representative, supported the compromise measures and voted with the North. None of these representatives delivered a major address on the question of secession. Only Congressman Riggs could in any way be called a supporter of the South; the Republican congressmen and Adrain supported the North.

vii

There were seventy weekly newspapers in existence in New Jersey in 1860 according to the United States Census of 1860. Twenty-three, or 32.9 percent of these newspapers, will be referred to and their positions on secession discussed.

Two newspapers advocated that New Jersey unite with the South. These were the Newark *Journal* and the New Brunswick *Times*.

Three newspapers wanted New Jersey to secede from the Union and join the other border states to form a central confederacy. One of the earliest newspapers to accept the idea of a central confederacy was the Monmouth *Democrat*. This was a Democratic newspaper that had originally endorsed Stephen A. Douglas but later supported the fusion ticket. On December 27, 1860, the Monmouth *Democrat* printed an editorial in which it favored a central confederacy as it was "better than to risk the results of a civil war." This same editorial was printed in the Hunterdon *Democrat* of January 2, 1861. As an introduction, Hunterdon's editor wrote:

Peaceful Secession—We agree with the following views taken from the Monmouth *Democrat,* in regard to Peaceful Secession.

This editorial stated:

We are in favor of peaceful dissolution, and opposed to all measures of coercion. If the Union cannot be preserved without shedding the blood of our brethren, it cannot be preserved at all.

It further argued that if the southern states withdrew their Congressional representation there would be no quorum, and a convention would have to be called to amend the Constitution. This convention would result in the formation of a central confederacy, for the middle states would never agree to a union with New England. The middle states would be the dominant power, standing between the fanatics of the South and North and compelling them to keep peace with each other. Such an adjustment would be far better than risking a civil war.

Both of these papers had originally supported Douglas. After the firing upon Fort Sumter, the Monmouth *Democrat* supported the government while the Hunterdon *Democrat* continued to support the South. Hunterdon's editor wrote:

> Those rights New Jersey has never denied to the South; her citizens have always been treated upon an exact equality with our own; and the question may yet have to be decided whether New Jersey will consent to remain divided by the arbitrary lines of black Republicanism, or adopt a Constitution which as sacredly regards the rights of others as it protects her own.[42]

The New Brunswick *Times,* in its editorial of March 14, 1861, also supported the idea of a central confederacy. The editor argued that the Southern Confederacy was "a fixed fact," and that the Union was divided. A central confederacy would save the Union by creating a third force around which the country could reunite. The New Brunswick *Times,* which had supported John C. Breckinridge in the election of 1860, now placed the blame for the secession movement on the Lincoln administration. It has

> forced upon all the conclusion that, sooner or later, the Border states will either unite with the Cotton States, or with the other States, and form a third or Central Confederacy.[43]

The states which might join such a confederacy were Virginia, Delaware, Maryland, North Carolina, Tennessee, Kentucky and Missouri.

> If New Jersey, Pennsylvania, part of New York, Illinois, Indiana, and a portion of Ohio would unite with it, it would be formidable in its character. . . .[44]

The editor stated the possibility of New Jersey's joining such a Confederacy:

> So far as our own State is concerned, we have no doubt she would at once take position with the conservative men of the Border States. New Jersey has no feeling in common with the ultraists of the South, who have been laboring for years to destroy the Union, and she has no sympathy with the ultraists of the North East, who are abolitionists at heart, and whose fanatical notions lead them to imagine that they are "doing God service," in carrying out doctrines which they know will dissolve the Union. We are "Middle Men" in this fight, and if the opportunity is presented, our masses will give unmistakable evidence of

this fact. . . . They cannot choose between these extremists, and, if called upon, they will repudiate both. . . .[45]

This editorial underscores the frustration of those persons who supported the idea of a central confederacy. They supported neither side and they wanted to prevent a war. This led them to a position permitting secession. However, those who advocated a central confederacy for New Jersey failed to contact people in other states who also supported the idea of a third nation.

Secessionist newspapers, for the most part, wanted to let the South go in peace. The newspapers that had either supported New Jersey's joining the South or a central confederacy were also anti-coercive. Once their positions became impractical, they hoped that the South would be permitted to leave the Union without a civil war. In addition to these were the newspapers which had originally supported the idea that the South not be forced to remain in the Union.

One of the earliest newspapers to present this idea was the Newark *Daily Advertiser,* which had supported Abraham Lincoln. On December 6, 1860, it printed an editorial entitled, "Let her Depart in Peace." While denying that a state had the right to secede from the Union, it took the pragmatic position that it was better for everyone to avoid a civil war.

> A state may possess no right of separation, and yet it may be wise and prudent for the confederacy, still remaining after such a disruption, to say to her "go in peace, in God's name, and trouble us no more, we wish you well."

The editorial further stated that, if conquered, a state would no longer be a state but a conquered territory. The United States, it continued, need not have the power to compel a state to remain against its will because,

> the Union was cemented by voluntary suffrage, and though meant to be permanent, cannot by genius of our policy be maintained by force. . . .

The Newark *Daily Advertiser* changed its opinion as the southern states seceded and as the Republican party adopted the view that it opposed any secession, peaceful or not. On April 8, 1861, just before the firing upon Fort Sumter, it printed an editorial opposing New Jersey's joining either the South or a central confederacy.

The Trenton *Daily True American,* which had endorsed Stephen A. Douglas, reported:

> An opinion seems to prevail with some people that it would be both right and possible to coerce the seceding States into adhesion to the Union; but it seems to us that the thing is easier said than done.[46]

This newspaper continued to attack the idea of coercion.

> If any State, by the voice of a majority of her people desire to separate her fortunes from those of the rest of the confederation, let her go by all means.[47]

This view persisted after the firing upon Fort Sumter.

> If the policy of coercion is persisted in, if the force of arms is to be still substituted for the force of reason, in less than sixty days the entire continent will be in a blaze of battle, the horrors of war will extend from the Lakes to the Gulf, from the Atlantic to the Pacific. . . .[48]

Considered disloyal, the *Daily True American* was barred from the mails in August of 1861.

The Monmouth *Democrat* of January 17, 1861, joined the other newspapers and argued that the South should be permitted to go in peace. It reprinted editorials from the *True American* advocating noncoercion of the South. Originally, this paper had supported the central confederacy.

The Paterson *Daily Register,* which had backed Douglas in the election of 1860, justified the right of secession on February 11 in an editorial:

> A peaceable division of the public property and an amicable separation, with treaty arrangements, which will prove mutually advantageous. We most heartily hope that such may be the case. If a nation like ours must be divided, for the sake of humanity and right let us not add the brutalizing horrors of war to an evil the magnitude of which is already sufficient to overwhelm us with dismay and consternation.[49]

The Sussex County *New Jersey Herald* supported John C. Breckinridge in the election of 1860 and advocated that the South be permitted to leave in peace.

> The only alternative presented therefore is peace or war. . . . the Southern people . . . [are] merely intent upon a quiet separation of their personal interest from our own. . . . To make war upon our Southern neighbors, who have been compelled to this act in consequence of Northern aggression, . . . is at variance with every principle of humanity, and will find but few advocates.[50]

The Mount Holly *Herald,* which had supported Douglas, argued that if force were used, Northern men would support the South:

> Myriads of Northern men would spring forth armed, not to battle their Southern relations and friends, but to strike down on a Northern soil that miscreant spirit willing to draw a blade or fire a gun in fraternal strife.[51]

The solution that the editor offered was that those states which wanted to do so should be permitted to withdraw in peace.

Two other south Jersey newspapers opposed the use of force: the Bridgeton *Pioneer* and the Camden *Democrat*. They felt that if New Jersey joined the Confederacy, it would become the battleground of any war between the North and the South. But,

> . . . New Jersey might find it very disadvantageous to join a Southern Confederacy, unless New York and Pennsylvania should accompany her.[52]

The fear that New Jersey would become a scarred state also dominated those who advocated the central confederacy.

The last newspaper in the State to advocate peaceable secession was the Jersey City *American Standard,* which had supported John Bell in the election.

Eight Republican newspapers denied the right of secession and felt that the Union should be maintained by force. They wanted laws enforced even with coercion, if necessary. Two additional newspapers supported the Union, the Cape May *Ocean Wave* and the Hackettstown *Gazette,* though not enough issues remain to determine their reasoning.

The oddest example of secession among the newspapers occurred in the case of the Toms River *Ocean Emblem,* which had supported Abraham Lincoln in 1860. Violently pro-Republican, it advocated that Ocean County secede if New Jersey or the United States compromised on the question of slavery.

> If the amendment to the Constitution proposed by the Border States' Senators and Representatives should be adopted we propose to the people of Ocean County that they meet in Convention at the Court House, in this village, and immediately adopt such measures as may be necessary to secede from the Union. . . . In short we have all the elements of independence. There is no reason why we should not become a great and a happy people. Let us secede.[53]

This editor, while demonstrating that he was a staunch Republican, accepted the idea that a county could secede from the Union.

When one analyzes these newspapers according to the candidates they supported in the election of 1860, the Democratic newspapers, especially those who supported Breckinridge, favored secession. Of the three Breckinridge newspapers, two wanted New Jersey to join the South and the third favored letting the South go in peace. Of the six newspapers that supported Stephen A. Douglas, two supported the central confederacy, one leaned toward that position (Camden *Democrat*), and the other three favored peaceable secession. No Democratic newspaper in New Jersey supported the use of force to hold the South in the Union. The one newspaper that supported John Bell opposed using coercion. Of the ten Republican newspapers, eight urged that force be used to hold the states in the Union. Only one favored letting the South go in peace—the Newark *Daily Advertiser,* which later changed its position. The exception to the rule among Republican newspapers was the *Ocean Emblem.* Three newspapers that supported the Union cannot be politically classified. In no other state of the Middle Atlantic region was there such a clear cut political division among its newspapers on the question of secession.

The geographical factor was an important one among the reasons that New Jersey newspapers wanted to secede. Secessionist activity took place mainly in the northern portion of the State where the institution of slavery was strong and where there were economic ties with the South. A second reason for newspaper support of secession was economic. Manufacturers feared losing the business of plantation owners or southern businesses. They also felt they would lose payment for past deliveries.

The Paterson *Daily Register,* a newspaper from a manufacturing area said, on February 11, 1861,

> if coercive counsels prevail among the advisors of the President elect, nothing can save our commercial manufacturing and business interests from the total ruin which must necessarily follow a bloody fratricidal war.

Paterson was the largest center for the manufacture of railroad locomotives in the United States.

Newark, the primary industrial city in New Jersey, was the location of two secessionist newspapers. The Newark *Advertiser* was the only Republican newspaper in the State to support peaceable secession. The Newark *Daily Journal* was the strongest secessionist newspaper in the State. Economic concerns were undoubtedly the major reason that these Newark newspapers wanted the South to be permitted to leave in peace.

Trenton, the state capital and a leading industrial center, had its secessionist newspaper, *The True American.* Specific cases of economic loss motivated secessionist sentiment. In Freehold, Monmouth County, which had a small slave population, the *Ocean Emblem,* a pro-Union newspaper, commented,

> Freehold "has already felt, and pretty seriously too, the effects of the unholy agitation of the slavery question. The Freehold Institute has already had from ten to fifteen students from the South, sons of wealthy planters; and having extravagant habits they spent annually large sums of money here." These young prodigals have all left for the sunny

south, and the village of Freehold, thus sacked, now mourns the loss! . . . . the greater loss of the large profits which the merchants and tradesmen were making out of their prodigality.[54]

A third reason for secession emerged with the hope that war could be averted by the peaceful secession of the southern states. This thinking prevailed especially in New Jersey where residents feared that the State would become the battleground for such a war as it had during the Revolutionary War. This was one of the motivating factors for forming a central confederacy. Fear of war was evident at the outbreak of the war. Governor Olden and the State authorities expected

> trouble in the southern counties, especially in Cape May, because of the close social and economic relations between that area and the South.[55]

Governor Olden put to use the telegraph line to Cape May and, at the same time, requested troops for Fort Delaware in the Delaware River near Salem. These actions emphasized the government's fear of an invasion of New Jersey.

viii

This fear also expressed itself in a book written by John Beauchamp Jones, the author of *A Rebel War Clerk's Diary*. In 1857 he began to edit a weekly, *The Southern Monitor,* a newspaper devoted to the interests of the South, which he published in Philadelphia. After the firing upon Fort Sumter he left Burlington, New Jersey, where he had been living and moved to Montgomery, Alabama, to serve in the Confederate Government as a war clerk. John B. Jones fled from New Jersey in 1861 because he feared for his life;

> for I well know that the first gun fired at Fort Sumter will be the signal for an outburst of ungovernable fury, and I should be seized and thrown into prison.[56]

After the war he returned to Burlington where he died in 1866.

Originally entitled *Border War: A Tale of Disunion,* published in 1859, Jones's fictional account that predicted warfare in New Jersey as a result of a civil war later appeared under the titles, *Wild Southern Scenes: A Tale of Disunion! And Border War!* and *Secession, Coercion, and Civil War: The Story of 1861.*

The novel depicted many episodes of battles and pillagings after the war broke out and spread into New Jersey. He presented a climate of anarchy and terror.

Predatory bands crossed the borders from both sides, and maintained a guerrilla warfare for plunder. In the North, strangers and sojourners, natives of the South, as well as citizens suspected or known to sympathize with the pro-slavery party, were subjected to many cruelties and sacrifices. Nor was it the guilty alone that comprised the victims. Advantage was taken of the prevailing exasperation by profligate, revengeful, and grasping wretches, to consummate the ruin of the rich, the exalted, and the purest members of society, who had unconsciously incurred their envy or hatred. The gutters ran with blood, and the waysides were strewn with the dead. Banks were pillaged, daring burglaries and remorseless assassinations were of frequent occurrence, and the vault of heaven was every night illuminated with the glare of conflagrations.[57]

According to Jones, when the war erupted Delaware and Maryland went with the South, leaving the Mason and Dixon Line the dividing point between the North and the South. He described Philadelphia at the outbreak of the war as a center of civil war:

Hundreds of free negroes, who had but a few hours before participated freely in the demoniacal saturnalia, were now lying dead and gory in the gutters, while the survivors of that miserable race were flying for refuge into the forests of New Jersey.[58]

The fear of runaway slaves prevailed before and during the war in New Jersey. This fear became vocal in the statements of those who supported the central confederacy or any form of secession. The central confederacy was created, in part, to prevent the possibility of great numbers of ex-slaves fleeing into New Jersey. Jones took satisfaction in predicting that the southerners would wreak vengeance against the Negroes and the Quakers, especially in south Jersey.

Jones and those who supported the South felt that many northerners, especially Democrats, would support the Confederacy. He has one of his characters attribute the strength of the southern sympathy to the fact that

. . . New Jersey, which runs down beyond the Southern border, always have sympathized with the slave States, and always will. Philadelphia is jealous of New York and New Jersey is fed by Southern travel.[59]

Once again the economic and pro-slavery feeling motivated support of the South in New Jersey.

While written as a work of fiction, its numerous publications would appear to have had a tremendous impact, especially since Jones was the well-known writer of a popular novel, *Wild Western Scenes*. This was Jones's subtle attempt to convince the people of New Jersey that a war against the South would mean their own ruin. Also, once such a war began, he predicted, numerous Jerseymen would fight for the South. Although he was wrong, he must have influenced many people during the secession crisis, especially those who supported peaceable secession. Peace was their answer to anarchy and terror; peace through joining the South, a central confederacy, or a peaceable secession of the South.

ix

Events that occurred in New Jersey following the firing upon Fort Sumter proved John B. Jones's thesis incorrect. The Confederate action created a wave of enthusiasm for the Union that had not existed before. Many persons who had supported the idea of compromise and opposed coercion now advocated that the Union be defended.

Charles Perrin Smith, a leading Republican and Clerk of the New Jersey Supreme Court, clearly showed the difference in attitude when he said:

In New Jersey it was declared that no troops should be raised, or, if raised, they would not be permitted to leave the State. They insisted that New Jersey's interest required that she should link her fortunes with the South. . . . Then followed the firing upon Sumpter [*sic*].[60]

According to Smith this was the turning point in many people's feeling about the war:

Thousands of people gathered in the streets—mournfully discussing the imperfect items and conjecturing as to the result. Suddenly there flashed over the wires, [the words] "The Flag is down, and the Fort in flames!" Then burst forth the long-pent patriotic enthusiasm! The cities suddenly became resplendent with flags! Then women and children vied in displaying National Colors, in badges, rosettes, and in every possible manner. Crowds paraded the streets, with drums and shouts, visiting the residence of supposed disloyalists and demanding that the [*sic*] "show their Colors."[61]

Certain newspapers reflected a considerable change of opinion as did many people at the news of the events that had occurred at Fort Sumter. Many newspapers that had once supported some form of secession reversed their positions and supported the Union, advocating that the nation should be defended.

An example of the typical newspaper reaction was the *New Jersey Herald*'s. The paper had supported Breckinridge in the election of 1860 and had advocated that the South be permitted to leave in peace. This paper after Fort Sumter printed:

Whatever previous justification there may be supposed to exist for maintaining a warlike attitude by the Confederate States towards the Government, this act has at once forfeited their claim to public sympathy or commiseration. These proceedings, so repelant [sic] and at war with every feeling of humanity, leaves [sic] but one course to be pursued by all true National men, and that is to sustain the flag of the Union.[62]

The two leading cities of New Jersey, Newark and Trenton, held large meetings of their residents to show their support for the government. These meetings were even endorsed by the leading businessmen. The Common Council of Newark voted unanimously to support the federal government and passed resolutions calling on the people to support the government and give up politics.

Robert F. Stockton, who had taken such a pro-southern position at the Washington Peace Conference, now supported the federal government and offered his services to Governor Olden. He wrote:

This is no time to palter about past differences of opinion, or to criticize the administration of public affairs. We are in the of an awful danger. [sic] We feel throes of political convulsion, which threaten to bring down to ruins the noblest fabric of Government ever constructed for the purposes of civilization and humanity.

Every citizen should feel that any sacrifice which he is called upon to make in such a crisis is as nothing. I am ready to do all I can to maintain our own rights and to preserve peace.[63]

However, the entire population of the State was not so enthusiastic for a war with the South. Certain newspapers remained opposed to coercing the South to stay in the Union, even after Fort Sumter. Both the New Brunswick *Times* and the Trenton *Daily True American* supported the government but blamed the war upon the Republican party. They called for a halt to the war and the arrival at a peaceful settlement.

The Paterson *Daily True Register* stated:

The contest, which has been forced upon us by the Administration will prove to be fruitless; and because it can terminate in no beneficial results, it is the more to be deplored. A very few days will now suffice to determine what will be the future course of the Republicans. They have provoked the fight, we shall now see whether they have the nerve to maintain it. The coercive policy, for which they prayed, is now inaugurated. Let them pursue it to the end.

It is most emphatically their fight.[64]

After war broke out, certain individuals, like John B. Jones, left New Jersey and joined the South. Their exact number cannot be determined.

Others remained in the North and refused to support the war. This was a time of decision in which each person had to determine his own position. During the patriotic furor following the firing upon Fort Sumter, most people supported the government. Mobs, as in the other Middle Atlantic states, forced known supporters of the position that the South should be permitted to go in peace to hoist the American flag.

x

During this period of crisis the secession movement in the State had to be dealt with as a powerful force. New Jersey was not only a border state but also a state with considerable economic and social ties with the South. Slavery existed in New Jersey, and its effects could not be underestimated as there was a geographic relationship between the secession movement and slavery. Neither is it coincidence that the area engaged in profitable southern trade also supported the secession movement. These economic and traditional factors made the cities and the Democratic party the two areas of greatest secession activity. But some Republicans in New Jersey also wanted the South to go in peace. Some members of the New Jersey Legislature, especially from the northern section of the State, supported measures either to make the war unpopular or to make New Jersey's part in such a war ineffective.

An unfortunate aspect of any discussion of New Jersey's role in the secession crisis is the lack of private papers containing views of the specific persons who are cited in this study. Newspapers are the sole source of the extent of the secession movement. These newspapers document the Democratic party's unanimous desire for some form of secession. Further, they reveal that the supporters of secession centered primarily in the cities and in northern New Jersey.

The secession movement's division into three forms weakened the movement. The reasons for the movement's failure in New Jersey were that its supporters could not unite behind a single form of secession nor could they establish any kind of an organization. No one attempted to call a convention of those persons who supported secession to mobilize their force effectively. The newspapers, while sharing editorials, failed to unite on a single position. But it is obvious from the numerous newspapers endorsing secession that a large number of persons supported it.

The most important single group of secessionists were those who wanted to see the South go in peace. But New Jersey, more than any of the other five Middle Atlantic states, supported the central confederacy. Those supporters of a central confederacy, however, did not contact individuals in the other states who also favored such a nation. Fear that New Jersey would become a battleground for a war between the North and the South motivated the thinking of persons who supported both of these movements.

The secession movement failed in New Jersey because of lack of leadership and the fact that individuals opposed to secession controlled the governor's office and the Legislature. A wave of pro-Union sentiment swept away the secession movement once Fort Sumter was attacked.

5
PENNSYLVANIA

i

DURING THE SECESSION CRISIS OF 1860–61, PENNSYLVANIA, A LARGE AND diversified state, was a leading manufacturing region which was still predominantly agricultural. With a cash value in farms three and a half times that of the capital invested in manufacturing, its two leading manufacturing items were iron and textiles. The iron mining, an important industry, was widespread throughout the State.

Pennsylvania was also known for its chemical, leather, heavy machinery and hardware products. Philadelphia, which possessed 46 percent of the State's manufacturing, was a center for sugar refining and hardware.[1] Pittsburgh was known as the "toolmaker of the West."[2] Western Pennsylvania was a large producer of salt. This economic diversification meant that Pennsylvanians would react in different ways to the secession crisis.

The population of Pennsylvania was also diversified. Approximately 11 percent was foreign-born white; this element was centered primarily in the cities of Philadelphia, Pittsburgh and Erie. The foreign born could also be found in large numbers in the coal mining regions. Two percent of Pennsylvania's population was free Negro. In 1860, there were no slaves in Pennsylvania. Twenty percent of the population lived in the county of Philadelphia; 6 percent, in Allegheny County. Lancaster County, the third largest county, accommodated 4 percent of the State's population. These three counties, therefore, contained 30 percent of the population of the State. The free Negroes were located primarily in the two major cities and in the counties bordering on Maryland as well as in the counties surrounding the city of Philadelphia.

Slavery as an institution in Pennsylvania was old, having begun even before William Penn arrived. In 1780 the State forbade the importation

125

of slaves, and from that point on the slave population declined. The act of 1780 established the principle of gradual emancipation so that,

> thereafter no child born in Pennsylvania should be a slave; but that such children . . . should be servants until they were twenty-eight years of age. . . . It abolished the old discriminations, for it provided that negroes whether slave or free should be tried and punished in the same manner as white people, except that a slave was not to be admitted to witness against a freeman.[3]

In 1790 there were 3,737 slaves residing in the State, most of them in Philadelphia and the southeastern counties. By 1800 the slave population had declined by 54.34 percent. There were few large holdings of slaves; the majority of owners had one or two.

By 1840 the slave population had dropped to 64 persons, and by 1850 the institution had disappeared from Pennsylvania.

> There is reason to believe that before 1850 a majority of the people of Pennsylvania were hostile to slavery anywhere.[4]

But they opposed any intervention into the areas where slavery existed.

In 1847 a so-called "personal liberty law" was passed by the Pennsylvania State Legislature. The law provided that a judge could not invoke the Fugitive Slave Law of 1793 and that a jailer could not confine a Negro who was brought to him as a runaway slave. It also provided that any individual attempting to capture a runaway slave would be subject to a fine and imprisonment.[5] This act in effect nullified the Fugitive Slave Law.

The act became controversial during the secession crisis, especially after the southern states pointed to it as a violation of the Constitution. Governor William F. Packer attempted to have the act repealed, but the Legislature refused.

Why did Pennsylvania have so few slaves? First the Germans and later the Quakers abhorred the institution; therefore, it died out quite early in the Philadelphia region. Second, Pennsylvania had cultivated no plantations, and slaves were not used to any extent in the mines. The areas of slave concentration from the period of 1790 to 1840 were in the counties of Lancaster, Franklin, Fayette, Adams and Cumberland, areas settled by the Scotch-Irish. These counties are located in south central Pennsylvania and along the Maryland border.

ii

The Democratic party in Pennsylvania was divided into three segments.

The pro-Buchanan group centered around the former State Chairman, Robert Tyler. The anti-Buchanan group was led by Richard Vaux and Lewis C. Cassidy, both of Philadelphia. They had refused to support the pro-Lecompton policy of the Buchanan wing of the party. A small group of Democrats was led by John W. Forney of Philadelphia, who after splitting with President Buchanan over the Lecompton issue supported Stephen A. Douglas.

At the Democratic State Convention held at Reading in late February 1860, the party was unable to decide on a presidential nominee. They sent an uninstructed delegation to the national convention, held at Charleston, South Carolina. There, the delegates voted for the Cincinnati platform then remained to cast the greater part of their votes for James Guthrie of Kentucky. Guthrie was the leading southern candidate,

> thereby contributing substantially to the failure of [Stephen A.] Douglas to secure the 203 votes needed for a nomination.[6]

The Democrats who had supported Stephen A. Douglas were powerful in western Pennsylvania. They strongly criticized the delegation to the national convention, led by Senator William Bigler, and went so far as to accuse him of being a secessionist. When the Democratic National Convention reconvened in Baltimore in mid-June, the majority of the Pennsylvania delegates continued to support James Guthrie. At the seceders convention the twelve Pennsylvania delegates present cast only four votes for John C. Breckinridge.

President Buchanan accepted John C. Breckinridge as the candidate of the Democratic party,

> because "he sanctions and sustains the perfect equality of all the states within their common Territories, and the opinion of the Supreme Court. . . ."[7]

The Buchanan wing of the party, therefore, supported Breckinridge. The Douglas forces began immediately to form a separate electoral ticket for the November election.

A fusion ticket established on August 9, would have permitted the electors to vote for any Democrat that could win the presidency. But if there was no chance for a Democrat to win, the electors could vote for whomever they personally supported. The militant Douglasites, led by John W. Forney, rejected this fusion move and continued to support a separate Douglas ticket.

The Republicans, or People's party as it was known in Pennsylvania, also suffered from internal discord, especially between the supporters of

Simon Cameron and Andrew Curtin, who was to be elected governor of Pennsylvania in 1860. At their national convention the Republican delegates supported Abraham Lincoln on the second ballot, after having first voted for Simon Cameron. Despite the splits within the party, the tariff issue and internal divisions in the Democratic party gave the Republicans the advantage. The Lecompton Constitution, the administration of President Buchanan, the question of the extension of slavery and the tariff were the major issues in the election.

While slavery was a central issue, the tariff issue was still more important. The Democrats' rejection of the Morrill tariff bill weakened their position in Pennsylvania. The importance of the tariff issue was clearly pointed out by the fact that both major parties chose pro-tariff men as their gubernatorial candidates. The Republican party chose Andrew G. Curtin, and the Democratic party chose Henry D. Foster.

Two elections took place in Pennsylvania in 1860, one for governor, in October, the other for the president of the United States, in November. In the October election, the Republican candidate, Andrew G. Curtin, defeated Henry D. Foster by a majority of 32,084. This was a defeat for a united Democratic party which had supported Foster. When the divided Democratic party faced Lincoln in November, the defeat was even greater. Lincoln carried Pennsylvania by a majority of 56,673. In the election for governor, the Democratic party carried 26 of the State's 66 counties, including Philadelphia County. In the November election the Democrats carried only 11 and lost Philadelphia County.

The Democratic party lost because the tariff was the prominent issue and the Republican party had a much stronger plank. After the defeat in October, many Democrats did not bother to vote in November because they felt that a Republican victory was certain. Another reason for the Democratic defeat was the division within the Democratic party. Even though it was divided between Simon Cameron and Andrew G. Curtin the Republican party had strong leadership. They had in addition two highly successful congressmen in John Covode of Westmoreland County, who had been investigating the corruption of the Buchanan administration, as well as Galusha A. Grow of Bradford County, a leading advocate of the Homestead bill.

The Republican party did its best in western Pennsylvania. It carried Pittsburgh with 66 percent of the vote and Allegheny County with 77 percent. Lincoln carried Reading with 55 percent of the vote. While he did well in the cities, he did as well in the rural areas, with 57 percent of the vote. The cities, with their interest in the tariff, and the rural areas, with their antipathy towards slavery, proved that a relatively united Republican party could defeat a disunited Democratic party.[8]

There was no Breckinridge vote to determine the strength of the Buchanan wing of the party. But the fusion ticket did its best in Reading and rural Pennsylvania with 40 percent of the vote and 28 and 25 percent in Philadelphia and Pittsburgh respectively. The fusion ticket did its poorest in Allegheny County where it received only 21.5 percent of the vote.[9]

The Douglas electoral ticket received only 16,765 votes in the entire State. While it received 12 percent of the vote in Philadelphia, it received only 1.5 percent of the vote in rural Pennsylvania. The combined Democratic party, therefore, received 42 percent of Reading's vote, 40 percent of Philadelphia's, 31 percent of Pittsburgh's, and 41.5 percent of rural Pennsylvania's. Thus, the Democratic vote averaged about 38.63 percent. Its weakest area was in the western part of the State.[10]

The Constitutional Union party of John Bell received only 12,776 votes in the entire State, making its best showing in Philadelphia with 9 percent of the vote. In rural Pennsylvania, it received only 1.3 percent of the vote. Its chief importance in the election was its nuisance value.[11]

iii

With the conclusion of the election of 1860, and the defeat of the Democratic party, the Democrats in Pennsylvania remained a divided party. However, the unity in their attitudes toward the South became obvious in the secession crisis. They opposed the use of force to keep the South within the Union. At the same time they did not favor uniting Pennsylvania with the South.

James Buchanan, as President of the United States, was the national leader of the Democratic party, and since he was from Pennsylvania, he took a great interest in his state's Democratic party. The former Chairman of the Democratic party in that State, Robert Tyler, supported Buchanan and shared his confidence. Other leaders of the Pennsylvania party who were close to Buchanan supported some form of secession. Buchanan's nephew-in-law was editor of the *Pennsylvanian,* which printed editorials stating that Pennsylvania should join the Southern Confederacy. Most of the Buchanan-appointed officials in the state of Pennsylvania supported some form of secession.

In December of 1860, President Buchanan, in two letters, recognized that states would withdraw from the Union and that he could do nothing to prevent it. These states, he felt, should be permitted to leave the Union. In a letter to James Gordon Bennett, editor of the New York *Herald,* after supporting the reenactment of the Missouri Compromise, he urged that:

if the merchants of New York would sit down calmly and ask themselves to what extent they would be injured by the withdrawal of three
or four cotton states from the Union; although they would come to the
conclusion that the evils would be very great, yet they would not destroy the commercial property of our great western Emporium.[12]

He wrote to Royal Phelps on December 22, that

> I cannot imagine that any adequate cause exists for the extent and
> violence of the existing panic in New York. Suppose, most unfortunately,
> that the cotton States should withdraw from the Union; New York
> would still be the great city of this continent. . . . But this great and
> enterprising brave nation is not to be destroyed by losing the cotton
> States, even if this loss were irreparable, which I do not believe, unless
> from some unhappy accident.[13]

President Buchanan justified this thinking in his famous Special Message
to the Senate and House of Representatives on January 8, 1861. After
denying the right of a state to secede from the Union, he pointed out that
the federal government did not have either the right to recognize the
independence of a state or retain a state by force.

> . . . the executive department of this government had no authority
> under the Constitution to recognize its validity by acknowledging the
> independence of such State. . . . It belongs to Congress, exclusively,
> to repeal, to modify, or to enlarge their provisions, to meet exigencies
> as they may occur. . . .
> I certainly had no right to make aggressive war upon any State and
> I am perfectly satisfied that the Constitution has wisely withheld that
> power even from Congress. *But the right and the duty to use military
> force defensively against those who resist the federal officers in the exe-
> cution of their legal functions, and against those who assail the property
> of the federal government, is clear and undeniable.*[14]

Buchanan felt that if the United States were attacked, it had a duty to
defend itself. Where is still retained the authority, it had a duty to defend
that authority. But where there were no longer forts or judges, then the
federal government could not reinstitute its authority by force. In a
memorandum of a conversation with Senator Clement C. Clay of Alabama, Buchanan referred to Fort Sumter and stated:

> I firmly believed [the fort] belonged to the United States, to act purely
> on the defensive, and if assaulted by the authorities of South Carolina,
> on them would rest the exclusive responsibility of commencing civil
> war. I believed South Carolina still to be a part of the Confederacy.[15]

He believed that South Carolina belonged to the Union because Congress
had not accepted the fact that it had seceded.

President Buchanan further developed his position in a message to Congress on January 28, 1861.

> Congress, and Congress alone, under the war-making power, can exercise the discretion of agreeing to abstain "from any and all acts calculated to produce a collision of arms" . . . .
> It is my duty at all times to defend and protect the public property within the seceding States so far as this may be practicable . . . preserve the public peace at this the seat of the federal government. . . . Defense, and not aggression, has been the policy of the administration from the beginning.[16]

Buchanan later wrote that when Lincoln issued his proclamation after the firing upon Fort Sumter, he used the same reasoning that Buchanan had stated in this message.

> Happily our civil war was undertaken and prosecuted in self-defense, not to coerce a State, but to enforce the execution of the laws within the States against individuals, and to suppress an unjust rebellion raised by a conspiracy among them against the Government of the United States.[17]

What the South failed to realize was that Buchanan and many other northern Democrats were advocating that it be permitted to go in peace. However, if the South attacked the United States, it was the duty of the United States to defend itself. Buchanan was not in favor of retaking forts, post offices and other government property, or of enforcing the laws in the South, but simply in defending the United States from attack.

Throughout the months of April and May, after leaving the presidency, Buchanan defended his position. He favored a policy of peace and felt that Fort Sumter would be abandoned by the Lincoln administration.[18] In a letter written to John A. Dix after the firing upon Fort Sumter, dated April 19, 1861, he said:

> Warning was repeatedly given that if the authorities of South Carolina should assail Fort Sumter this would be the commencement of a civil war and they would be responsible for the consequences. The last and most emphatic warning of this character is contained in the concluding sentence of W. Holt's final and admirable answer to W. Hayne on the 6th February. . . . I perceive that you [Dix] are to be President of the Great Union meeting. Would it not be well in portraying the conduct of South Carolina in assaulting Fort Sumter to state that this had been done under the most solemn warnings of the consequences and refer to this letter of W. Holt. Nobody seems to understand the course pursued by the late administration. . . . The Present administration had no alternative but to accept the war initiated by South Carolina or the Southern Confederacy. . . .[19]

The positions of James Buchanan and Abraham Lincoln divided on the question of *de facto* secession. Buchanan did not recognize the right of secession nor the right of the United States to force a state to stay within the Union.

> If South Carolina should attack any of these Forts she will then be come [*sic*] the assalant [*sic*] in a war against the United States. It will not then be a question of coercing a State to remain in the union to which I am utterly opposed,—[but] between independent Governments, if one possessed a fortress within the limits of another and the latter should seize it, without calling upon the appropriate authorities of the power in possession to surrender it this would not only be just cause of war but the actual commencement of hostilities.[20]

Buchanan used this analogy of two independent states and a fortress to point out that the South was an independent nation and that he was recognizing *de facto* secession and, at the same time, denying the *de jure* right of secession.

The South never seemed to understand the subtle difference between defense and offense as stated by Buchanan and many northern Democrats.

President Buchanan's Attorney General, Jeremiah S. Black, who was also from Pennsylvania, took the same position as Buchanan on the question of secession. After the federal officials within a state resigned and no one would accept their positions, there could be no federal authority. There would be no one to enforce the laws and no courts to interpret the laws. Once this condition existed, the federal government could not force its authority upon the people of that state. Buchanan had refused to authorize the use of troops. He stated that

> troops would certainly be out of place, and their use wholly illegal.

Black pointed out that the President could only execute the laws to the extent of the "defensive means." He believed that Congress had to consider for itself whether it had the power to attack. Black felt that the people who wrote the Constitution and those who ratified it would have opposed the use of force "as a means of holding the States together." When it came to a question of defending itself, the Attorney General argued that the government had such a right,

> to preserve itself . . . by repelling a direct and positive aggression upon its property or its officers cannot be denied.

But that this was a

> different thing from an offensive war to punish the people for the political misdeeds of their State government. . . .[21]

He concluded succinctly that

> the States are colleagues of one another, and if some of them shall conquer the rest, and hold them as subjugated provinces, it would totally destroy the whole theory upon which they are now connected.
>
> . . . the Union must utterly perish at the moment when Congress shall arm one part of the people against another for any purpose beyond that of merely protecting the General Government in the exercise of its proper constitutional functions.[22]

Black agreed with Buchanan that defending the property of the United States from attack was a legitimate function of the United States government.[23] He also realized that if some states were permitted to secede, others would follow.

> . . . if no force is used, and the cotton-states can show the others the road to independence and freedom from abolition rule without fighting their way, every slave state will regard the question as one of free choice to be governed by their sympathies.[24]

Black and Buchanan advocated allowing those states that so desired to leave the Union in peace and not permitting the use of force to hold them in the Union, provided that they did not attack United States property. This was a *de facto* recognition of secession.

During the first part of the secession crisis the Governor of Pennsylvania was William F. Packer, a Buchanan Democrat who broke with the President over the Kansas question and refused to support the Lecompton Constitution. He had assumed the office of Governor in 1858. Packer advocated repeal of the State's personal liberty law and urged the Legislature to permit southern masters the right to retain their slaves in Pennsylvania for a temporary period. The Legislature failed to support him. He also urged that an amendment to the United States Constitution be passed to extend the 36°30′ line to the Pacific but, at the same time, he opposed the right of secession. To him the compact theory of the Union was "clearly erroneous."[25] The federal government was a sovereign body and as such had the

> right to enforce its laws and decrees by civil process, and, in an emergency, by its military and naval power.[26]

He was more emphatic:

> Every attempt, upon the part of individuals, or of organized societies, to lead the people away from their allegiance to the government, to induce them to violate any of the provisions of the Constitution, or to

incite insurrections in any of the States of this Union, ought to be prohibited by law, as crimes of a treasonable nature.[27]

In his Annual Message, he concluded that

the people of Pennsylvania are devoted to the Union. They will follow
its stars and its stripes through every peril.[28]

In no way could Packer be labeled a secessionist.

The former Chairman of the Democratic Executive Committee of the
state of Pennsylvania was Robert Tyler, son of the former President.
Tyler had been Chairman of the Democratic Executive Committee in
1858 and 1859. A strong supporter of Buchanan, he had been appointed
Prothonotary of the Supreme Court of Pennsylvania. Tyler vigorously
opposed the use of force to maintain the states in the Union. He stated that

should the Government of the Union ever be perverted into an instrument of oppression and insult to the people of Pennsylvania, I should
unhesitatingly denounce it and oppose it with the most unrelenting
enmity.[29]

It was up to each state to determine for itself whether it had just cause
to leave the Union. Whether these states once separated would again be
reunited, he felt, depended upon whether or not warfare between the
two sections had begun. War would prevent the reconstruction of the
Union.

To Tyler the framers of the Constitution did not grant

the power to the Federal Government to make war upon a State and to
crush the people beneath the weight of a military yoke. I am therefore
unalterably opposed to coercion as some persons daintily describe the
act of civil war.[30]

In a letter referring to a meeting which opposed coercion, Tyler wrote,

I most cordially approve of your explicit declaration in this respect.[31]

He hoped that the difficulties with the South might be compromised. He
even suggested that the United States adopt the Constitution of the Confederate States.[32]

When a civil war began, he wrote that:

the Border States [should] join the Southern Confederacy within one,
two or three years, it would then become a most serious question to
determine the political status of Pennsylvania and New Jersey in that
relation.[33]

This letter, written on the day of the attack upon Fort Sumter, manifested an unrealistic optimism toward the South unshared by his fellow Pennsylvania Democrats. Once war began, the border states were held in the Union, and there was no chance or desire on the part of Pennsylvania or New Jersey to join the South.

Robert Tyler's life was threatened shortly after the firing upon Fort Sumter when a mob ran him out of Philadelphia. He arrived in Richmond about May 11.[34] During the war he lived in Richmond and acted as Register of the Southern Confederacy. He retreated with Jefferson Davis in 1865 and left him at Charlotte, North Carolina. After the war he settled in Montgomery, Alabama, where he became Chairman of that state's Democratic party.

George W. Woodward, Chief Justice of the Supreme Court of Pennsylvania, also supported peaceful secession. Soon after the election in November, he wrote that the North had broken the bonds of the Constitution, and

as a Northern man I cannot in justice condemn the South for withdrawing from the Union. I believe they have been loyal to the Union formed by the Constitution—secession is not disloyal to that, for that no longer exists. The North has extinguished it.[35]

If war does occur, he said, "I wish Pennsylvania could go with them."[36] He felt that Buchanan was following the right course of action.

I hear that he insists on execution of the laws in all states that remain in Union, but that he will not resist secession. That is exactly right.[37]

Coercion was not the remedy to end secession. ". . . coercion is not to be thought of as a preventive."[38]

Woodward took a legalistic position to defend the same actions that Buchanan, Black and Tyler advocated—the peaceful secession of the southern states.

Another leader in the Democratic party, John W. Forney, wrote to J. Alexander Fulton, editor of the Kittanning *Mentor* and a supporter of Breckinridge, that he was opposed to coercion of South Carolina. Forney, who had endorsed Stephen A. Douglas, supported the Crittenden compromise and stated that "it is idle to talk of coercion."[39] He saw no reason for civil war.

Victor E. Piollet, a leading citizen of northeastern Pennsylvania and a friend of Buchanan, wrote soon after the election in November that the Republican party dare not attempt the subjugation of the Southern people by the Sword.[40]

He favored the secession of the South:

> . . . they must now go forward to actual Secession or be forever subjugated through the fortunes of the ballot box.[41]

Once secession began then some compromise could be reached by the nation as a whole. A month later he wrote that the South was right and that "Secession . . . is their right, and their duty."[42]

By the end of December he became more vehement.

> The Southern States ought all to go out of the Union before the fourth of March and seize the capital as it is in their section and let Abraham Lincoln be Inaugurated in the Section that elected him. . . .[43]

This pro-secessionist sentiment can also be seen in the many letters received by Senator William Bigler. One such letter was written by John F. Means of Clearfield, who said that if coercion was used it

> will only arraign the Conservative masses with the Democrats against them [supporters of coercion] in every state in the North and Middle States.[44]

The predominance of the letters to William Bigler supporting the idea of peaceful secession, and the fact that they were retained by a Democrat, reaffirms the fact that the Democratic party in Pennsylvania favored the idea of permitting the southern states to leave the Union in peace.

Pro-secessionist feeling within the Democratic party became public when it met in a state convention in Harrisburg on February 21. Over 350 delegates passed resolutions approving compromise and opposing coercion. The convention passed a series of resolutions: each state was sovereign; the federal government did not have the right to interfere with domestic institutions of each state; states were bound by the Constitution to deliver up fugitive slaves; the Crittenden compromise should be adopted; Pennsylvania should abolish its personal liberty law; and

> we will, by all proper and legitimate means oppose, discountenance, and prevent any attempt on the part of the Republicans in power to make any armed aggression upon the Southern States; especially so long as laws contravening their rights shall remain unrepealed on the statute books of Northern States.[45]

These resolutions were passed "without a single dissenting vote."[46] A delegation was sent to Washington to present these resolutions.

Before this state convention, meetings were held in the various counties of Pennsylvania. On February 11, the Northampton County Democratic party met in Easton and adopted a resolution which

> utterly repudiated the idea of employing the military force of the Federal Government to coerce submission on the part of the seceding States. . . .[47]

Three days later in Lancaster County the Democratic convention adopted a resolution against coercion.

This is reaffirmed by the Republican party's comments about the Democratic party. The Pittsburgh *Gazette* stated on December 17, 1860 that

> nearly all the democratic [sic] papers in the North openly sympathize with and aid, as far as they can, the Disunionists of the South.[48]

On January 16, this same newspaper specifically mentioned the Democratic party of Pennsylvania as a disunionist party. The Philadelphia *North American* of March 27, 1861, reported that

> the controlling majority of the democratic [sic] party are disunionists, and in full accord with the purposes we have here named. At the south the slave oligarchy is at actual war, and here the disunion democracy support and defend that war.[49]

The Lancaster *Union* stated on April 3, that

> "the Democratic party" in the North, complicated in the same plot and operating by its unscrupulous policy, clearly foreshadowed at Harrisburg on the 22d of February, of opposing the policy of the National Administration and of yielding to every Southern action. . . .[50]

The leadership of the Democratic party as well as most of its rank-and-file favored a policy of no coercion.

Relatively few Democrats favored Pennsylvania's joining the South. The position taken by Buchanan and his Attorney General, Jeremiah S. Black, appears to have been the position of most Democrats in Pennsylvania. Whether it was the local Democratic party at the county level, the State Convention or the leaders themselves, or even the Democratic newspapers, the unanimity appears to be unquestionable. The party favored letting the southern states secede without any attempt on the part of the federal government to enforce the laws, or to force these states to stay in the Union. Any use of arms by the federal government to hold, retain, or retake forts, arsenals or post offices was condemned by the Democratic party of Pennsylvania.

iv

While most of the Republican party opposed any form of compromise with the South and demanded that the forts be retaken by force, some prominent Republicans, primarily in Philadelphia, favored peaceable secession. The Philadelphia Republicans were not so avid in their support of force as those in other areas of Pennsylvania.

Andrew G. Curtin, a Republican, was elected Governor in October 1860. In his Inaugural Address he emphasized that he opposed any form of secession, including *de facto* secession.

He accepted Daniel Webster's definition of the Union as a sovereign body acting directly upon the people and not through the states.

> No part of the people, no State nor combination of States, can voluntarily secede from the Union, nor absolve themselves from their obligations to it. To permit a State to withdraw at pleasure from the Union, without the consent of the rest, is to confess that our government is a failure. Pennsylvania can never acquiesce in such a conspiracy, nor assent to a doctrine which involves the destruction of the government.[51]

Curtin believed that the federal government had the right to enforce the laws.

> It must have power adequate to the enforcement of the supreme law of the land in every State. It is the first duty of the national authorities to stay the progress of anarchy and enforce the laws, and Pennsylvania, with a united people, will give them an honest, faithful and active support. The people mean to preserve the integrity of the national union at every hazard.[52]

The Democrats and persons who favored peaceable secession considered this policy coercion.

Curtin immediately sent investigators to the southern states to determine the seriousness of their secession statements. His agents traveled secretly and reported from the South.[53] Governor Curtin was convinced from the information he received from his agents that war was inevitable.[54]

When Lincoln stopped in Harrisburg on his way to his inauguration, Governor Curtin pledged the support of Pennsylvania in defending the Union.

> But, sir, when conciliation has failed, read our history, study our traditions. Here are the people who will defend you, the constitution, the laws and the integrity of this Union. . . .[55]

Not only did Curtin believe philosophically that the Union should be defended, but he felt that the militia would be needed in the near future, and he took all steps towards improving it.

Governor Curtin's position was similar to that of many other Republicans who were advocating force to uphold the integrity of the Union. The Speaker of the Senate, Robert M. Palmer, stated

> that Pennsylvania would never consent to disunion and that she would resist every effort to destroy the constitution or the Union.[56]

The political party differences were to become clearer when the State Legislature held its session from January 1 until April 18, 1861.

The Republicans controlled both houses of the Legislature and were able to elect Edgar Cowan and David Wilmot to the United States Senate. Both opposed a conciliatory policy toward the South.

George Rush Smith of Philadelphia introduced the first piece of major legislation concerning secession. It was a joint resolution that adopted

> the sentiment and language of President Andrew Jackson . . . "That the right of the people of a single State to absolve themselves at will, and without the consent of the other States . . . cannot be acknowledged; and that such authority is utterly repugnant, both in principles upon which the general government is constituted, and the objects which it was expressly formed to attain."

The resolution continued that

> the Constitution of the United States of America contains all the powers necessary to the maintenance of its authority, and it is the solemn and most imperative duty of the government to adopt and carry into effect whatever measures may be necessary to that end; . . .

It concluded with the resolve that

> all plots, conspiracies, and warlike demonstrations against the United States, in any section of the country, are treasonable in their character, and whatever power of the government is necessary to their suppression should be applied to that purpose without hesitation or delay.[57]

George R. Smith's resolution passed the Senate on January 11, by a 27–6 vote. Five additional affirmative votes were recorded on January 14. The negative votes were from various parts of the State. The same resolution passed the House of Representatives 68–24. The negative votes were cast by representatives from Philadelphia, its suburbs and the southern tier of counties. Those opposing the Smith resolution were Democrats.

On April 12, the Pennsylvania House of Representatives approved a bill entitled, "An act for the better organization of the militia of the Commonwealth," which was approved 76–21. The same voting pattern existed. After the firing upon Fort Sumter five members changed their vote to the affirmative. The Senate approved this bill the same day by a vote of 27–6. No senators from Philadelphia voted against it, and four voted in the affirmative. The negative votes were scattered across the State. After Fort Sumter, these senators entered their reason for voting against the bill in the *Journal*. They objected to the excessive power to be given to the military commission and took a position that resembled neutrality or peaceful secession. They stated that:

> It is our unquestioned duty as *Legislators* to put this State in a condition to repel invasion, to suppress insurrection, and to defend our borders in time of war. . . . [and as a state to] support the General Government, to protect the public property, and to enforce the laws. At the time the bill was under consideration, no such requisition had been made, either directly or indirectly, to the knowledge of the undersigned.[58]

Delay in preparing the militia for war led to accusations of aiding the enemy. But they simply opposed the use of the militia without legislative approval or for any purpose except invasion or attack upon the federal government. They did not consider the states' seizures of forts and arsenals either an invasion or an attack upon the federal government.

v

Governor Andrew G. Curtin appointed seven Republicans to represent Pennsylvania at the Peace Conference held in Washington. The Pennsylvania delegation had "a conservative majority [which] favored conciliation."[59] Nevertheless, the Democratic party objected to the selection of all Republicans. They objected especially to the appointment of David Wilmot, a radical anti-slavery man. However, the delegation from Pennsylvania voted for every provision of the compromise.

David Wilmot, addressing the Peace Conference, stated,

> . . . the right of secession cannot be conceded. . . .
> I think it high time that the Constitution was made unequivocal upon the subject of secession.[60]

Two other delegates from Pennsylvania predicted ruin for the South. A. W. Loomis of Pittsburgh referred to the border states and predicted that if they did join the South, they would encounter the "vortex of ruin."[61] Thomas E. Franklin of Lancaster offered a resolution that refused to recognize the constitutional right of secession.

Two members of the delegation referred to Pennsylvania as a border state, and Thomas White, of Indiana, Pennsylvania, stated that

> if there is to be war; civil, unnatural war, whose country is to be devastated, whose fields laid waste and trampled down? They are those of the border States. . . .[62]

James Pollock of Milton, also predicted that Pennsylvania would be the battleground of such a civil war. Thomas White went further than any of the other Pennsylvania delegates and seemed to advocate peaceable secession.

> If the seceded States will not come back, if the other Southern States cannot bring them back, then, are we in any worse position? No, sir! we are not. We desire to place ourselves right before the world. Then, if some States will not stay in the Union, on their heads be the responsibility.[63]

The Pennsylvania delegation, while made up exclusively of Republicans, represented a cross section of the party's viewpoints. Wilmot represented the radical wing and White represented a wing that favored peaceful secession. Between these individuals stood the majority who feared a civil war and advocated compromise. Nevertheless, this delegation did not represent the viewpoint of the people of Pennsylvania. The Democrats were not represented. Only one person was from a border county and Wilmot was the only member from the northeast section of the State.

vi

The Republican party dominated the Congressional delegation from Pennsylvania. Of the four men who served in the United States Senate during this period of crisis, three were Republicans and one was a Democrat. At the beginning of this period Pennsylvania was represented by Republican Simon Cameron and Democrat William Bigler. They were replaced by Edgar Cowan and David Wilmot, both Republicans.

Simon Cameron, born in Lancaster County, was a Democrat until 1854 when he helped form the People's party. He was elected to the United States Senate in 1857. Abraham Lincoln appointed him Secretary of War, and he consequently resigned from the Senate in 1861. Cameron built an effective political party in Pennsylvania and controlled it through the use of patronage. His voting record was pro-northern, but he favored compromise with the South.

For a short period of time Simon Cameron stood out in sharp relief,

much in contrast to his Republican colleagues, in expressing a conciliatory attitude toward the South. Certainly he did not condone the secessionist movement, but he believed Crittenden's solution would furnish
a satisfactory basis for a peaceful settlement. However, he would have
liked to see the thirty-six–thirty line restored but not extended into the
territories[64]

Edgar Cowan of Greensburg, in southwestern Pennsylvania, was elected
to the Senate in 1861 to replace William Bigler. A native of Westmoreland County, he had been a presidential elector in the 1860 election. He
had defeated David Wilmot to gain election to the United States Senate
because Cowan was considered more moderate. Cowan can be considered
a coercionist. Writing to Simon Cameron in December he said:

> That is a singular term of Mr. Buchanan that a State cannot be coerced
> —but is not that along side the question—cannot the traitors who live
> in a state be punished without inquiry as to whether they are few or
> many—enough to control the State or only enough to take an arsenal?
> It seems to me the State herself is secure, but her people why cannot
> they be brought to their senses. . . .[65]

The third Republican to serve as senator during this period, David
Wilmot, practiced law in Bradford County. He had been a leading anti-
slavery man and author of the famous "Wilmot Proviso." Wilmot was
one of the founders of the Republican party, and he had been elected to
the Senate to fill a vacancy created by the resignation of Simon Cameron.
In March of 1861 he delivered a speech in Philadelphia in which he made
his position clear:

> We are met by an armed rebellion in a portion of the Republic. I believe
> that the policy of the Administration will be peaceful; that it will
> exhaust every peaceful means to restore quiet to the country without
> the employment of force. . . . No man can tell what day will bring
> forth, and it is a matter of the highest importance that we give all the
> aid we can to the Government. . . .[66]

Wilmot lived up to his reputation as a rabid Republican ready to use
force if necessary. None of the three Republican senators from Pennsylvania advocated peaceable, or any other form of secession. While Cameron
urged compromise, he was ready and willing to use force against the South.

The only Pennsylvanian who served as a Democratic senator during
this period was William Bigler. He had supported Buchanan in his
Lecompton policy. His voting record was divided evenly between those
favoring South and North, and he was in favor of compromise with
the South.

Senator Bigler delivered a speech to the United States Senate on December 11 urging the establishment of a convention of the states to amend the Constitution to arrive at a compromise with the South. Although he had little hope that the Congress would achieve a compromise settlement, he urged the South to permit the North time to settle the dispute. Bigler believed that Northerners

> would go very much further than their representatives on the Republican side believed, in order to accomplish this desirable end.[67]

In his speech he assured the South that in Pennsylvania "no war of aggression is intended by the people of that State. . . ."[68]

In January Bigler introduced a bill requiring the federal government to hold a referendum on the proposed compromise amendments to the Constitution permitting the people the opportunity to vote on the major issues that divided the North and the South. In a speech to the Senate on January 21, Bigler reiterated his previous position and, after denying the right of secession, he made it clear that he opposed war.

> . . . I deprecate with all my heart the remedy they pursue, and am prepared to resist it by all proper and peaceful means in my power.[69]

The Constitution provided means for redressing grievances with the convention system for amending the Constitution. The use of force would have resulted in the secession of fifteen states and then the Union would be destroyed.

> . . . secession is the worst possible remedy for the evils complained of by the southern States, and coercion the maddest of all the remedies suggested for secession. . . . Such a war would be one of extermination. Neither side could ever conquer. . . . I am for peace; and I am ready to grant anything in reason to reconcile the discontented States and the offended people. I am ready to implore them to remain in the Union; I am ready to fight for their constitutional rights to the last hour; but to shed a brother's blood in a fratricidal war, I shall be ready—never! never![70]

In the same speech Bigler urged acceptance of the Crittenden compromise and concluded, that

> Pennsylvania will never become the enemy of Virginia. Pennsylvania will never draw the sword on Virginia; and she is no less affectionate to her other sisters.[71]

In a letter to James Buchanan a day before the firing upon Fort Sumter, Bigler wrote, war seems to be inevitable. . . . Mr. Lincoln is about to initiate Civil War.[72]

He told Buchanan that his policy was correct and that time would vindicate him.

Clearly, William Bigler, along with the other Democrats, supported the idea of peaceable secession. He opposed war for the pragmatic reasons that it would further divide the nation and make reconstruction impossible. He not only opposed the use of force to retain the South, but he also felt that the Republican administration's policy would start a civil war.

vii

As was the case in 1858, the congressional election of 1860 in Pennsylvania was an overwhelming Republican triumph. Only five of the 25-man Pennsylvania congressional delegation were Democrats.

Of the five Democratic congressmen, only one was from Philadelphia, Thomas B. Florence, whose voting record favored the South. On January 19, he introduced a series of resolutions, one of which stated that

> no State, or the people thereof, shall retire from this Union without the consent of three fourths of all the States.[73]

In February in a speech to the Congress, he supported the Crittenden compromise and the proposition put forth by Senator Bigler that the people vote on a compromise.

There were two Democratic congressmen from the northeastern part of Pennsylvania. William H. Dimmick had a poor voting record, making his position difficult to ascertain. Jacob K. McKenty voted five times favoring the South. He also supported every attempt at compromise. In explaining his vote on the Adrain resolution, he stated:

> Our political affinities and sympathies have been always with the South; but I do not believe there is a single man in my district that does not sustain the President [Buchanan] in his course. . . . [his action] is merely defensive; and, sir, if the last page of our nation's history is to be a bloody one, let the responsibility rest with those who will make it so.[74]

John Hickman had been elected to the thirty-fourth and thirty-fifth Congresses as a Democrat, to the thirty-sixth as an Anti-Lecompton Democrat, and in 1860 he ran for Congress and won on the Republican ticket. Therefore during the secession crisis, he was still serving as a Democratic congressman. He represented Chester County, favored the North, and opposed any attempt at compromise.

The last Democratic congressman, William Montgomery of Washington, also had a voting record favoring the North.

The composite picture of the Democratic members of the House from Pennsylvania is confusing. As politicians, none was a leader, and none took an active role during this period of crisis. Members favoring the South were either from Philadelphia or the northeastern part of the State. However, since there were so few, it is difficult to make even a generalization. None delivered a lengthy speech on the subject of secession: therefore, Democratic views must be determined from the voting records.

Of twenty Republican congressmen, all voted consistently for the northern viewpoint. Although most Republican congressmen voted for compromise, the three congressmen voting consistently against attempts at compromise were Thaddeus Stevens of Lancaster; Galusha Grow of Glenwood, and Samuel S. Blair of Hollidaysburg.

Twelve of these twenty congressmen expressed themselves on the issue of secession. Only Edward J. Morris of Philadelphia opposed the use of force to maintain the Union. He favored a compromise with the South, and believed that

⅔rds of the Republicans are against all reasonable compromise and I might say against any compromise whatsoever.[75]

Morris hoped to settle the slavery question with a constitutional amendment that would have prohibited Congress from acting upon the subject. He favored the compromise put forward by the Committee of Thirty-Three but opposed the right of secession.

As to the question of force, he believed that the federal government should hold its forts, and regain those already lost but not force the South into submission.

The idea of coercion is misrepresented. No one proposes to march the Federal armies into the seceding States, to subjugate them back into the Union. We know that it is utterly impossible to force into submission to the Union a people who are opposed to it.

Congressman Morris felt that such a war, if won, would only produce "reluctant allegiance from citizens . . ." He opposed the idea of a war with the South because of the "greater expenditure of money" and the "greater waste of life." Yet he wanted the federal government to collect the customs revenue and to "maintain possession of the more important forts and arsenals." He failed to explain how this might be accomplished without force. He stated that

above all, it should not permit the national flag to be dishonored.

This was a key phase after the attack on Fort Sumter. Congressman Morris and many other Pennsylvanians who had been urging that no force be used now felt that the honor of the United States was at stake when Sumter was attacked.[76]

The importance of Congressman Morris is that he was the only Republican congressman from Pennsylvania who opposed the subjugation of the South. He represented a section of the city of Philadelphia and was later appointed by President Lincoln as the United States Minister to Turkey.

Two Republican congressmen, George W. Scranton of Scranton, and John W. Killinger of Lebanon, urged that a compromise be arranged with the South. But they wanted the federal government to take a stand against secession. Congressman Scranton owned major interests in railroads, iron manufacturing and coal mining. He supported the idea of compromise with the South and praised William Seward after his conciliatory speech in the United States Senate.

You see now that if Seward is right then I have been right from the commencement of this controversy,[77]

he wrote in January. Nevertheless Scranton opposed the idea of peaceful secession because he opposed the possibility of division of the United States.

John W. Killinger, the only Republican congressman from Pennsylvania to vote with the South on the issue of censure, favored a compromise to hold the border states.

In my judgment, the Republican party can well afford to meet the propositions submitted to this Congress by the border State members, in a liberal and conciliatory spirit. . . .

All your legislation is founded on compromises. Every concession, every amendment, every modification, is a compromise; and if you resorted to the dread arbiter of civil war to settle your difficulties, you would finally come to a compromise.[78]

Opposing the idea of secession, he believed that the laws must be enforced and that the disloyal element in the South must be punished.

Members of the Republican delegation to Congress who wanted a compromise as much as Edward J. Morris came from the city of Philadelphia, its suburbs, or the northeastern section of the State, where the secession movement was the strongest. But all the Republican congressmen from northeastern and southern Pennsylvania did not approve of compromise. Other Republican congressmen from these areas, Galusha A. Grow, Thaddeus Stevens, and Edward McPherson, were party leaders representing the Republican viewpoint: that is, they opposed compromise and secession in any form. Their positions were firm and no occurrence during the crisis would make them vacillate.

The remaining members of the Republican congressional delegation from Pennsylvania opposed any form of compromise with the South because they felt it would weaken Republican principles. They also opposed any form of secession, urging enforcement of the laws of the United States. If enforcement meant coercion, then coercion should be used. The *Congressional Globe* reported an example of this type of thinking, expressed by James H. Campbell of Philadelphia.

> . . . I hold it next to treason, at a time like this, to claim that the Union of our fathers is dissolved. Every true man, every native and adopted citizen, should rally around her altar and swear to maintain the Union, without reservation, in all peril, and in every contingency. . . .
> Let every effort be made to preserve our nationality intact—every star upon our flag, every acre within our limits. . . .[79]

This meant the use of all possible force, even war.

viii

Newspapers of Pennsylvania indicated the strength of the secession movement in the State. According to the United States Census of 1860, there were 279 weekly Pennsylvania newspapers. Many of the smaller newspapers have not survived. Of the 279 newspapers, the 62 obtained by the author included views on the question of secession—that is, about 23 percent of the newspapers existing at that time. Those obtained represent all geographic areas of the State and include all the major newspapers. Of the 62 newspapers, 23 were Democratic (one of these began after the election); 31 were Republican, 1 supported the Constitutional Union party, and 8 either supported no candidate in the election of 1860 or the issues no longer exist for the election period. About 74 percent of the Democratic and about 26 percent of the Republican newspapers supported some form of secession. The lone newspaper endorsing the Constitutional Union party in 1860 opposed a war with the South. Of the newspapers which either could not be determined politically or were independent, 25 percent favored secession. The secession movement was indeed strong within the Democratic party and significant in the Republican party.

The five newspapers that supported John C. Breckinridge all favored secession. As early as November the Philadelphia *Morning Pennsylvanian* urged that the slave states be permitted to leave the Union, and

> that occurring, it will then have to be determined whether the Middle States will consent to remain in association with the New England States, and whether the empire of the Northwest will remain as it is, or set up for itself.[80]

The *Pennsylvanian* advocated letting the South go in peace and urged the middle states to form a central confederacy.

The Harrisburg *Patriot Union* wanted compromise with the South and Pennsylvania's repeal of its personal liberty law. It opposed the spending of money to reform the militia system. On November 7, 1860, this newspaper carried an article supporting peaceable secession. The *Patriot Union* blamed the Republican administration for dividing the country in April and advocated that the Democratic party have nothing to do with a war with the South.

> If this Administration wickedly plunges the country into civil war, it will be a war between the Republican party and the Southern States. . . . In such a conflict the Northern Democracy can have no sympathy with the Government. . . . If the Administration is bent upon having a fight, let it be understood that they created the difficulty and their partisans must carry on the war. Northern Democrats can never shoulder a musket or pull a trigger against those whose rights they conscientiously believe have been trampled upon. If this is treason, it is treason against the Chicago platform, and in behalf of the majority of the American people; treason for the Union, and against its enemies. If this is treason, make the most of it.[81]

This newspaper continued to call for compromise to avoid the dissolution of the Union. After the firing upon Fort Sumter, the *Patriot Union* supported the Union, because

> the Confederate States have taken the initiative in war . . . deeply as we condemn the defiant attitude of the Republican party towards the South, we are not prepared to countenance or submit to such an indignity to the authority and the flag of our country.[82]

The Easton *Sentinel* took the same stand, blaming the Republican party for the dissolution of the Union and urging that the South be permitted to go in peace. After Fort Sumter, this newspaper supported the federal government. The *McKean County Democrat* favored compromise but felt that the South should depart in peace, stating that war meant no possibility of reconciliation. Such reconciliation, though, might mean "the exclusion of the New England States."[83] They placed the blame upon the Republican party and the New England states. These newspapers could not see the Union as something to be saved at any cost, as did many Republicans. After Fort Sumter, the McKean County *Democrat* predicted the end of the Union.

> From the recent events at Charleston [*sic*] war, we fear, is inevitable. Civil War of course ends the Confederacy. . . . we are now forced into a war against the known wishes of the masses.[84]

The pro-Breckinridge newspapers urged that the South be permitted to go in peace. Most of them, however, after the firing upon Fort Sumter, supported the Union.

Eleven newspapers endorsed Stephen A. Douglas. Of these, six asked for some form of secession while three supported the use of force to retain the South. The other two are difficult to categorize. The most rabid, pro-secession Douglas newspaper was the Bedford *Gazette,* which blamed the division within the country upon the Republican party.

> If the Constitution is to be overridden by the Chicago Platform, if business and trade are to be prostrated, internal peace and domestic tranquility sacrificed, and dictatorships given to military chieftains, simply because this Republican Administration is unwilling to yield to a fair and honorable compromise with the South, then we are for revolution, peaceful if it can be, forcible if it must. . . . the steady and true-hearted yeomen of Pennsylvania, will rise in their might, and in the name of the Great Jehovah, hurl from power and existence a party that has perverted the Constitution. . . .[85]

After Fort Sumter, the Bedford *Gazette* at first accused the Lincoln administration of having caused the war, but a week later called on Democrats to aid the Union, probably because the editor saw the upsurge of Union support that was sweeping across Pennsylvania.

Typical of the pro-secessionist, pro-Douglas newspapers was the Clinton *Democrat.* Its editor wrote,

> the clamor for coercion was at all times a senseless one, because it was impossible and because any attempt at it was sure to prove abortive and would only make the breach wider.[86]

The other pro-secessionist Douglas papers argued similarly that the writers of the Constitution had not intended for the federal government to be endowed with the right to use force against the states; therefore, the two sections should be permitted to depart in peace. The Republican party was held responsible for the war.

The three Douglas newspapers that approved of the use of force were the Lancaster *Inquirer*, the Philadelphia *Press*, and the Lycoming *Gazette*. They wanted Abraham Lincoln to hold Fort Sumter but emphasized that a compromise should be reached with the South. The federal government should maintain itself, by force if necessary. The Philadelphia *Press* stated:

> Yet should generous treatment fail, it recognized that "harsher measures" must be adopted.[87]

It is obvious that these newspapers and their supporters were not willing to let the South go in peace.

Two pro-Douglas newspapers with views on secession difficult to determine are the Wilkes Barre *Luzerne Union* and the Lewistown *True Democrat*. The *Luzerne Union* urged that force be used.

> We have surrendered much for the sake of peace, and from the faith we have entertained in the power of reason to supplant passion. It is all vain. We must now maintain the Union at all hazards.[88]

However, the same newspaper later supported the resolutions of the Pennsylvania Democratic Convention which were in direct contrast with the above editorial. Since only a few editions of the *True Democrat* exist, it is difficult to state its views accurately.

Five of the other seven Democratic newspapers opposed the use of force to retain states within the Union. Either these newspapers endorsed no candidate, or they began operations after the November election. These newspapers would not condone a war with the South. They predicted that no Democrat would fight in a civil war brought about by the Republican party. The Gettysburg *Compiler*, in a prophetic statement, wrote,

> . . . "enforcing the laws" in States which have formally withdrawn from the Union, would be exactly synonymous, in practice with Coercion. Coercion is Civil War; and Civil War would be the Consummation of Our Woes—say the *Journal of Commerce*, and so say we.[89]

After the attack upon Fort Sumter these newspapers called upon their readers to stand by the government in the war against the South.

Two newspapers that had endorsed the Democratic fusion ticket, the Uniontown *Genius of Liberty* and the Hanover *Citizen*, supported the use of force to retain the states in the Union. While these newspapers did not want a civil war with the South, they were unwilling to see the South leave the Union, even if it meant war.

Among the thirty-one Republican newspapers, seven endorsed peaceable secession. The Philadelphia *Inquirer* wanted the Republican party to compromise with the South. Without compromise, the nation would be divided permanently. This newspaper called upon the middle states, from New York to Missouri, to unite in order to save the Union.

> The powerful tier of Middle States cannot be too frequently reminded that their prompt and proper action in favor of conciliation may confine secession to a comparatively small number of the extreme Southern States, and greatly soften the shock of dissolution, if it must come.[90]

This was by no means a call for a middle states confederacy, but simply for a unity of action. It nevertheless published a letter in December which advocated a middle confederacy.

In December the Philadelphia *Inquirer* wrote a prophetic editorial which the South should have noted more carefully. It recommended peaceable secession provided the South did not attack the United States.

> No proposition to coerce an aggrieved State, as long as justice is denied, can ever meet with favor. The hearts and the voices of the people would repudiate any such measures. While your wrongs remain without redress, there can be no union of the Northern people to coerce you, unless you provoke it by some act that will outrage their sense of right or their self respect. In this lies your safety and your best assurance of justice. But if you permit the infatuated demagogues who have taken this revolutionary business in hand in South Carolina, to assault Fort Moultrie, or sacrifice its little garrison in accordance with the murderous threats in the Charleston *Mercury,* the North will rise in arms like one man.[91]

A few weeks later, the Philadelphia *Inquirer* called the firing upon the *Star of the West* an act of war and urged the government to take some action. When the federal government did not go to war with South Carolina the newspaper returned to its peaceable secession position, taking the position that two nations were now an inevitability. After the defeat of the Crittenden amendments, the *Inquirer* predicted a division of the Union at the Mason and Dixon line.

> Secession or division here is inevitable. . . . They ought to be treated as virtually separated, that we may establish pacific relations with them. . . .
> Civil War in such circumstances is mere folly. We have no place in our system for conquered provinces. The Free States cannot be political slave owners.[92]

By April the Philadelphia *Inquirer* was calling upon the Montgomery government to ascertain the southern will and, on that basis, arrive at a truce with the United States. If this were not done, then the United States government would have to defend the people of the South against the Southern Confederacy. After the firing upon Fort Sumter the *Inquirer* reiterated its position of December, calling upon everyone in the North to defend the United States government. The Philadelphia *Daily News* concurred.

Another major Republican newspaper that advocated a peaceable secession was the *Pennsylvania Daily Telegraph* of Harrisburg. Its support of peaceable secession lacked continuity because it vacillated between advocating the use of force and suggesting that the South be permitted to leave in peace. This Republican newspaper took a strong Republican viewpoint at the beginning of the secession crisis; it opposed any form of compromise with the South, arguing that such compromise would be an abandonment of Republican principles. In January it called upon the federal government to use force to maintain the Union.

> If nothing but a fight will answer the purposes of the rebels, much as all true patriots would regret it, a fight they can have.[93]

By March it was defining the use of the word coercion as self defense and as a means of maintaining the government. But by April it recommended peaceable secession.

> War with the seceded States will not bring them back into the Union. . . . Such a recognition of peaceable secession would not increase the danger and difficulties by which we are already surrounded, nor would it affect any more than they have been affected, the destiny and development of the free States. In the present juncture, a resort to arms seems utterly impracticable.[94]

Three Republican weekly newspapers supported the idea of peaceable secession. The Muncy *Luminary* recommended that the southern states be permitted to leave in peace and hoped that eventually they would return to the United States. The Johnstown *Cambria Tribune,* after stating that a war with the seceding states could not bring them back into the Union, called for the recognition of the Confederacy.

> We are rather inclined to favor the policy of recognizing the Southern Confederacy as being *our* choice of the two evils—disunion or civil war. . . .[95]

The Easton *Free Press* thought it better to let the South go in peace than to give in to Confederate ultimatums. All of these newspapers, after Fort

Sumter was fired upon by the Confederacy, supported the Union and urged the defense of the "flag."

Two Republican newspapers located in Philadelphia vacillated in their positions toward the South. The *Daily Evening Bulletin* and its weekly counterpart, *The Saturday Bulletin,* stated in March that as nothing could be gained by a war with the Confederacy,

> we are not going to fight about it, that is certain; for then we should be substituting the sword for the popular will, and a government forced upon the people by the sword could never be maintained in this country. . . .[96]

They recommended that a national convention be called to decide whether the Union should be divided and, if so, the terms of such a division. But before the firing upon Fort Sumter, in the first two weeks of April, this newspaper advocated that the government defend itself against the South.

> The Federal Government has done everything that could be done to conciliate them, and it can yield nothing more, unless it yields everything.[97]

The *Philadelphia North American and United States Gazette,* published by Morton McMichael, a leading Republican in Pennsylvania, also vacillated on the issue of war upon the South. This newspaper blamed the crisis upon the Buchanan administration and called secession "worse than treason. . . ."[98] But by April, it no longer endorsed the use of force.

> We have said that it was because the folly of this course of costly warfare even its atrocity, that the administrators of the law have hesitated as to what should be done, and have chosen to avoid any needless test of their right to control affairs at any one point.[99]

The Republican newspapers which supported peaceable secession and those which vacillated on the issue were only a minority of the Pennsylvania Republican press. At least twenty-two Republican newspapers consistently defended force, if it were necessary, to uphold the Union. Most of these newspapers advocated no compromise with the South. They consistently favored a policy of coercion, which they defined as defending the principles of the Republican party, and a policy of self-defense against the South, which was seizing United States forts, arsenals, and post offices. They demanded that the government take a firm position, enforce the laws, and retake government property. Yet it is significant that a minority of Republican newspapers recommended peaceable secession, especially the Philadelphia newspapers. This minority group within the Republican party was important and seemed to be growing.

Eight newspapers either supported no candidate in the election of 1860 or their editions for the period of the election no longer exist. Two of these opposed the use of force, the *Public Ledger* and the *Palmetto Flag,* both of Philadelphia. Like its other counterparts in Philadelphia, the *Public Ledger* vacillated on the issue of force. At first, it wanted the laws enforced and called South Carolina's secession an act of rebellion. This was its position in December. By January it was arguing for compromise. By March, the *Public Ledger* was stating that

> a course of precipitancy, or of force, without regard to circumstances, might establish the power of the government, but it could not recommend its justice or its wisdom. It would reconcile nothing, . . .[100]

By April, this newspaper was once again recommending force to defend the Union because the Confederacy was arming itself, and all attempts at conciliation had failed.

When one examines the secession newspapers geographically, one discovers that with a few exceptions they centered in major cities or along the southern tier of counties. Philadelphia had the greatest number of secessionist newspapers, but Harrisburg and Easton had two and three respectively. Small-town papers in the western, central and northern parts of Pennsylvania opposed the notion that the South should go in peace. The exceptions to the geographic pattern of secessionist newspapers were mostly Democratic newspapers that supported their party's point of view. The same geographic generalizations apply to the Pennsylvania congressmen.

ix

A definite division of opinion separated the people of Philadelphia and Pittsburgh. Philadelphians had strong economic ties with the South and therefore strongly supported the idea of peaceable secession. At the same time economic conditions tied the destinies of their Pittsburgh counterparts to the western states, so that people in the latter city favored the federal government and opposed peaceable secession.

A. K. McClure, the Republican leader, summed up Philadelphia's economic position and its relationship with the South when he wrote:

> Philadelphia was then the great emporium of Southern commerce, and her merchants were compelled to face the fearful problem of sacrificing millions of dollars due from their Southern customers.[101]

With the beginning of the secession crisis economic stagnation and a recession crippled Philadelphia. By the end of November the banks of the city had suspended specie payments, and unemployment figures rose.

A sharp recession had set in because of the decline in the rich southern trade. Shipowners, dry goods merchants, textile manufacturers saw . . . . an economic crisis in the near future. During the winter and early spring bankruptcies began in Pennsylvania . . . with the predominance of cases in Philadelphia. Philadelphia newspapers were looking for a curtailment of southern trade, "fully one-half." In Philadelphia alone rich capitalists had built up a thriving trade with the South that spelled prosperity: Baldwin locomotives were in use on every southern railroad; Philadelphia wagons and carriages were a byword in the South; printer's type, textbooks, and Bibles had afforded a lucrative source of trade. Now before the end of November, Philadelphia banks had suspended specie payments. Old credit accounts of the South had been left without settlement, and the money of the cotton crops had gone to purchase war materials, food, clothing—but purchases were made from entirely new business houses. Thus in Pennsylvania unemployment and suffering spread, so that by December, 1860, there were nearly 20,000 unemployed in Philadelphia.[102]

By January the workingmen of Philadelphia were feeling the effects of this recession, and they held a mass meeting. Supporting the Crittenden compromise, they sent a delegation to Washington to recommend the adoption of its resolutions. They hoped that if conditions between the North and the South could be compromised, the city's economy would improve. The Philadelphia *Inquirer* commented on the conditions of the working people of Philadelphia.

There is at this time scarcely a large manufacturing establishment in Philadelphia working full handed—many are running at half time, and some even less. Full forty per cent of the operatives of the city of both sexes, are to-day either wholly out of employment or upon short allowance.[103]

George W. Curtis, a noted abolitionist, was to lecture at the People's Literary Institute, but Mayor Alexander Henry wrote to all the officers of the Institute, asking them to cancel this meeting.

To scotch the idea that the city was abolitionist, the municipal Council chose the day of Curtis's lecture for a great demonstration of cordiality to the South. All business was to be suspended for two hours and delegations of factory workers were to parade to Independence Square.[104]

At the meeting, called by Mayor Henry, numerous speakers advocated a policy of conciliation, and resolutions were passed condemning the personal liberty laws. Yet no resolution condemned secession as illegal or unconstitutional. The most violent speech was delivered by Judge George W. Woodward. Judge Woodward had been elected to the Pennsylvania Supreme Court in 1852 and held that position during the Civil War. He said that the government could not prevent secession.

Leaders of the Democratic party in Philadelphia favored some form of secession. They did not hold the Union sacred. The leaders expressed themselves both at a convention held in the city and in their letters. They were more emphatic in their position concerning secession than the state Democratic party leaders. Most of the men appointed to positions by Buchanan supported his point of view or favored peaceable secession. They denied the federal government's right to defend itself. Many seemed to be waiting for the permanent dissolution of the United States so that they could decide whether to join a specific section or to form a central confederacy.

H. B. Robinson, writing to Hendrick B. Wright in December states,

> [after] leaving out office holders, there seems to be a general disgust towards the President, he is openly charged as being in collusion with the members of Congress from the Seceding States. . . . But for the *Pennsylvanian* and office holders, and W.[illiam] B. Reed and R.[obert] Tyler. [*sic*] I think things would not be so bad they openly preach Secession. I have stoped [*sic*] my *Pennsylvanian*. . . . I will not support a Tory sheet in our midst.[105]

A mass meeting was held on January 16, 1861, at National Hall. Resolutions were adopted including the following:

> That in the deliberate judgment of the Democracy of Philadelphia, and, so far as we know it, of Pennsylvania, the dissolution of the Union by the separation of the whole South, a result we shall most sincerely lament, may release this Commonwealth to a large extent from the bonds which now connect her with the Confederacy, except so far as for temporary convenience she chooses to submit to them, and would authorize and require her citizens, through a Convention, to be assembled for that purpose, to determine with whom her lot should be cast, whether with the North and the East, whose fanaticism has precipitated this misery upon us, or with our brethren of the South, whose wrongs we feel as our own; or whether Pennsylvania should stand by herself, as a distinct community, ready when occasion offers, to bind together the broken Union, and resume her place of loyalty and devotion.[106]

According to the Philadelphia *Inquirer,*

> when the Chair put the question, the vote "aye" was about as loud as the vote "nay," but the Chair decided the resolution carried.[107]

The Chairman for the Committee on Arrangements for this meeting, Vincent L. Bradford, was president of the Philadelphia and Trenton Railroad Company. He wrote to President Buchanan that

> if the present Union cannot be preserved (for it cannot be maintained by military Force employed against nearly half of its confederate states), will not a Northern and Southern Confederacy, living in terms of amity and trading with each other, on most favored nations, be all but in name, one people and nation. . . .[108]

On January 25, he suggested that Buchanan

> evacuate all forts in the South before March 4th in the seceding states in order to remove "all causes of offense or irritation to the People of the South. . . ."[109]

Obviously, Vincent L. Bradford favored at least peaceable secession, if not joining the South.

A leading Democrat and friend of President Buchanan, J. B. Baker, Collector of the Port of Philadelphia, is quoted by the New York *Tribune,* as having

> openly justified the secession of the South as proper, and charged the whole blame upon the North.[110]

In a letter to Buchanan, Baker stated that

> the sentiments here among democrats [*sic*] is decidedly against re-inforcing [*sic*] the Charleston Forts. It looks like war, against which there is a strong opposition by your friends.[111]

George M. Wharton, a friend of President Buchanan who had spoken at the January mass meeting, took a more moderate position. For him secession was a last resort. The Constitution of the United States, he argued, took precedence over that of the states. While he opposed any use of force to suppress a state, the

> defence of the rights of the General Government and adequate, nay, absolutely certain, protection of her property, is very different from aggression upon the rights of S. Carolina.[112]

His position was similar to Buchanan's—only Congress had the authority to act, not the executive.

James Campbell, who had been in President Pierce's cabinet, stated that

> the Democracy of the North are not for coercion, and if it be attempted, party lines will be drawn tighter than they have ever been in this

country, and we shall be backed by every man of conservative feelings; and the coercionists must soon go under; and thus they will discover when the fight commences.[113]

William B. Reed, who took part in the January meeting at the National Hall, was a leading Democrat. He stated that the reason the meeting was held

was to dissuade and oppose military coercion, and the inauguration of civil war by the act of the Federal Government. . . .[114]

In his autobiography he admitted that he wrote the controversial resolution adopted at that meeting.

It embodied my opinions when danger of disruption was at a distance. It expresses my opinions now, when it is a hideous reality.[115]

The reasoning behind the resolution was,

that the separation, once accomplished . . . each State, without any act of its own, but literally by the force of circumstances, would be "released," and, being released, falls back on its own sovereignty. The resolution asserted this, and no more; and the time will come when it will be accepted as truth.[116]

At this same meeting, Reed stated that

Pennsylvania will, whether she is detached or not—whether she is compelled for a time to go with the North, or the South, or stand by herself, she will, if she is true to her own honored history, be always ready to pacificate and reconcile and reconstruct, even if the ruin be complete. . . .[117]

Reed placed his hope in the middle states. Obviously a peaceable secessionist who opposed the use of force, he felt that they could halt the coercion of the southern states. He even hoped that Pennsylvania might join the South. To Reed, there was nothing sacred about the Union, it could be broken and, once that happened, each state would go its own way.

The Democrats in Philadelphia, even more so than those in the State, opposed the use of force to retain the South. The same can be said about Philadelphia newspapers. The meeting at the National Hall in January seemed to express the viewpoint of many of the leaders of the Democratic party in Philadelphia. Most of these men assumed that the Republican government would attack the South. Once this happened the Democratic party would oppose such a move either verbally or by force.

The Republican party in Philadelphia found itself divided on the issue of secession. Mayor Henry, a Republican, favored a conciliatory policy toward the South and urged that criticism of the institution of slavery cease. At the same time, at Union meetings held in Philadelphia, resolutions adopted opposed peaceable secession. The Philadelphia Republican newspapers, as mentioned previously, by the beginning of April opposed the use of force to coerce the South. The Republican party in Philadelphia seemed to lack direction.

Philadelphian Sidney George Fisher, member of a wealthy merchant family, while supporting no political party wrote an article for the Philadelphia *North American* entitled, "Legalized Secession," which appeared on December 31, 1860. This newspaper was edited by Morton McMichael, a leading Republican. Fisher's thesis was that

since secession appeared inevitable, he thought it best to give it legal status by passing certain laws. "Let us therefore open the door wide to our southern friends, and say to them, 'depart in peace, we will not detain you against your will'. . . . To cry Union when there is no Union, is like crying peace, peace, when there is no peace."[118]

He wrote in his diary on January 14:

Are these states to be allowed to stay out? I suppose so, for they can only be brought back by force and coercion, which everyone agrees will not be attempted.[119]

Referring to the Republican party, Fisher wrote on April 1:

Called at McMichael's [editor of the Philadelphia *North American*]. He says he thinks the administration has no plan and, such is the position of affairs, can have none. He thinks the border states will all go. He saw Mr. Chase, a member of the Cabinet, a few days ago, who told him the only thing left now was to call a convention of the people and let them decide how the Union was to be divided. . . .[120]

This made Fisher happy because it seemed to approve legalized secession. McMichael's printing of Fisher's article and his comment on Chase's position emphasized his approval of peaceable secession. The Philadelphia *North American,* during these last two months of the secession crisis, approved of letting the South go in peace.

The religious denominations in Philadelphia also opposed the policy of coercion. The Old School Presbyterian General Assembly met in Philadelphia in May 1861. Their stand in favor of the Union was opposed by members from southeastern Pennsylvania.

. . . in Philadelphia this denomination was pro-southern and for compromise and in western Pennsylvania opposed to secession and slavery.[121]

This reiterates the difference in viewpoint between Philadelphia and western Pennsylvania.

> A pacific and legal withdrawal of the South from the North was the view of the editor of the *Friend* (Quaker) of Philadelphia in March.[122]

The Philadelphia *Inquirer* aided the Quakers in this goal.

The newspapers of Philadelphia advocated peaceable secession as did the Democratic leaders and the religious organizations. This support for letting the South go in peace was widespread throughout the city. The economic relationship with the South previous to the secession crisis and the consequent depression played a significant role in fostering secessionist sentiment.

Pittsburgh, whose people opposed secession, was a center for trade with the West. The sentiments of Pittsburgh became vocal when the United States War Department attempted to send arms to southern forts.

On December 23, 1860, the arsenal at Pittsburgh received the order to ship 100 twenty-pound cannons to New Orleans, from where they would be sent to Texas. A telegram to President Buchanan signed by five leading citizens of the city asked that he countermand the War Department order. A mass meeting was held on December 27, and the speakers included Congressman James K. Moorhead. All condemned the removal of the guns to the South.

> Several resolutions were adopted by an almost unanimous vote, declaring the loyalty of the citizens of Pittsburgh to the Union; . . . deprecating any interference with the shipment of arms under the orders of the Government, however inopportune or impolitic the order may be. . . .[123]

While this mass meeting disapproved of mob action, it nevertheless condemned sending arms to the South. Once the War Department rescinded the order, Mayor George Wilson of Pittsburgh congratulated the federal government in words

> expressive of the grateful feeling which now animates all classes for an act of the Government at once so well timed and judicious. . . .[124]

Union meetings in Pittsburgh held throughout the month of January expressed support for the Union. Such actions contradicted the opinions being expressed at the same time in Philadelphia.

x

After the firing upon Fort Sumter, there was an almost universal feeling throughout Pennsylvania that the "flag" and the Union must be defended. Former President James Buchanan wrote to Edwin Stanton expressing the views of many people of Pennsylvania, that

> the first gun fired by Beauregard aroused the indignant spirit of the North as nothing else could have done and made us a unanimous people. I had repeatedly warned them this would be the result. . . .[125]

The pro-Union mob became a brutal force in Pennsylvania, as in so many other states. In Easton they forced Philip Johnson, the congressman from that district, to profess his loyalty to the Union. They then marched to the *Sentinel,* a local newspaper, and destroyed its office. Later the mob wrecked two other newspaper offices. In West Chester, rowdies entered the office of the *Jeffersonian* and stole its type. A mob was active in Philadelphia. H. B. Robinson wrote to Hendrick B. Wright that

> the excitement here to day [sic] is on the increase. Earnest inquiries have been made to day [sic] for Bob Tyler and V. L. Bradford they have been notified that they had better be on their guard. The mob seized today the office of the *Palmetto Flag* and threw the papers into the street. They marched about town and compelled the people to put out the Flag of the Union. They compelled the Merchants Hotel to bring out the Union Flag. Nearly all of the public buildings are decorated with the Flag a report is in circulation that Gen. Patterson is to be mobbed to night [sic] I would not be surprised if it were so, disunionists have to haul down their colors and keep quiet [sic] do not be surprised if the next news you get from here informs you that some of the Southern sympathizers have been hanged an outraged people will not [sic] longer tolerate treason.[126]

H. B. Robinson did not despair that these secessionists were attacked or that they were required to fly the flag for reasons of safety.

Sidney George Fisher also commented in his diary that well-known secessionists were assaulted in the streets and that everywhere he went he saw flags. He commented that

> they are necessary to protect the houses of persons suspected of "secession" opinions from insult by the mob.[127]

Fisher detested the fact that the city was under mob rule and that businesses continued to fail.

> The town, [he said,] is in a wild state of excitement. Everybody is drilling.[128]

He contemplated joining the army but was advised against it for reasons of health.

But not everyone in Pennsylvania gave up pro-secessionist feelings. On April 22, Governor Curtin ordered the arrest of Lieutenant Sennifer as a spy. Stationed at Carlisle Barracks, Sennifer had been sending messages to the Confederacy.

Furthermore fear of spies was especially emphasized when secession flags were run up Pennsylvania flagpoles late at night.[129]

M. S. Buckley wrote to Simon Cameron that the Port Richmond Artillerists, in Philadelphia, refused to offer their services to the government and that the Irish of the city were saying that "if they were to fight at all they would go with the South."[130] The fact that some men, especially Robert Tyler, later joined the Confederacy, showed the extent of their convictions.

Trading with the South continued after the firing upon Fort Sumter. Confiscations of materials destined for the South continued through April and May. Municipal authorities or extra-legal committees set up for the purpose in various Pennsylvania towns seized these illegal goods. One such committee was the Committee of Public Safety, established at a mass meeting held in Pittsburgh on April 15.[131]

On the whole, however, the majority of the people of Pennsylvania supported the Union after the firing upon Fort Sumter. Before this action by the Confederates, a distinction had been made between coercion and protecting the forts. Once the Union was put in the position of defending itself against an attack made by the Confederacy, however, the question of coercion was no longer valid.

Now placed in a position where it had to support either the aggressor, the South, or the Union, the Democratic party chose the Union. Buchanan spoke for the majority of Pennsylvanians who had urged that the South be permitted to go in peace. Once the Confederacy attacked Fort Sumter, he urged that the Union be defended.

xi

There never was a danger that Pennsylvania would join the South. Those who supported such a position did so only after they believed that the Union was permanently divided. Furthermore, few individuals supported a central confederacy. On the other hand many wanted to see the South permitted to leave in peace. In the states of Maryland, Delaware and New Jersey there was a very active secession movement. Within Pennsylvania it was confined primarily to the city of Philadelphia, the southern border and in some areas of northeastern Pennsylvania.

Of the five Middle Atlantic states Pennsylvania had the weakest secession movement. Its institution of slavery had disappeared early, and only the southern border and Philadelphia had strong ties with the South. The central areas and the western region of the State did not support secession.

In Philadelphia the Municipal Council, the Democrats and even some Republicans supported peaceable secession. The Philadelphia Democratic leaders even went further than most of the statewide leaders and would not allow the federal government the right to defend itself.

The Democratic party led the fight for peaceable secession. Its leaders, with the exception of the Governor, wanted the South to leave the Union without a war. In the Pennsylvania Legislature and in the United States Congress the Democrats opposed measures that would strengthen the government or permit the federal government to retake its forts and post offices.

Those who advocated peaceable secession did so in the belief that the use of force was futile. To them war could not restore the Union; it would only permanently divide the nation if it had not already been permanently divided. They also feared that Maryland would join the Confederacy and Pennsylvania would be the battleground. They also feared that the Democratic party would not support such a war and that the Republicans would have to do the fighting. There was concern, too, that the Pennsylvanians would battle among themselves and a civil war would erupt within the State. These fears were assuaged after the firing upon Fort Sumter when the Democratic party supported the Lincoln administration and Maryland did not secede.

The fact that the South attacked a United States fort destroyed the secession movement. The honor of the country had to be defended. The organizations which had argued for the peaceable secession of the South were undermined by the South's aggressive action.

6

NEW YORK

i

THE STATE OF NEW YORK WAS DOMINATED BY NEW YORK CITY, WHICH
contained about one-fourth of the State's population. Therefore, the State
presents a situation differing tremendously from that of the other four
Middle Atlantic states. New York State was made up of sixty counties,
many of them small in population and importance. Of the fifteen most
populated counties, twelve had a valuation of estate, real and personal,
of over $40 million. Of the twelve only two, Oneida and Onondaga, were
diversified, with both agriculture and manufacturing. The leading agricultural counties were Dutchess, Jefferson, Monroe, St. Lawrence, and
Westchester, while Albany, Erie, Kings, New York and Rensselaer led in
manufacturing. Three counties with large populations, but not leaders in
either agriculture or manufacturing were Oswego, Steuben and Ulster.
Three counties, agricultural centers, but not among the fifteen most populated were Cayuga, Columbia, and Orange.

New York City was the manufacturing, commercial, and shipping center
of the United States.

Many New York firms had found their greatest market in the slave
states. This was especially true for those selling the cheap cotton goods
used as clothing for the slaves, although many luxury articles found a
ready market among the planters. So great was the trade with the
South that some companies advertised themselves as "Exclusively for
the Southern Trade." When the South began a boycott and showed a
reluctance to pay its debts prosperity began to give way to panic.[1]

The merchants were afraid that secession would eliminate their markets
in the South and prevent the collection of money owed by southern buyers.

164

It was estimated by a special committee of the New York state Chamber of Commerce that the debts owed to New York merchants by creditors in the seceding states amounted to not less than $150 million.[2]

Yet buyers in the South believed that they spent excessive amounts of money for New York goods, and that the city's merchants and manufacturers were profiting enormously from their purchases. Southerners believed that they could influence New York commercial interests by refusing to make payments due or to buy from the New York market.

Besides the manufacturers and merchants, the shipping interests in New York wanted to maintain the peace. They were concerned that their ships would be attacked and sunk if a war broke out, and they feared the loss of coastwise shipping.

New York dominated the coastal trade and any disturbance would check the prosperity of these shipping lines. As the breach widened, the South made it quite obvious that they would inflict untold harm, directly or indirectly, on the Northern shippers and merchants.[3]

An overwhelming economic tie bound the State, especially New York City, to the South. Social and traditional ties strengthened the bond. One area was the exception—the "burned over" district of upstate New York, known for its religious and social revivals. This section had strong sympathies with New England, and also family connections with the midwest.

In colonial times New York State slave owners were legion, and slavery continued there until just twenty years before the beginning of the Civil War. New York had

the largest and most important slave system in colonial times north of the Mason-Dixon Line.[4]

The State provided an excellent example of urban slavery, where slaves working next to free whites and acquired a variety of special skills.

The Dutch West India Company introduced slaves into New Netherlands in 1626. They were imported to New York

to work on the farms, public buildings, and military works for which free workers were not available. It is doubtful whether New Netherlands would have survived without these slaves, for they provided the labor which ultimately transformed the colony from a shaky commercial outpost into a permanent settlement.[5]

When the British captured New Netherlands in 1664, slavery continued and the slave population multiplied. Slaves were concentrated in New York City and surrounding counties.

By 1746 Negro slaves accounted for 15 per cent of the total New York population.[6]

The Quakers initiated anti-slavery activities, when, in 1771 at their annual convention, they adopted an anti-slavery resolution. This resolution urged the members to free their slaves as their religious duty.[7] When the Revolutionary War began, anti-slavery sentiment increased. Ideologically it was difficult to support both the "Declaration of Independence" and human bondage. But it was

the British occupation of southern New York [that] thoroughly disrupted slave relations.[8]

The British offered freedom to slaves who sought asylum with them, and in 1781 the New York Assembly passed a law that freed all slaves who had served in that State's militia. The result, therefore, undermined the slave system in New York.

Following the war, anti-slavery laws became popular. Measures were introduced that limited and finally ended slavery. In 1785 the Legislature had prohibited the importation of any Negro slave and, three years later, it outlawed the slave trade. Organized in 1785, the New York Manumission Society won support for an emancipation bill. In 1799 the New York Legislature passed a law that established the system of gradual emancipation.

The law freed all children born to slave women after July 4, 1799, the males become free at the age of twenty-eight, and females at the age of twenty-five.[9]

This act was followed by a bill passed in 1817 that freed all slaves born before July 4, 1799 on July 4, 1827.[10] This meant the virtual extinction of slavery in 1827.

The increase in the free population made slavery uneconomical as a system of labor.

In 1771 the ratio of slaves to whites was about one to seven, whereas in 1786 the ratio had declined to one to twelve.[11]

In 1790 New York had 21,324 slaves, which increased ten years later to 30,343, the highest number of slaves that New York ever possessed. By 1820, New York's slightly more than 10,000 slaves showed a 33 percent decrease since 1810. By 1830, 75 slaves remained in the State, ten years later, there were only four.

The bulk of the slaves belonged to masters in the Hudson Valley and the counties that today make up the city of New York.

The election of 1860 split both the Republican and Democratic parties in New York. While the Republicans united behind Abraham Lincoln, the factional Democratic party was attempting to establish a fusion ticket and therefore failed to mount a successful campaign.

The Democratic party had three major factions, the Albany Regency, Tammany Hall, and Mozart Hall. The regular state organization, led by the Albany Regency, and closely connected to the New York Central Railroad, was centered in upstate New York. Its chairman, Dean Richmond, was the vice-president of the New York Central Railroad. Other leaders were Erastus Corning, president of the New York Central and a wealthy iron manufacturer; William Cassidy, editor of the Albany *Atlas and Argus;* ex-Governor Horatio Seymour; and Peter Cagger, secretary of the Democratic State Committee. August Belmont, who was the American agent of the Rothschild fortune, managed the money for the party.

The Tammany Hall organization, centered in New York City, lost some of the power it had and would regain in the future. Its leader, Isaac V. Fowler, past Postmaster of New York, absconded with over $150,000 in May 1860, leaving the faction with no single powerful leader. Mozart Hall, run by Fernando Wood, controlled New York City Hall. Fernando Wood was assisted by his brother, Benjamin, editor of the New York *Daily News.* The New York *Herald* also supported Mozart Hall.[12]

Dean Richmond led the New York delegation to the Democratic National Convention in Charleston, made up of his organization and Tammany's. Fernando Wood challenged the seating of this delegation, and lost. The New York delegation consisted of about thirty persons who opposed Stephen A. Douglas, and forty persons who supported him. However, with the unit rule in effect, the entire New York vote was cast for Stephen A. Douglas and against the southern platform.

> Had the New York delegation been uninstructed or the Wood delegation seated, the Southern rights platform would have been adopted by the convention.[13]

Thirty-five New York votes were cast for Stephen A. Douglas. John Cochrane was a leader of the delegation which voted for Douglas. The anti-Douglas faction was led by Daniel S. Dickinson of Binghamton, who hoped to receive the presidential nomination in the event of a deadlock. His supporters characterized his position

> as a Northern man who had consistently clung to Southern views for years.[14]

Dean Richmond had earlier gained Dickinson's support

> with a promise of solid support for Dickinson for President—and then
> gagged them [Dickinson's delegates] by a rigid unit rule at the Charleston convention in April.[15]

For this reason Daniel S. Dickinson refused to join Dean Richmond and form a fusion ticket of Democratic electors in the November presidential election.

The southern delegates were defeated in their attempt to change the platform of the Democratic party to support the extension of slavery into the territories. These southern delegates withdrew from the convention and held their own at Charleston. which has been referred to as the "seceders" convention. New York was represented there. However. only two votes were cast for Dickinson. Most of the delegates felt that it was inappropriate to take part because of their instructions from the state convention. When this convention later met in Richmond, New York was again represented.

The regular Democratic Convention adjourned to Baltimore where New York cast its thirty-five votes for Stephen A. Douglas. August Belmont, a Tammanyite (the Tammany organization supported Stephen A. Douglas), was elected to the National Executive Committee. He was also elected chairman of the pro-Douglas Democratic National Committee. A significant Douglas supporter, Horatio Seymour, was a former governor who later opposed war with the South. Mayor Fernando Wood of New York City, and his Mozart Club, preferred Breckinridge. But on July 6, Wood issued a manifesto, in which he stated that while he preferred Breckinridge, he knew Breckinridge

> could not win in the North. . . . Wood had decided to vote for Douglas, and he urged all to save New York from Lincoln.[16]

Fernando Wood led the fight for a fusion ticket in the November election.

The Breckinridge supporters were primarily officeholders, which again showed the attitude of the Buchanan segment of the party.[17] The Breckinridge supporters met in convention in Syracuse on August 8, where they nominated James T. Brady for Governor and chose a set of electors pledged to Breckinridge. They realized that New York City had social and commercial relations with the South.[18] They hoped to capitalize on this support.

> The federal patronage was utilized for the Breckinridge ticket: Collector Schell and Surveyor Hart, of the port of New York, and Sub-Treasurer Cisco attended Breckinridge meetings.[19]

James Gordon Bennett, editor of the *Herald,* backed Breckinridge and urged his readers not to support any fusion with the Douglas Democrats.

The Douglas Democrats held their convention on August 15 in Syracuse. Both the Tammany and Mozart Hall factions were seated, much to the disgust of the Tammany Club. William Kelly was nominated for Governor. The Douglas Democrats worked out a fusion ticket with the Constitutional Unionists, who were supporting John Bell for President, giving the Bell men ten electors.

Several attempts at fusion between the Breckinridge and Douglas supporters, made in early September, failed. When Stephen A. Douglas spoke in New York, he opposed fusion with the Breckinridge men. He said:

> I am utterly opposed to any union or any fusion with any man or any party who will not enforce the laws, maintain the constitution, and preserve the Union in all contingencies. . . .[20]

But this did not end the efforts towards fusion. A meeting was held in Cooper Institute on September 17, called by Joshua Henry, a prominent merchant "in the southern dry-goods trade."[21] A committee of fifteen was formed to establish a fusion ticket. It resulted in the division of the New York electors as follows: eighteen Douglas, ten Bell and seven Breckinridge electors. But since this was mid-October, it was too late. The victory of the Republican party in Pennsylvania made a Democratic presidential victory a matter of wishful thinking.[22] The Breckinridge faction of the party also refused to withdraw its candidate for Governor, James T. Brady.

The election was a complete victory for the Republican party. Abraham Lincoln received 362,367 votes while the fusion ticket received 313,790 votes, making Lincoln's majority 48,577. The fusion ticket carried only ten counties, all in the Hudson Valley or New York City with the exception of Sullivan County, located in southeastern New York just west of the Hudson Valley. Of these ten counties seven had had a significant slave population. Lincoln was able to carry four of the former slaveholding counties. The Republican candidate for Governor Edwin D. Morgan won by a majority of 45,577, and received 64,482 more votes than the fusion candidate, William Kelly. The Breckinridge candidate for Governor, James T. Brady, ran a poor third with only 19,310 votes.

The key to the Republican success can be found in the votes that the American party members gave to Lincoln.

The 1859 election had indicated that the "Americans" held the balance of power between Republicans and Democrats. . . .[23]

In 1856, Millard Fillmore had polled 124,000 votes in New York or 21 per cent of the whole. . . . if enough of the nativists voted for Bell, Douglas would carry New York.[24]

While Millard Fillmore did not support Lincoln, many Americans did. Two major American newspapers, the Albany *Statesman* and the Buffalo *Commercial Advertiser* endorsed Lincoln.

. . . the greater part of those who supported Fillmore in 1856 voted for Lincoln in 1860.[25]

At the same time, many upstate Democrats voted for Lincoln rather than casting their votes for an opposing faction within their own party.[26] The result was that the fusion ticket damaged the possibilities of a Democratic victory, as much as it helped unite the party.

The great mercantile interests of New York City were for the most part a source of strength to the anti-Lincoln ticket. It was the merchants who took the lead in effecting the fusion.[27]

The merchants held out the promise of money to unite the Democratic party in the presidential election. Mayor Fernando Wood, of New York City,

expressed concern for commerce, though also for manufacturing and agriculture—"its handmaiden." He thought that the issue of slavery in the territories was trivial beside the important issue, "our continued commercial prosperity."[28]

The fusion ticket

received 65% of the New York City returns, and 58% in Brooklyn, while in upstate rural New York Lincoln amassed 58% as against 42% for fusion.[29]

The fusion ticket carried the cities of Troy and Albany while Lincoln carried Buffalo, Rochester, Syracuse, and Utica. Brooklyn voted for the fusion ticket because a "substantial anti-Negro sentiment"[30] existed there. The large immigrant population of Brooklyn and the anti-Negro sentiments of the influential leaders of the community account for this vote.

The Republican party fared better in the election of 1860 than in 1856. While Fremont carried New York he had lost twenty-seven counties. In almost all of the counties that Lincoln lost, he received more votes than Fremont. Lincoln was a more popular candidate than Fremont, and the Republican party was better organized in 1860.

The whole State showed a Republican gain over the figures of 1856 of almost 100,000 votes.[31]

Nevertheless, a proposed constitutional amendment, which would have given the suffrage to Negroes, was defeated by over 140,000.

As the vote against the amendment exceeded the vote for the fusion electoral ticket by 30,000, many supporters of Lincoln must have cast their ballots against an extension of negro suffrage.[32]

Lincoln's election in New York, therefore, did not mean equality for the Negro, and it is significant that those areas that had possessed the greatest slave populations voted against the Republicans.

iii

After the election of 1860, the Democratic party in New York continued to be divided among its three factions: The Albany Regency, Tammany Hall, and Mozart Hall. On January 18, 1861, the Democratic State Committee issued a call for a convention to be held on January 31 in Albany. While this convention was called by the Albany Regency, all factions of the Democratic party attended as well as supporters of John Bell. According to Horace Greeley

> it was probably the strongest and most imposing assemblage of delegates ever convened within the State. Not less than thirty of them had been chosen to seats in Congress, while three of them had been Democratic candidates for Governor. . . . There was a large and most respectable representation of the old Whig party, with a number who had figured as "Americans." No Convention which had nominations to make, or patronage to dispose of, was ever so influentially constituted. All sympathizing State officers and members of the Legislature were formally invited to participate in its deliberations.[33]

In its call for the convention, the Democratic State Central Committee stated:

> In this emergency conservative men of all classes call upon our time-honored party, which at this moment represents the views and feelings of a majority of the people of New York, to co-operate with patriotic citizens elsewhere, and especially with the efforts of the "Border States," in putting down the agitations and conspiracies of the Secessionists of the South and the ultra Republicans of the North.
>
> The honor and interests of our own State also call for action on our part, to check schemes of corrupt legislation which are already engendered under pretexts of military and coercive projects.[34]

The convention was run by the Albany Regency, and its president was Judge Amasa J. Parker. Parker had been the Democratic candidate for governor in 1856 and was a Supreme Court justice who lived in Albany. Eight major speeches were delivered, the first by Parker who said that the people of New York wanted a policy of compromise and a peaceful settlement of the dispute.[35] In another speech Horatio Seymour also supported conciliation and declared that it was "madness" to raise an army to "occupy" the South.[36]

On the second day, Lyman Tremain, declared

> that not only would the Democracy of the State not join in a civil war on the South but they would interpose [itself] to prevent it; not only would the Republicans have to fight such a battle without them but in spite of them.

He said it was unconstitutional for the governor to raise an army to fight the South and plunge the State into debt.[37]

James S. Thayer felt that the seceded states could not be brought back by force and advocated peaceable secession.

> What, then is the duty of the State of New York? What shall we say to our people when we come to meet this state of facts? That the Union must be preserved. But if that cannot be, what then? *Peaceable separation.*[38]

James S. Thayer, at a meeting during the winter of 1860–61, said that if the federal government attempted to use force,

> we will reverse the order of the French Revolution, . . . by making those who would inaugurate a reign of terror, the first victims of a national guillotine.[39]

Not only did Thayer support peaceable separation but also the use of force against the federal government if it attempted to hold the states in the Union.

Samuel J. Tilden, another speaker, also opposed coercion declaring that

> he, for one, would resist under any and all circumstances, the use of force to coerce the South into the Union. . . .[40]

Ex-Chancellor Reuben H. Walworth also protested any attempt to bring about a civil war. Alex B. Johnson expressed similar views, stating that the people of New York State were against coercion as a means of maintaining the Union.[41]

The only pro-Union speech was given by George W. Clinton, from Buffalo, son of DeWitt Clinton and a supporter of John C. Breckinridge. He referred to secession as unlawful and rebellious. He spoke for the preservation of the Union and its property even if it meant war.[42] His speech received applause, which revealed a group of individuals whose sentiments had not been expressed until that time. But the majority supported the views of the previous speakers who endorsed peaceable separation of the Union.

The resolutions adopted were not so outspoken as the speakers. They supported the Crittenden compromise and condemned coercion. According to the Brooklyn *Daily Eagle* the desire not to "weaken the moral force of the convention" resulted in a moderate set of resolutions, but

> as the resolutions were sufficiently emphatic in a condemnation of a resort to arms and the duty of appealing to the people, and of staying the Southern revolution by conciliation, those who felt disposed to insist on a more unequivocal expression of opinion, thought it better to "take the good to [*sic*] God provided them," than to hazard any action which might lead to even a seeming difference of opinion. On the cardinal points involved in the present controversy the convention was a unit.[43]

Horace Greeley expressed the view that this convention strengthened the southern states in their attitude towards secession. The speeches and resolutions of the convention

> were hailed by the engineers of Secession as proof positive that they would either not be forcibly opposed at all, or would have no difficulty in overcoming, by the help of their sympathizing friends and allies in the Free States, any resistance to their purpose that might be offered. Mr. Roscoe Conkling attests that, when the proceedings of this Convention reached Washington, they were hailed with undistinguished exultation by the Secessionists still lingering in the halls of Congress; one of whom said to him triumphantly, "If your President should attempt coercion, he will have more opposition *at the North* than he can overcome."[44]

The sentiments of the Democratic party were clearly presented in this convention and their effect can be seen in Greeley's statement. Other newspapers agreed with Greeley. The New York *Daily News* wrote that the Democratic party of New York would not permit coercion. The New York *Journal of Commerce,* concluded that the convention opposed the use of force to maintain a state in the Union.[45]

August Belmont, one of the most influential men in the Democratic party, wrote letters to southern Unionists and businessmen attempting to hold the southern states in the Union. He urged the North to make concessions to the South. In November, opposing the idea of secession, he wrote that

> the idea of separate confederacies living in peace and prosperity on this

continent, after a dissolution of the Union, is too preposterous to be entertained by any man of sound sense, and the slightest knowledge of history.

Secession means civil war, to be followed by a total disintegration of the whole fabric, after endless sacrifices of blood and treasure.[46]

This letter not only points out that Belmont disapproved of the right of secession as impractical but also that he opposed the idea of coercion to hold states in the Union. As the crisis became increasingly evident and more states left the Union, he printed and mailed out hundreds of copies of John P. Kennedy's pamphlet, *The Border States*.[47] In a letter to John J. Crittenden, Belmont referred to *The Border States* as a pamphlet, which contained suggestions that

> are practical and statesmanlike, and I hope they may find an echo in your State, and in Virginia.[48]

While Belmont opposed the use of force to retain the southern states, he also disagreed with Fernando Wood's idea that New York should secede and become a free city. He continued to hope for a peaceful settlement but after Fort Sumter fell, he supported the Union.

Another leading Democrat, Horatio Seymour, who had already served one term as Governor, would be reelected during the Civil War. He wrote to Senator John J. Crittenden that he supported the Kentuckian's compromise and hoped that it would be submitted to the people for a vote.

> In the event of the northern vote going against the compromise measures of Crittenden, the middle states "would be amply justified, before the world to posterity in casting their lot with their more southern brethren."[49]

He presented the best statement of his views on the question of secession in his speech at the Albany Democratic Convention. The North, he argued, could not win a war with the South, and that some sort of compromise was therefore imperative.

> The question is simply this: Shall we have compromise after the war, or compromise without war?[50]

He opposed force as a weapon to hold the states in the Union as simply impossible. The idea was anathema.

Samuel J. Tilden took a leading part in the fusion electoral ticket of 1860. During the secession crisis, he actively supported attempts at compromise. Even before the election of Lincoln, he predicted if we elect Lincoln, and we invite those perils which we cannot measure; we attempt in vain to conquer the submission of the South to an impracticable and intolerable policy. . . .[51]

He urged conciliation. In January he endorsed calling a national convention to propose amendments to the Constitution. In his speech to the Democratic Convention in Albany he stated:

I do firmly believe that coercion is no remedy for the present state of things. . . . to attempt coercion, you will surely fail. . . . my hand shall never be raised against our brethren of the South.[52]

However, when John O'Sullivan, a Democrat living in Paris, stated that he was trying to buy arms for the South, Tilden did not answer his letter.[53] After the fall of Fort Sumter, Tilden supported the government.

One of the great enigmas of the Democratic party during this period, John A. Dix, was appointed Secretary of the Treasury in the Buchanan cabinet. He gave orders to a special agent who was sent to the South to return two revenue cutters. These orders were that

if any person attempts to haul down the American flag, shoot him on the spot.[54]

While he took this position as a member of the cabinet, before his appointment he had supported the peaceable secession of the southern states.

In a letter to New York's Governor Edwin Morgan, on December 20, 1860, the Secretary of the New York congressional delegation, John B. Haskin, stated that his delegation had met and passed a resolution favoring the enforcement of the Constitution although the New York City congressmen were not present at this meeting. In his letter Haskin called upon Morgan to express Unionist sentiments in his annual address, so

that those who are now engaged in the work of destroying the federal government may know that New York at least will never submit to the doctrine of secession as recently enunciated by Messrs. O'Conner [sic], Dix and Tilden.[55]

John A. Dix had supported John C. Breckinridge. Throughout the months of November and December 1860, he tried to persuade the southerners not to secede until the northern Democrats could bring the majority of northerners to accept southern rights. He believed earnestly that the South was deserting their supporters in the North, leaving them to face the Republicans alone.[56]

By January he wrote Horatio King, Postmaster General in Buchanan's cabinet, that

> the feeling here is strong and undivided in regard to sustaining the administration to stand by Major Anderson, to protect the public property, and to enforce the revenue laws. . . .[57]

On January 15, he assumed the position of Secretary of Treasury and soon issued his famous order to shoot anyone who attempted to take down the American flag.

If Dix seemed to change his position radically, he did not. Although he favored the peaceable secession of the South, at the same time he felt that the southern states should not seize United States forts or stop the enforcement of the revenue laws. As late as March 15, he wrote William Seward that if the southern states were permitted to leave the Union they should return the money, ships and equipment they had taken from the United States.[58] In a memorandum written by General Dix himself, in 1875, he expressed the point of view that if the South had not used violence, the North would have permitted them to leave the Union peaceably.

> . . . many of us never thought it possible that a violent separation from the Union would be attempted. . . . As for myself, I never dreamed of the coming war; I detested abolitionism . . . my sympathies were with the South, and I had no doubt of their right, if they chose, to free themselves gently from those bonds which held us together. Under these impressions I voted for Breckinridge and Lane. . . .[59]

Dix's son wrote,

> It was his [father's] opinion that a separation, if sought by the South through peaceful means alone, must be conceded by the North, as an evil less than that of war.[60]

iv

Mayor Fernando Wood of New York City was best known for his recommendation that when secession became a reality, New York should become a free city by breaking away from the United States as well as from the State.

There had been several proposals that New York City secede even before Mayor Wood's statement.

> During the campaign of 1860, the Union electoral committee had warned that a Republican victory would force the New York merchants to organize a free city in order "to retain even the smallest part" of the Southern and Western trade.[61]

This was followed in December by a series of statements that there were individuals who wanted to make New York a free city. Edward Bates, in his *Diary* entry for December 8, 1860, mentioned the existence of such a group. Two days later Democratic Congressman Daniel Sickles from New York City said,

> in the event of secession in the South, New York City would free herself from the hated Republican "State" government of New York and throw open her ports to free commerce.[62]

The New York *Leader,* which had supported Stephen A. Douglas, mentioned that there was a plan to separate the city of New York from the State. The New York *Express,* presented similar views, while the New York *Herald,* stated that a

> secret meeting of its promoters is to be held today. . . . The object is in the event of a secession of the Southern states, to throw off the yoke of the Western part of this state, and make New York a free city.[63]

In an article that favored making New York a free city, the *American Railway Review* quoted a prominent New York banker[64] as favoring such a plan. All of these preceded the message delivered by Fernando Wood, and all had the same premise.

On January 6, 1861, Mayor Wood delivered the famous message in which he expressed his desire to see New York a free city once the Union was dissolved. Yet he opposed the obtaining of this freedom through violence. At the same time he believed that the United States was a compact of sovereign states and that

> it cannot be preserved by coercion or held together by force.[65]

His reasons for creating a free city were that New Yorkers could maintain their trade with both the North and the South and that the New York State Legislature was usurping the city's power and suppressing its rights.

> . . . judging from the past, New York may have more cause of apprehension from the aggressive legislation of our own State than from external dangers. . . .
> The Legislature, in which the present partizan [sic] majority has the power, has become the instrument by which we are plundered to enrich their speculators, lobby agents, and Abolition politicians.[66]

Third, the city of New York would be economically more prosperous outside of the Union than within.

As a free city, with but nominal duty on imports, her local Government could be supported without taxation upon her people. Thus we could live free from taxes, and have cheap goods nearly duty free.[67]

His plan revolved around the dissolution of the Union and the popular support of New Yorkers in general, and it gained particular interest from the merchants engaged in trade with the South.

Only three New York City newspapers supported the idea: the *Daily News,* his brother's newspaper, the New York *Morning Express,* and the *Day Book.* The New York *Herald,* which usually supported the Mozart faction of the Democratic party failed to endorse Wood's scheme. The other New York newspapers ridiculed the plan. The Albany *Atlas and Argus,* the spokesman for the Albany Regency, argued that New York City was economically tied to the State by the Hudson River, the Erie Canal and the New York Central Railroad. Secession from the State,

> would dwarf the great city to reduce it to the level of the German Free towns. Its destiny is with the State; and the greatness of the State is tributary to its own.[68]

Except for the merchants the Wood plan won little support.

There was comment in the South about New York City's becoming a free city. The Louisiana Legislature referred a letter from a citizen of Brooklyn asking Louisiana to extend an invitation to New Jersey and southern New York to unite with the Southern Confederacy, to its Committee on Federal Relations.[69] George Fitzhugh wrote an article for *DeBow's Review,* February 1861, urging that New York City become the "Republic of New York." He pointed out that New York City had considerable trade with the South which would be endangered if it stayed with the North.

> When she sets up for herself, her free-trade policy will give offense to none, make friends of all. . . . The South is accustomed to deal in New York, and although she *can* live independently of her, will feel no disposition to withdraw from a steadfast and a powerful friend, especially, when to do so would only subject her to great temporary privation. For European trade New York is best situated: she almost now monopolizes it, and will not lose it, unless she comes under Yankee rule, and offends the South.
>
> . . . there is no reason, that we can see, why she and a few adjoining counties might not contain a prosperous and enlightened population of ten millions. . . .
>
> Should New York fail to erect herself into a free port and separate republic; should she remain under the dominion of the corrupt, venal wire-workers of Albany, and of the immoral infidel, agrarian, free-love democracy of western New York; should she put herself under the rule of Puritans, the vilest, most selfish, and unprincipled of the human

race; should she join a northern confederacy; should she make New England, western New York . . . her masters; should she make enemies of her Southern friends, and deliver herself up to the tender mercies of her Northern enemies, she will sink to rise no more.[70]

This was typical of the thinking that motivated southerners to pressure for New York City's independence.

This pressure was especially severe upon the merchants of the city. The *Journal of Commerce* of November 5, 1860, stated that:

There are a million and a half mouths to be fed daily in this city and its dependencies; and they will not consent to be starved by any man's policies. They will sooner set up for themselves against the whole world.[71]

John A. Kennedy, the Superintendent of Police of New York City, on January 22 seized the steamer *Monticello,* bound for Savannah, Georgia, carrying muskets. This episode became a major incident and, before it was over, Governor Edwin Morgan apologized to the state of Georgia. Several New York vessels were seized in Savannah and held as hostages. United States Secretary of War Joseph Holt refused to support Kennedy and the *Monticello* was finally released. Kennedy was a staunch Union man who did not trust Fernando Wood. In December he had written Governor Morgan, that

I have been informed, through a source on which reliance may be placed, that Mayor Wood is arranging with others to make an open demonstration in favor of Secession.[72]

Mayor Wood wrote an apology to the Governor of Georgia and pointed out that he had no control over the police of his city. Wood said that

if I had the power I should summarily punish the authors of this illegal and unjustifiable seizure of private property.[73]

After this episode with Georgia, Mayor Fernando Wood continued to oppose the use of force. When Abraham Lincoln stopped in New York City on his way to Washington, Wood said:

To you, therefore, . . . we look for a restoration of fraternal relations between the States—only to be accomplished by peaceful and conciliatory means—aided by the wisdom of Almighty God.[74]

On April 4, the Mozart Hall General Committee passed a series of resolutions that were

opposed to every form of menace, restraint, or coercion under whatsoever pretext of enforcing law, collecting revenue, or retaking property, which may lead to a conflict with the seceded States. . . .[75]

Both of these statements placed Wood and his organization in opposition to the use of force. The Mozart Hall resolutions appear to accept the "seceded States" as an accomplished fact.

The Albany *Atlas and Argus,* the newspaper of the Albany Regency, had supported Stephen A. Douglas in the election of 1860. As early as December 15, this newspaper stated that

> when, however, the Southern States become *de facto* a separate Confederacy, we shall consider the present Union at an end in all its parts. Then New York will seek to gather around her, in mutual relations of friendship, the States that will naturally seek her alliance, and will open her ports and offer her internal lines of communication to their use. She will preserve her own freedom and give to her sister confederates and to the world the boon of freedom of trade.[76]

By January it was opposing the use of coercion that would result in a civil war. By the middle of February it was supporting peaceable secession, stating that it would lead to a settlement and a reconstruction of the Union. This newspaper continued to oppose the use of war as a means to unite the country. On March 20, it published a letter signed by "Pride," which took the position that the United States was destroyed and that the Confederate States would be a permanent entity. The letter recommended that New York become an independent nation, which in "Pride's" opinion, would be the

> richest and most prosperous State in Christendom. Let us then, in New York, take the matter seriously in hand, weigh and consider the advantages of an independent existence for our favored State . . . and to abandon once [and] for all, the indulgence of hopes of a reconstruction of a Union we once loved, but which has perished forever.

While the Albany *Atlas and Argus* opposed Wood's idea of a free city, it supported the secession of the State.

While the New York City Democratic party, the center for secessionist activities, encouraged a free city, other segments of the party hoped that the state would become independent. Almost all the major Democrats opposed the use of force to retain the South within the Union.

v

The small American party that existed in the state of New York was led by Washington Hunt. Hunt wrote in December of 1860, that

I am for saving the Union by conciliation and against civil war. When the federal tie is broken it cannot be restored by shedding the blood of our brethren.[77]

Millard Fillmore, who had been the party's presidential standard bearer in 1856, hoped for a compromise. He opposed both the right of secession and civil war.

The Republican party was split into two wings. One segment, which had once supported the Whig party, was led by William H. Seward, Thurlow Weed and Henry J. Raymond, editor of the New York *Times*. The anti-Seward segment of the party was made up of former free-soil Democrats led by Horace Greeley, William Cullen Bryant, and David Dudley Field.[78] Field had been the Republican candidate for the United States Senate in 1857 and was later to be a United States Supreme Court Justice.

It is interesting to observe that the leadership of both segments of the New York Republican party favored a policy that would have permitted the South to go in peace. The Seward-Weed faction, represented by Thurlow Weed and Henry J. Raymond, and Horace Greeley of the anti-Seward faction, took a similar position—one that would have recognized *de facto* secession. However, the rank and file Republicans tended to support Lincoln's position of no compromise and the use of force.

Thurlow Weed was the editor of the Albany *Evening Journal,* and had supported Abraham Lincoln in the election of 1860. As the secession crisis deepened, Weed argued for the extension of the Missouri Compromise line and the compensation for fugitive slaves by those counties where violence prevented their recovery by their masters. The result of this policy led to his being attacked by the more radical Republicans who did not favor any form of compromise. On the other hand, New York businessmen and some of his former opponents praised his suggestions. August Belmont wrote approvingly to Weed of his suggestion.[79]

From some of his former supporters Thurlow Weed was receiving letters urging that the South be permitted to go in peace. Weed himself appeared to adopt this policy by March of 1861. In the Albany *Evening Journal* of March 18, 1861, he wrote that secession would lose its glamor and the states would return to the Union.

. . . the People of the Gulf States will discover the real character of the entertainment to which they were invited. And then the Leaders of Rebellion will be called to an account. These leaders dread nothing so much as to "be let alone, severely." They have prepared themselves for War, and do all they can to provoke it. The Government, on the other hand, will endeavor to preserve Peace. Unless the Insurgents resist the execution of the Laws there will be no collisions.

Weed disagreed with the Lincoln administration's use of its patronage power and its tariff policy. He felt that Lincoln could have reduced the tariff and appointed leading individuals from the border states. If this were done, Weed concluded, it would have brought the secession states back in "the course of a couple of years."[80]

By April, Weed had taken the position that

> the refusal to permit the ordinary supplies to be sent to Fort Sumpter [*sic*] was an act of war—as much so as a bombardment, and more inhuman.[81]

He now placed the blame for the forthcoming war upon the South and felt that the southerners were the aggressors.

Not all of Weed's supporters favored his earlier policies of compromise or of permitting the South to go in peace. Governor Edwin D. Morgan, who belonged to the Seward-Weed faction of the party, opposed compromise with the South. Governor Morgan in his annual address, delivered on January 2, 1861, said that no state could voluntarily withdraw from the Union, that this was disunion and "treason" which the government had to arrest and punish.

> The laws of the United States must be executed; the requirements of the Constitution must be obeyed.[82]

He argued for the repeal of New York's 1840 statute permitting fugitive slaves the right of a jury trial, which he felt was unconstitutional. He called upon other states to repeal any law that might be considered a personal liberty law, and yet he opposed the extension of slavery into the territories.

Henry J. Raymond, editor of the New York *Times,* advocated a policy that resembled Thurlow Weed's. Soon after the November elections, Raymond wanted a compromise with the South, which would reimburse the owners of fugitive slaves. He hoped that such a compromise would prevent the border slave states from seceding. He based his entire policy upon the southern Unionists, who, he felt, would eventually rise and overthrow the secessionists. By the end of November he favored peaceable secession. The southern people had the right to decide for themselves what course they would take in this period of crisis. He also said that these states could not be retained by force.[83]

By February, he stated that the Union must be preserved and that there was no right of secession. The South, he felt, could bring about war if it wished, but the federal government should not provoke war. The Lincoln administration was indeed following the correct course. In March, while he opposed peaceable secession, which according to him would cause war, he opposed coercive policies that would force the states to stay in the Union.

> The true policy of the Government is unquestionably that of *masterly inactivity*. The object to be aimed at is, the conversion of the Southern people from their Secessionism. . . .[84]

Just before the firing upon Fort Sumter, Raymond was lending his total support to the administration regardless of the consequences. If it meant war, that was better than surrender.[85] Henry J. Raymond's policy vacillated on the issue of secession from

> unconcern, compromise, watchful waiting, and compromise again, [it] relied steadfastly on the development of Southern Unionist strength, first to prevent secession and later to limit that movement to the seven states of the relatively defenceless Lower South.[86]

By the time of the firing upon Fort Sumter he steadfastly supported the Lincoln administration.

Horace Greeley, an opponent of Seward and Weed, wrote to Abraham Lincoln on December 22, 1860, opposing the right of secession.[87] But while opposing the abstract right of secession, he wrote that a

> political community large and strong enough to maintain a National existence—have a right to form and modify their institutions in accordance with their own convictions of justice and policy. Hence if seven or eight contiguous States (not one small one) were to come to Washington saying, "We are tired of the Union—let us out!"—I should say, "There's the door—go!" and I think they would have a *right* to go, even though no one recognized it.[88]

He recognized the right of revolution, whereby a strong group of people could win its freedom. Do not fight them, he argued, but let them go. Yet if the seceding states attacked the United States, then the North would have the right to defend herself.[89] Greeley made it clear that:

> We shall never have peace nor equality in the Union till the Free States shall say to the Slave, "If you want to go, go. . . ."[90]

To Greeley there was no longer any point in discussing the question,

> The Cotton States *are going*. Nothing that we can offer will stop them.[91]

What he opposed more than secession was another compromise with the South.

> I fear nothing, care for nothing, but another disgraceful backdown of

the Free States. That is the only real danger. Let the Union slide . . .
but another nasty compromise whereby everything is conceded and nothing secured will so thoroughly disgrace and humilate us that we can
never again raise our heads. . . .[92]

James Ford Rhodes, a late-nineteenth-century historian who believed
that the sole cause of the war was slavery, made an interesting observation
about the strength of Greeley's views in the New York Republican party.

. . . a respectable minority of Republicans were inclined to a similar
view in the last months of 1860. That Greeley came near being nominated United States senator [sic] by the New York Republican caucus
in February, 1861. . . .[93]

Horace Greeley's sincerity is shown in a letter to William H. Herndon,
Lincoln's law partner, on December 26:

I would have liked very much to talk peace and fraternity—begging the
Secessionists to look toward a peaceable separation; but our friends will
not listen to any thing [sic] but fight, so I shall have to let them have
their own way.[94]

The South was buoyed by Greeley's statements, J. L. Pugh and J. L.
McCurry reported to the Alabama Convention in January that

the opinion generally obtained in Washington that the secession of five
or more States would prevent or put an end to coercion, and the New
York Tribune, the most influential of Republican journals, concedes
that the secession of so many States would make coercion impracticable.[95]

When Greeley later supported the Union he was not changing his position as so many have accused him of doing. He was simply accepting the
idea that the South would not secede in peace and that war was therefore
the only alternative. The government

must deal justly with the North as well as the South; must recover the
property which belongs to both in the Union, to neither without it;
and must assert its own authority, or be forever a subject for derision
to the civilized world. . . .[96]

The seizure of federal property moved Greeley towards this position because, to him, this was an act of aggression by the South.

One of the members of Greeley's faction of the Republican party,
William Cullen Bryant, editor of the New York Evening Post, printed an
editorial criticizing the idea of peaceful secession soon after Greeley's
famous editorial. As Allen Nevins cites:

No government could have a day of assured existence, he wrote, if it tolerated the doctrine of peaceable secession, for it could have no credit or future. "No, if a State secedes it is in rebellion, and the seceders are traitors."[97]

Among the Republicans, some who opposed the institution of slavery would have liked to see the South leave the Union. An abolitionist Republican, Gerrit Smith, said on February 6, that

our States cannot be held together by force, and should not if they could.[98]

These abolitionists felt that the country was better off without the corrupting influence of the South.

While these are the views of some Republican leaders, many members disagreed with them. Most Republicans favored a strong position that would defend the Union from the secession of the South. John E. Wool, who had been born in New York State and was commander of the Army's Department of the East, opposed amending the Constitution and recommended that the United States forts be strengthened. Ezra Cornell, writing to a friend in the South, said:

we at the North [are] condemning the treason. . . .[99]

Even the rank and file Republicans in New York City urged that a firmer policy be taken towards the South. The radical anti-Seward Young Men's Republican Union wrote Lincoln that they

utterly disown and repudiate the idea that peaceable *Secession* is possible, and that the permanency of this *Union* is dependent upon the whims or wish of any single *city, state,* or *section.* . . .
. . . that we endorse, in advance, any action proposed by the *incoming administration* which shall present a *firm unyielding front of opposition* to traitors and which shall indicate a policy devoted solely to the *enforcement of the Laws, the up-holding of the Constitution and the perpetuity of the Union.*[100]

The Republican party within New York was therefore split between those who supported Lincoln and his policy of no concessions to the South and most of the leaders who at some time during the crisis wanted the South to go in peace.

vi

The New York Legislature convened in January 1861 with the Republicans holding a substantial majority. Major resolutions and bills were introduced that affected New York's position toward secession, one of them stating that:

> The insurgent State of South Carolina . . . by firing into a vessel ordered by the government to convey troops and provisions to Fort Sumpter, [sic] virtually declared war. . . .[101]

The New York Legislature was determined to preserve the Union and that they would give

> whatever aid in men and money he [Buchanan] may require to enable him to enforce the laws and uphold the authority of the Federal Government. . . .[102]

The resolution also praised the border states that had not seceded. This resolution received only two negative votes, both from New York City legislators. In the New York Senate this resolution was amended to include a section stating that treason existed "in one or more of the States of this Union. . . ."[103] The only senator to vote against it came from Sullivan County. In February, a bill appropriating $500,000 to equip the militia passed the Legislature with the Republicans voting for it; the Democrats, with but one exception, against it.

On April 15, 1861, a bill was introduced into both houses that provided equipment for

> the volunteer militia, and to provide for the public defence.[104]

There were six votes against it in the Assembly, all from New York City assemblymen, and in the Senate two negative votes, from senators from Kings and Queens Counties. Where the Democratic party had been almost united when they opposed such a bill in February, only the New York City area legislators provided the negative votes after the firing upon Fort Sumter.

Francis Kernan, the Democratic leader in the New York Assembly, who was from Niagara County, stated on April 16,

> that because he believed there was danger of attempts on the national capital, he favored furnishing the federal government with means to repel such an aggression. "But," he continued, "I am opposed to, and I trust the National Government will not attempt to carry an aggressive war into the Southern States. Such a war will neither preserve or restore the Union. . . . If, then, we cannot adjust our differences now by concessions which will make us one people, is it not better to separate peaceably?"[105]

Therefore the votes for this bill to provide troops and equipment did not mean that everyone that voted for it favored a policy of coercion against the South. But it was the New York City representatives who consistently voted against any measure to improve the arms of the New York militia.

Governor Morgan sent a special message to the Legislature urging that it send a delegation to the Washington Peace Conference. Opposition arose within both houses, led by the supporters of Horace Greeley who consistently opposed any compromise with the South. Eleven delegates were selected, including Republicans, Democrats and Constitutional Unionists. When it came to the final vote in February of 1861, the delegation at the Convention was evenly split: five were for the compromise resolutions and five opposed. Absent was David Dudley Field, who was arguing a case before the United States Supreme Court. Field, a member of the Greeley segment of the Republican party, had opposed the propositions proposed by the Convention and would have voted against them, and thus broken the tie.

Of those individuals representing New York at the Washington Peace Conference, two spoke out on the question of war and secession. Greene C. Bronson of New York City, a Democrat, introduced an amendment that opposed the use of force to maintain the Union, while at the same time refused to recognize the right of secession.[106] Amaziah B. James of Ogdensburg said that if the North were forced to defend the government it would do so, but that ". . . the North proposes no civil war."[107] The division within the state of New York can easily be seen in this eleven-man delegation. It was divided on the question of secession and compromise.

vii

At the same time the New York delegation in the United States Congress was divided, but the majority were pro-war and anti-compromise. New York was represented by two Republican United States Senators. Preston King, from Ogdensburg, represented the upstate Republicans. He had been a Democrat but broke with that party over the issue of slavery in Kansas and Nebraska. During the secession crisis he remained a staunch Republican and opposed any compromise with the South. He wrote Thurlow Weed a vigorous letter condemning Weed's compromise plan. King asked Weed:

> are you willing to be instrumental in making the proposed amendments of Mr. Crittenden enclosed herein or any thing like them a part of the Constitution of the United States—It is possible you do not see the magnitude of the evil to spring from your favoring such a proposition. . . .[108]

His votes in the United States Senate are indicative of his beliefs. He voted with the North four times and twice against compromise. He never supported the South or compromise.

The more famous Senator from New York was William H. Seward, who was to resign and become Abraham Lincoln's Secretary of State. A close friend and political partner of Thurlow Weed, he was also from upstate New York. William Seward delivered two speeches in January of 1861 in which he denied the right of secession and expressed the opinion that the federal government should not permit the southern states to leave the Union. To Seward, no compromise could be made, but Congress should redress any legitimate grievances that the states might have. He urged Congress to prohibit the interference with the institution of slavery where it existed, but at the same time opposed the extension of slavery. The only way that the

> Union can be dissolved, [is] not by secession, with or without armed force, but only by the voluntary consent of the people of the United States, collected in the manner prescribed by the Constitution of the United States.[109]

He urged that the President maintain the Union by all the authority at his disposal.

On January 31, he made his position clearer. He predicted that after compromise attempts had failed,

> then, this Union is to stand or fall by the force of arms, I have advised my people to do, as I shall be ready to do myself: stand in the breach, and stand with it or perish with it.[110]

Seward argued that force would be the only means to preserve the Union. Seward voted against the Crittenden compromise, and he also voted three times with the North, none with the South.

New York State had thirty-three representatives in the United States House of Representatives. Twenty-four were Republicans, eight were Democrats, and one was a member of the American party. All of the Republicans supported their party and voted with the North. Of the eight Democrats, five (all from New York City) voted with the South. These five congressmen, plus the American party's congressman, also from New York City, presented a proposition to Congressman James Humphrey, the New York State member of the Committee of Thirty-Three. It would have extended the Missouri Compromise line and compensated the owners of fugitive slaves who could not be recaptured. The five Democratic congressmen from New York City who supported the

South were either not candidates for reelection in 1860 or were defeated in that election.

John Cochrane, one of the Democratic congressmen from New York City, favored the extension of the Missouri Compromise line and introduced a series of resolutions to that effect. Included in these resolutions was one that stated that

> the Constitution of the United States being an agreement between the sovereign States . . . any attempt by the Federal Government to compel by force a sovereign State to the observance of the constitutional compact would be to levy war upon a substantial Power, and would precipitate a dissolution of the Union.[111]

By March he had accepted the fact that the South would leave the Union and that the northern states would be free to form their own confederations:

> It can hardly be supposed—the entire South withdrawn that the whole North will consent to remain in a confederation—of power under its present adjustment. . . .[112]

Two days later in Richmond, Virginia, Cochrane

> promised that New York would sustain Virginia in any policy it adopted. . . .[113]

He supported the idea that New York City would secede when the Union was broken. John Cochrane supported all compromise attempts as well as the South in almost every measure except the Adrain resolutions. These resolutions praised Major Anderson at Fort Sumter and declared the United States Constitution the supreme law of the land.

Congressman Daniel Sickles, a Democrat from New York City, delivered a speech in the House of Representatives on December 10, 1860, on the question of secession. He opposed the use of force to retain states in the Union, making it clear that

> when the call for force comes—let it come whence it may—no man will ever pass the boundaries of the city of New York for the purpose of waging war against any State of this Union. . . . the Union can be made perpetual by justice; but it cannot be maintained an instant by force.[114]

Sickles recognized the right of secession

> as the last dread alternative of a free State when it has to choose between liberty and injustice. In our Federal system the recognized right of se-

cession is a conservative safeguard. It is the highest constitutional and moral guarantee against injustice; and therefore if it had been always and universally acknowledged as a rightful remedy, it would have contributed more than all else to perpetuate the Union, by compelling the observance of all their obligations on the part of all the States. The opposite dogma, which is so extensively believed at the North, that no matter what wrongs a State may have to endure, it may and ought to be compelled by force to remain in the Union, even as a conquered dependency, is a most dangerous error in our system of government, and has contributed largely to the existing anarchy.[115]

He placed the responsibility for arriving at a peaceful settlement on the Republican leaders since they controlled not only the executive branch of the federal government but also many northern governorships and legislatures. Yet he believed that the Republican party was unwilling to arrive at any peaceful settlement.

In this speech he put forth his views on the secession of New York City from the state of New York. He felt that New York City would remain in the Union as long as it could, but

. . . she will never consent to remain an appendage and a slave of a Puritan province.

According to Sickles, the city would take such action only after the Constitution was destroyed. He took the same position as Fernando Wood: that this independence would be as much from Albany as from the Union. The result would be a free city open to world commerce.[116]

A week later, on December 17, Sickles offered a resolution that would have provided a method by which a state could peaceably withdraw from the Union.[117]

Congressman Sickles voted almost consistently with the South except in the case of the Adrain resolutions, which he supported. He reasoned

that my constituents are inflexibly opposed to coercion employed against a sovereign State . . . they regard the act of Major Anderson as one done within the spirit of his instructions, and from patriotic motives; and that it is the sworn duty of the President, according to his oath, to preserve the Union. . . .[118]

Sickles began to lessen his support for the South when he felt the southern states were becoming aggressive. He believed that the laws should be enforced where it was possible. However, he felt that while the laws should be enforced, they could only be enforced upon individuals and not states.[119] He criticized the southern states for seizing forts, arsenals and post offices, which he defined as acts of war.

That, sir, is not and cannot be peaceable secession. . . . These acts, whensoever or by whomsoever done, are in themselves overt acts of war. And, sir, when sovereign States, by their own deliberate acts, make war, they cannot cry peace. When they employ force, they cannot declaim or protest against coercion.[120]

He made the distinction between the South leaving the Union in peace and its acts of war, that is

. . . I have said it before, and I repeat it now—you could not recruit a regiment that would ever march from the frontier of New York into any southern State for the purpose of employing coercion upon its people in the exercise of their legitimate political rights. Never, never! But the men of New York would go in untold thousands anywhere to protect the flag of their country. . . .[121]

Sickles also pointed out that a divided country would damage the commercial interests of the nation. He quickly gave up the idea of secession, and supported the government of the United States when he felt that the South insulted the flag, seized United States property and abandoned its northern allies.[122]

Congressman Daniel Sickels finally ceased to support the South. He gave as his reason southern aggression. Reviewing the secession movement he concluded that the South, as he, had undergone many changes.

In November it was peaceable secession. We could agree to that. I am for it. In January, it was forcible secession; and then, sir, your friends in the North were transformed into timid apologists. In February, it is spoilation and war. And I say, in the presence of the new and last phase of the secession movement, that it can have no friends in the North; it can have no apologists in the North; and there will soon be no exception to the general denunciation which it must encounter from the loyal and patriotic citizens of this country.[123]

After the firing upon Fort Sumter Daniel Sickles wrote to Secretary of War Simon Cameron and pledged the city of New York's and his own support.

The city of New York will sustain the Government. The *Herald* will declare to-morrow for the Administration. Democrats are no longer partisans. They are loyal to the Government and the flag. The attack on Fort Sumter has made the North a unit. We are at war with a foreign power.[124]

Sickles raised a regiment of volunteers and during the Civil War rose to the rank of Major General of the Volunteers, distinguishing himself in many battles.

The three other Democrats were anti-Lecompton Democrats, who had refused to support Buchanan on the question of slavery in the Kansas and Nebraska territory. None of the three returned to Congress in 1861. John H. Reynolds and Edwin R. Reynolds both voted with the North and against compromise. John B. Haskins, the third anti-Lecompton Democrat who represented a congressional district near New York City, denied the right of secession and supported the coercion of the southern states as enforcement of the laws. He also opposed compromise with the South.[125]

George Briggs from New York City was elected as a member of the American party to the House of Representatives in 1858, but he was not a candidate for reelection in 1860. He voted for compromise, and consistently with the North, never supporting the South. In a speech to the House he said that

> there is no such thing as a peaceful secession of any of the States of this Union; that secession is revolution, and revolution is war. A portion of the States of our Confederacy are now in a state of insurrection and rebellion against the Government. . . .[126]

Supporting the use of force against these states, while at the same time recommending the extension of the Missouri Compromise line, he argued for compensation to owners of fugitive slaves who were not recovered.

In 1858 Luther C. Carter was elected to the House of Representatives as a Republican and also as an American party candidate. However, two years later he was defeated for reelection. A resident of Long Island City, he was engaged in agricultural pursuits. Carter voted with the North, and once for compromise and once against it, the latter being the report of the Committee of Thirty-Three. He opposed the Crittenden amendments and considered secession tantamount to rebellion. His position was closer to that of the Republican party than to that of the American party.

Of the remaining twenty-three Republican Representatives, sixteen voted consistently with the North and against compromise while seven voted with the North but favored compromise. No Republican congressman voted with the South.

Of the sixteen Republican congressmen who were against any form of compromise, three advocated peaceable secession of the South while the remaining thirteen refused to recognize the right of secession and demanded that the laws be enforced. Opposing peaceable secession, they argued that no state could leave the Union on its own initiative unless it received the approval of the other states. One of these congressmen, Roscoe Conkling, summed up their position when he said,

> there are three ways in which the people of a State can cut themselves

loose from their Federal allegiance. The first is by an amendment of the Constitution, as provided for in the Constitution itself. The second is, by the consent, not of the remaining States, but of the people. . . . third is, by that right or power which . . . all men have to defy their Government, and if they succeed, to live, and live perhaps as patriots and heroes; but if they fail, to die, and die as rebels and as traitors.[127]

These thirteen congressmen constantly referred to southerners as traitors, considering their actions a rebellion against the government. Their remedy for the situation was force.

Three Republican congressmen supported the idea that the South should be permitted to leave the Union in peace. Two of these men took positions similar to those of the abolitionists. Charles B. Sedwick of Syracuse believed that free and slave states could not live together in peace. He believed that the attempt to unite the two sections of the country into one nation was a failure because of the

irreconcilable difference between free and slave institutions; and if States that maintain both systems remain under the same Government, one or the other must yield.

He said that he would agree to a separation of the slave territory from the United States if they went peaceably, provided they assumed their just part of the United States debt. Sedwick would permit the slave states to remain only on the condition that they agreed to compensatory emancipation.[128]

Congressman Charles H. Van Wyck of Bloomingburg, in the Hudson Valley, took the same stand as Sedwick. After urging a convention of all the states to arrive at a method of peaceable secession, Van Wyck concluded that

if the people consent, let the cotton States depart. Then let us vote millions to purchase the slaves of the border States as fast as either of them may desire to sell; then, let us purchase for them a home in Central America. . . .[129]

He opposed any compromise.

Alfred Wells of Ithaca, advocated the peaceable secession of the South to prevent war. After asserting the right of revolution, which he believed was inherent in the Declaration of Independence, he said,

that the poorest argument that could possibly be presented, is this idea that we can conquer the South by force of arms on the field of battle. . . . I never can give up the conviction of my mind that it would be brutal and inhuman butchery . . . believing, as I do, that all men are created equal. . . . I would rather make a peaceful division than shed a drop of blood. . . . I would carry coercion . . . no further than was absolutely necessary to protect the vital interests of the North. . . . Let her go. I would use no more force against her than is absolutely necessary for self-preservation and the protection of the great interests of the country. I would let time work its effects upon her. . . .

. . . Peace! wait; shed not blood. Let not these cannon that run along our streets send forth their showers of grape and canister. . . .[130]

Of the seven Republican congressmen who supported the North and favored compromise with the South, all lived in upstate New York except James Humphrey, who was from Brooklyn. Of these seven, only two expressed themselves on the issue of secession. James Humphrey, who signed the majority report of the Committee of Thirty-Three, rejected the right of secession and he predicted that departure of the South would result in war. Congressman George W. Palmer of Plattsburgh, urged that the laws be enforced. While these men supported compromise with the South, none supported secession.

All Republican congressmen, with three exceptions, favored the policy of coercing the South by force. Their preponderance of strength, with the exception of those representing New York City, gave the New York delegation a pro-war, anti-compromise posture.

viii

The secession of the southern states directly affected the merchants of New York City. Not only were they losing their markets, but they were also gaining uncollectible debts. They felt that the South had betrayed them. When the South took a more belligerent position towards the United States government, New York merchants found themselves in an awkward position. After all, they had defended the South at the beginning of the secession crisis. The merchants insisted on compromise and concessions by the United States government to prevent the secession of the border states. At the same time they urged that the seceded states be left alone. Many merchants thought that peaceable secession would not affect the economic position of New York City. Some argued that a policy of compromise would hold the border states in the Union and that peaceable secession would eventually lead to a reuniting of the two sections.

One group of merchants, which decided that it would make an effort to prevent a war with the South, met in the offices of Richard Lathers on Pine Street in New York City in December 1860. The persons who had been invited to this meeting were largely Democrats plus a few Bell men.[131]

Lathers was a native of South Carolina who had moved to New York City in 1848 as a commission merchant for the sale of southern products.

He was also President of the Great Western Insurance Company and a director of the Erie Railroad. In an attempt to halt the secession of South Carolina, he sent a letter to four of its leaders on November 28, urging that they use their influence to stop South Carolina's actions. He pointed out that

> the argument seems irresistible in favor . . . [of staying] within the Union rather than resorting to the untried and hazardous experiment of a revolution, which, if unsupported by other southern states, presents evils of a magnitude disagreeable to contemplate, even if a peaceful solution of the question could be relied on. Besides, you withdraw all your power from the federal government, and leave your friends less able to assert your rights, or protect their own in the coming congress. . . .[132]

Lathers referred to General John A. Dix and Charles O'Conor as persons who

> earnestly desire that the South shall be united for the coming contest under the new administration; and, failing in a peaceful solution of the issues, under a joint demand of a Southern convention of the States aggrieved, they will regard secession as the only remedy left for the South, and the North as powerless to resist it.[133]

Charles O'Conor was a leading New York lawyer who defended the institution of slavery. He spoke at the Pine Street meeting and, after defending the South, said that

> a political Union of distinct organized communities thus opposed in moral sentiment, can only be upheld by force. . . . Therefore, gentlemen, whilst I deplore secession as much as any man who breathes, whilst I deplore secession as fraught with the greatest evils, I have looked upon it as an inevitable event whenever those who detest the life and conversation of the Southern people acquire political control over the central government at Washington. . . .[134]

Those who attended the Pine Street meeting formulated their ideas into an address and a series of resolutions which they published. They stated that:

> Should the efforts "to procure a redress of existing wrongs" fail, should it become apparent that others were not disposed to concede "what is due to you, as members of a confederacy, which can only be preserved by equal justice to all," then the merchants of New York would be prepared to uphold the right of the South to part in peace. But let the parting be carried out as becomes "reasonable men" (at least reasonable business men).

. . . let us divide what we possess on the one hand, and what we owe on the other, and save the Republic—the noblest the world has seen—from the horrors of civil war and the degradation of financial discredit.

. . . . But we earnestly entreat our Southern brethren to abstain from hasty and inconsiderable action. . . .[135]

In the address and resolutions they presented not only the principle of peaceable secession but also a plea for time to rectify difficulties between the North and the South.

The resolutions passed at this meeting also called upon the North to return fugitive slaves and to repeal the personal liberty laws; they asked that a policy of popular sovereignty be followed in the territories, and that the South not act in haste.

A delegation of New Yorkers was appointed to meet with leaders of the South and present the Address and Resolutions. Millard Fillmore and Greene Bronson, who were appointed, did not go. This left Richard Lathers to travel to the South alone.

Richard Lathers journeyed southward on a mission that was doomed to fail and met Governor Joseph Brown of Georgia and Jefferson Davis, but, when he reached New Orleans, he was ordered to leave the city as an "alien enemy."[136] In a speech to Jefferson Davis at Montgomery, Alabama, Lathers attempted to prevent secession, and said:

In my opinion secession is a reckless disregard of the judgment of the world and of the sympathy and efforts of your friends at the north, who for years have defended your constitutional rights, often to their own sectional disadvantage. . . .[137]

Taking much the same stance as in New York City, he pointed out to the southern leaders that secession would fail, it would only mean abandoning their northern friends.

Philip Foner, the historian of the merchants in New York City during this period of crisis, concluded that the Pine Street meeting

is especially important for it reveals clearly the views of a great many merchants early in the secession crisis.[138]

Foner believed that

it can be definitely stated that a majority of the New York merchants at first upheld the right of secession.

In fact, it might even be said that not a few Republican merchants shared this view.[139]

For example, Abram S. Hewitt, a leading industrialist in the states of

New York and New Jersey, wrote to one of his mills before the election of Abraham Lincoln and said,

> if Lincoln is elected, secession is certain.[140]

In early January, he advocated holding a general convention that would arrive at terms for a peaceable secession. At the same time he was writing to friends in the South urging them not to secede and to abandon northern Democrats like himself, who had defended the South. He told Colonel E. Houstoun, President of the Pensacola and Georgia Railroad Company, that

> all my political friends are using every effort to induce the public mind to give up the idea of coercion and to take to that of peaceable separation.[141]

At the same time he argued that the South must stop attacking forts, which he was sure would bring on civil war. He hoped that politicians would arrive at some sort of compromise which would unite the country.[142]

Hewitt did not stop the sale of iron to the South, as one of his biographers alleged. In February he wrote that

> the sale of iron to the south gives me no uneasiness, but I would not like to manufacture actual implements of warfare under present circumstances.[143]

He was a person who hoped that warfare could be prevented and that the South would be permitted to leave in peace. Yet, at the same time, he would not prevent the sale of iron to either side as long as it was not for armaments.

His partner, Peter Cooper, who had endowed Cooper Union, was also in favor of the South's seceding in peace. Writing to Abraham Lincoln in March, Cooper urged that a compromise with the South be arrived at, and that peaceable measures be used. He felt that force would not bring a reconstruction of the nation,

> to overcome them [the South] by force will require a long and desolating war spreading death, debt and demoralization far and wide threw [sic] our country.[144]

Samuel F. B. Morse, along with many leading New York businessmen, organized the American Society for Promoting National Unity in March of 1861. The purpose of this society was to organize the merchants into an organization that would disseminate sound and wholesome teachings, to conciliate differences and restore peace and harmony.[145]

In late January 1861, the New York Chamber of Commerce sent a delegation of twenty-five members to Washington to present a proposal for compromise, but their mission failed. They were indicative of the men who, while refusing to take a position on secession, urged compromise. After the firing upon Fort Sumter these New Yorkers supported the government.

John M. Brower, a leading shipping merchant, addressed the New York Chamber of Commerce on March 31 and predicted that

> if the Union is really gone, each state of the North will ere long begin to consult its own interests, before permanently binding itself to new systems. . . . The City of New York, the fountain spring of the state in commercial and financial resources, with her free trade arms open to and in sympathy with the trade and exchanges of the world at home and abroad, would enjoy for herself and her state, unbounded correspondence and prosperity. But fasten her to the restrictive policy of the North, with nearly two-thirds of the Atlantic and Gulf sea-coast and an equal proportion of the exports cut off, and she would wither and decay.[146]

The merchants and businessmen of New York City tried to prevent war at first by compromise and then by attempts at peaceable secession. War would damage business severely and they used every method they could to prevent it.

ix

There were 337 weekly newspapers in New York, according to the 1860 United States Census. Of these, it was possible to locate and determine the positions on secession taken by 98 dailies or weeklies and three monthlies.

Of these 101, 46 newspapers endorsed some form of secession. None of them favored New York's joining the South. However, the Albany *Atlas and Argus* wanted New York to join a central confederacy. Twenty-four opposed the use of coercion and argued that the South be permitted to leave the Union. An additional seven opposed coercion of the South but did not advocate that the South be permitted to go in peace, even though the end result would be the same. Three New York newspapers recommended that New York City secede, they were the New York *Morning Express, Day Book,* and *Daily News.*

Eight upstate newspapers took a middle position. They advocated what they called a "peaceful policy." This policy consisted of opposition both to the right of secession and war with the South. These were newspapers which had endorsed either Stephen A. Douglas or John Bell in the 1860 presidential election and now did not want to support the Lincoln administration.

Three other newspapers took an ambiguous position that implied that they favored peaceable secession. Among these was the *Douglass' Monthly*, printed by Frederick Douglass, which took the typical abolitionist position.

Geographically the largest group of the secessionist newspapers was located in New York City, the Hudson Valley or the southern border of the State. The balance were scattered throughout the State. Those counties possessing secessionist newspapers also boasted a significant amount of manufacturing. Only one of the larger agricultural counties had a secessionist newspaper.

Politically, almost half of the secessionist newspapers supported the Democratic party's candidate. Only four endorsed Lincoln in the election of 1860, one of these being an abolitionist newspaper. The rest of the papers either advocated no candidate or endorsed John Bell.

Of the 101 newspapers located, 13 did not identify with a political candidate. These were mainly religious, literary, business, or legal newspapers that catered to a specialized audience and therefore did not give space to political issues. Eleven of these were published in New York City.

The Lincoln administration could count on 42 newspapers which advocated that coercion be used to hold the states in the Union. Of these, 13 were located in New York City. Three-quarters of these newspapers had endorsed Abraham Lincoln in the election of 1860. Only three had supported a Democrat.

There was an even division among the Republican and Democratic newspapers. The Republicans wanted to coerce the South, while the Democrats opposed the use of force. Almost half of the secessionist newspapers were located in New York City. Yet, of the 45 newspapers printed in that city, 13 wanted to use force against the South. Therefore, a significant minority in the city of New York supported coercion even though this does not show in the votes of its politicians.

Primarily it was the areas that had manufacturing or had had slavery or had ties with the South which now endorsed secession. These were the some areas in which the Congressmen who argued for secession were located.

x

There were some supporters of the South in New York City who made their positions clear during the secession crisis, and after the outbreak of war they supported the Confederate states. New York City was closely connected to the South through its business dealings, and its Democratic political leaders. The relationship, therefore, between many New Yorkers and southerners was close.

> . . . many businessmen in New York were boasting of aiding the South by selling to the seceded states material of war.[147]

Sidney Webster of New York City wrote to Caleb Cushing, a leading Massachusetts Democrat, that if the southern states created a strong government

> with provision for admission of new states then I feel sure that middle states would join the South, New York would come in, and all the other states necessary to a powerful and happy nation.[148]

Reports circulated that revolution would erupt in New York City to take the city out of the Union and make it either a free city or to unite it with the South in the Confederacy. It was reported

> that a group of secession sympathizers were planning to seize the Brooklyn Navy Yard was widely believed. Some said that twenty thousand men under [James] Kerrigan were to do the deed, while others said Marshal Rynders was the leader and that he had ten thousand followers.[149]

Workers at the Brooklyn Navy Yard had been laid off from work because, as some said, they were part of a plot to seize the Navy Yard.

> In order to defend the yard practically all the police in Brooklyn, four regiments of militia, some harbor police, and about a hundred marines were held ready, but of course there was no attack.[150]

James Kerrigan was elected as a Democrat to the United States House of Representatives in the election of 1860. He had accompanied the Walker filibustering expedition to Nicaragua. (William Walker had seized Nicaragua in 1855, reintroduced slavery into the country and tried to have Nicaragua annexed to the United States.) On December 13, the New York *Herald* printed an advertisement that was signed by Kerrigan. It read:

> The Captains of all the Volunteer companies in the city of New York, are requested to send a communication to the undersigned . . . stating the name of the company and the number of men under their command, for the purpose of perfecting a military organization to protect the

municipal rights of the citizens of the country, in the event of a revolution in the country.[151]

Kerrigan was summoned before the United States Grand Jury in January, but claimed that he was not forming an organization to overthrow the government. Superintendent of Police John A. Kennedy testified that he knew of no secret military organizations in the city.[152] Later Kerrigan became Colonel of the 25th Regiment, New York Volunteer Infantry, and William H. Russell

found them unlike the other troops on reviews: "The men were silent as they march past, and did not cheer for President or Union."[153]

John Forsyth, a Confederate commissioner negotiating with the United States government, wrote to Jefferson Davis on April 4:

While in New York last week, I learned some particulars of a contemplated revolutionary movement in that city.[154]

Forsyth explained about the free city movement and the plot against the Brooklyn Naval Yard and stated that the

military of the city had been felt and found responsive; the mayor of the city, while not taking a leading part from considerations of policy, will at the proper time throw his whole power into this movement. Several army officers are in it, two of the principal ship-builders and the leading merchants and capitalists of the city. The movement is to be divested of everything like party aspects, and among the conspirators are several who, although never Republicans, voted for Lincoln. . . .[155]

Philip Foner, historian of the New York merchants and the Civil War, argued that

if the plot did exist, then it is very likely that G. B. Lamar, President of the Bank of the Republic, Samuel J. Anderson, a merchant in the Southern trade, Emanuel B. Hart and Augustus Schell of the Custom House, John M. Brower, the shipping merchant, . . . John A. Parker of the Great Western Insurance Company, Dr. Louis A. Sayers, . . . Isaiah Rynders, Fernando Wood, and the entire Mozart Hall General Committee were active in it.[156]

While this plot failed to materialize, because of information supplied them by Forsyth and from the New York City newspapers, the leaders of the South were undoubtedly aware of its existence.

Two members of the New York City street commission became generals in the Confederate Army: Mansfield Lovell, and Gustavus W. Smith, who was "prominent in Democratic political circles."[157] Both men had attended the New York State Democratic convention in January of 1861.

On January 15, an anti-coercion meeting was held at Brooks Hall, New York City. The leaders were pro-southern and opposed the use of force to retain any state. Among the vice-presidents of this session were Gustavus W. Smith and Mansfield Lovell. According to John A. Kennedy, hand bills passed out before the meeting had announced that the purpose of this meeting was to

> put down the Black Republicans who are forcing our brethren of the South to secede.[158]

Kennedy believed that Mayor Fernando Wood had sponsored the meeting; no proof substantiates the accusation.

The Brooks Hall meeting adopted a resolution stating that

> we are firmly and unalterably opposed to any and every attempt on the part of the Government or people of the North to coerce the Southern States, or any one of them, into submission to the will of the majority of the North . . . that we will, by all proper and legitimate means, oppose, discountenance, and prevent, the Republican party from making any aggressive attempt, under the plea of "enforcing the laws," and "preserving the Union"; upon the rights of the Southern States.[159]

The *Evening Day Book,* a pro-southern newspaper, reported that thousands had attended the meeting.

Meetings such as this led the South to believe that they had considerable adherents in New York and that they could count on this support if war broke out.

xi

When the Confederacy fired upon Fort Sumter extreme patriotic reaction engulfed the entire state of New York. The nation was attacked, and the sentiment was expressed that it was time to unite and defend the United States. The hopes of a New York City revolt did not materialize. Almost all segments of the population of New York State supported Lincoln's call for troops. On April 20, a mass meeting was held in Union Square attended by 50,000 persons.[160] Men of all political stripes urged defense of the federal government and the use of force against the South.

The Democratic party, which had advocated the peaceful secession of the South, now supported the Lincoln administration. Tammany Hall adopted resolutions that declared that the Democracy, as one man, were "heartily united to uphold the constitution, enforce the laws, maintain the Union, defend the flag, and protect the Capital of the United States. . . ."[161]

It even raised a regiment. Daniel Dickinson, the former United States Senator and candidate for the Democratic presidential nomination in 1860, and who was also a member of the Albany Regency, said:

> For myself, in our federal relations, I know but one section, one Union, one flag, one government. That section embraces every State. . . .[162]

Even Fernando Wood said,

> whatever may be or may have been individual positions or opinions on questions of public policy, let us remember that our country now trembles upon the brink of a precipice, and that it requires a patriotic and honest effort to prevent its final destruction. Let us ignore the past, rising superior to partisan considerations, and rally to the restoration of the Constitution and the Union. . . .[163]

The merchants urged that the Union be defended and that the people unite behind their government. The New York Chamber of Commerce passed a series of resolutions including the passage that

> this Chamber, forgetful of past differences of political opinion among its members, will, with unanimity and patriotic ardor, support the Government in this great crisis. . . .[164]

Peter Cooper, a leading iron manufacturer who had supported peaceable secession, joined the great Union demonstration on April 20 and argued that the South was responsible for the war. Abram S. Hewitt, also a previous advocate of peaceable secession, and a partner of Peter Cooper, ordered a flag to be flown over his Trenton Iron Works. Writing on April 19, he pointed out that although he regretted the war,

> northern men feel that the time for forbearance is past.[165]

However, Samuel F. B. Morse, who had led the American Society for Promoting National Unity, still hoped for peace.

> There is such an overwhelming horror oppressing me in the thought of brother arraying against brother, that I cannot rest an idle listless spectator of such an unnatural strife, with not a single effort to arrest it.[166]

Morse was an exception, as most merchants now supported the war against the South.

Gazaway B. Lamar, President of the Bank of the Republic, was surprised by the pro-war feeling sweeping New York City.

> Strange as it may seem, . . . it is true that the people of this city who have professed to sympathise [sic] with the South have recently changed their expressions to hostility, some for one cause and some for another. . . . Even many influential Democrats have changed and there are very few reliable.[167]

Sidney Webster confirmed this view when he wrote:

> The war feeling here is uppermost and it will not permit any criticism of the Lincoln proclamation or of the duty of Congress, if the comment is unfavorable to the administration. The despotism of opinion is absolute today.[168]

In New York a few newspapers which had supported secession still urged that the South be permitted to go in peace. Most of these papers were located in New York City, and all of them had supported Democratic candidates in 1860. But as public sentiment in favor of the war reached its peak, these newspapers slowly began to support the administration.

As in the other Middle Atlantic states, the support for the war swept across New York following the firing upon Fort Sumter. Politicians, merchants and newspapers who had supported the South now urged that these states be brought back into the Union by force. When the Confederacy fired upon Fort Sumter, the peaceful secession movement ended in New York.

xii

New York had a significant secessionist movement, particularly that of the peaceable secessionist persuasion. The State had close economic and social ties with the South and had strongly supported slavery in the first decades of the nineteenth century. The state Democratic party, while divided on both local and national personalities, represented the entire spectrum of that party nationally. The Democratic party, with all of its factions, opposed the use of force to hold seceded states in the Union. There were supporters for a free city of New York in the Democratic party, especially Fernando Wood and Daniel Sickles. The Albany Regency supported the idea of a central confederacy. All the Democratic congressional representatives from New York City supported peaceable secession.

Within the Republican party some of the leadership of both segments, the Greeley and the Weed factions, endorsed *de facto* secession by arguing that the South should be permitted to leave in peace. Henry Raymond of the *New York Times* echoed this sentiment. However, before the firing upon Fort Sumter, almost all of the Republicans were supporting the administration of Abraham Lincoln.

The merchants of New York City did not want war because such a war would endanger their business interests. This led them to urge that the South be permitted to leave in peace.

The South felt that it could rely on New York City, if not the entire State, for support. But the firing upon Fort Sumter drastically changed opinion within the State. A few individuals who had previously backed the South moved south, but most remained behind and supported the federal government, at least for a while.

There was a definite correlation between the areas that had been the centers of slavery and the Democratic fusion ticket—New York City and the Hudson River Valley—and the areas that had supported the secession movement. There was also a correlation between the areas that could be considered manufacturing centers and the secession movement. As in the other Middle Atlantic states, the secessionists could be found in the sections of the State linked by economic, social and political ties with the South. Those who believed in the traditional philosophy of States' rights also endorsed the secession movement in New York. The Democratic party was the strongest supporter of the idea of peaceable secession. With but few exceptions the Democratic political leaders, their papers, and their supporters, along with the manufacturing and commercial interests, wanted to permit the South to secede in peace.

7
CONCLUSION

CERTAIN GENERALIZATIONS CAN BE MADE ABOUT THE SECESSION MOVE-
ment in the Middle Atlantic states. First, it had the support of the Democratic party in all of the states. The greatest secessionist activity came from
the areas that had supported Breckinridge or Douglas in the election of
1860. Some leaders of the Republican party, especially in New York,
were willing to see the South go in peace, at least for a short time during
the period of the secession crisis. Second, the secession movement centered
in those areas linked to the South by economic, cultural and social ties.
The large cities of Baltimore, New York and Philadelphia were centers
of secession, and the movement correlated directly with traditional regions
of slavery where slavery persisted during or prior to 1860.

Since the five states encompassed a vast area, various geographic regions
reacted differently. The secession movement in the states nearest the South
favored joining the South. Those persons who wanted to join a southern
confederacy did not simply oppose coercion, they were also sympathetic
to the South. New Jersey had the largest central confederacy movement.
Strong secession movements were also present in New York City and the
Hudson Valley. Upstate areas of New York and western Pennsylvania
leaned least toward secession.

Of the three forms of secession, peaceable secession was the most popular, dominating the others in all five states. The reasons for supporting
peaceable secession were based primarily on a fear that a specific state or
even a community would become a battleground in a war between the
North and the South.

Franklin Pierce, former President of the United States, wrote to Jefferson Davis that:

Without discussion [sic] the question of right, of abstract power to
Secede, *I have never believed that actual disruption of the Union can*

206

occur without blood; and if, through the madness of Northern Aboli-
tionism, *that dire calamity must come,* THE FIGHTING WILL NOT BE
ALONG MASON'S AND DIXON'S LINE MERELY. IT [WILL] BE WITHIN
OUR OWN BORDERS, IN OUR OWN STREET, BETWEEN THE TWO CLASSES
OF CITIZENS TO WHOM I HAVE REFERRED. *Those who defy law and
scout Constitutional obligations will, if we even reach the arbitrament of
arms,* FIND OCCUPATION ENOUGH AT HOME.[1]

A letter from Edward Everett, who had run with John Bell on the
Constitutional Union party ticket in 1860, was read at a Union meeting
in Boston in February.

If the Border States are drawn into the Southern Confederacy the fate
of the country is sealed. . . . We must look forward to collision . . .
not alone between the two great sections of the country, but between
neighboring States. . . . To expect to hold fifteen States in the Union
by force is preposterous. The idea of a civil war, accompanied as it
would be, by a servile insurrection, is too monstrous to be entertained
for a moment.[2]

Furthermore, an epidemic of secession among the southern states and
the vast area of secession frightened many people into extreme pessimism.
They could see only the futility of trying to force the southern states to
rejoin the Union. Others argued that a war would destroy the economy
of their states or cities. They preferred to let the South go and to continue
their reciprocal trade. Still others insisted that the United States Constitution did not allow the federal government the right to coerce a state to
remain in the Union against its will.

Why then did the secession movement fail in the Middle Atlantic states?
It failed primarily because of the lack of leadership and the lack of a
vehicle for legal expression of opinion. Governor Hicks of Maryland,
hoping for a central confederacy, refused to call the Legislature into
session. Governor Burton of Delaware was ineffective, and the Delaware
Legislature was pro-Union. In New Jersey, Pennsylvania and New York,
the legislatures and the governors supported the Union. This meant that
the secessionists had to act independently. But no single leadership group
arose in any of the states to guide the secession movement. Secessionists
simply talked and wrote editorials, waiting for advantageous events to
materialize. Maryland waited for Virginia; Delaware waited for Maryland; New Jersey waited for ubiquitous recognition of the end of the
Union. The delay supplied Lincoln with enough time to carry out his
plan. When he acted, all hope for the secession movement was obliterated.

If a single institutional factor could explain the failure of an effective
secession movement in the Middle Atlantic states, it would be its ineffec-

tive leadership. Other factors included the lack of conventions called for the expression of secessionist views as well as inadequate means of communication among secessionist supporters in the different states. For example, the central confederacy had advocates in each of the five states but no unifying system of communication among these individuals. With the existence of various and fragmented forms of secession, sympathizers divided their energies and their proselytizing and weakened their cause. They fought against each other and against the Unionists.

The most important psychological factor for the failure of the secession movement lay in the belief that once war began, peaceable secession was impossible. The peaceable secessionists had argued that it was better to let the South go in peace than to have a war. The fear that their states would be turned into a battleground of conflict provided the argument for letting the South go in peace. To secede after the firing upon Fort Sumter would have made their communities the natural theaters of war for the Union Army marching to the defense of Washington. War, at this point, would have defeated their whole purpose.

The South damaged its own cause when its militants seized forts, arsenals and post offices, which undermined their northern supporters. When the South finally attacked Fort Sumter, the northern outcry against this direct act of aggression eliminated any hope of northern support for the South. Men who had consistently supported the South's right to go in peace now openly advocated defense of the Union without necessarily changing their views on slavery or their political affiliations.

As Joel T. Headley wrote during the Civil War:

Every where [sic] threats had been heard that if the republican [sic] party endeavored by any unconstitutional act to carry out its hostility to slavery, there would be an uprising at the north. . . . Indeed, it was clear to the careful observer, that if the south managed discreetly, the party would have more trouble at the north than at the south. What course would this powerful opposition take now, was a question fraught with life and death to the administration. But there was no time given for arguments and appeals and attempts to conciliate. Political animosities vanished—party lines disappeared and all opposition went down like barriers of mist before the rising patriotism of the people.[3]

John Dix, who had once supported peaceable secession, wrote:

It is by no means improbable that if a separation had been sought by the slave-holding States persistently, and through peaceful means alone, it might have been ultimately conceded by the Northern States in preference to a bloody civil war, with all its miseries and demoralization. But the forcible seizure of arsenals, mints, revenue-cutters, and other property of the common government, and the attack and capture of Fort Sumter, put an end to argument as well as to the spirit of conciliation, and aroused a feeling of exasperation which nothing but the arbitrament of arms could overcome.[4]

This same feeling was expressed in the city of Philadelphia:

So many Philadelphians distinguished coercion from defense that the city's reaction to a call for troops would have been very different, had Sumter not first been attacked.[5]

The attack on Fort Sumter made the difference between northern support of the Lincoln administration's war measures and its refusal to assist this administration. Even the abolitionist wing of the Republican party, especially in New York, had argued during the secession crisis that the South, with its slaves, should be permitted to leave the Union. It now insisted that since the South had begun the war, the North should turn it into a crusade against slavery. Gerrit Smith, of New York, said, that

a few weeks ago I would have consented to let the slave states go without requiring the abolition of slavery. . . . But now, since the Southern tiger has smeared himself with our blood, we will not, if we get him in our power let him go without having drawn his teeth and claws.[6]

Why then did the South attack Fort Sumter? Were the Confederate leaders so unfamiliar with their supporters in the North? The southern leaders counted on the support of their northern allies. They had seen and heard what the Democratic leaders and the merchants of the North had to say about coercion. As a result the South felt that it would be permitted to leave in peace. President Buchanan noted this when he said that

the people of the cotton States, unfortunately for themselves, were also infatuated with the belief, until the very last moment, that in case they should secede they would be sustained by a large portion if not the whole Democratic party of the North. . . . In this delusion they were also greatly encouraged by sympathy and support from influential and widely circulated Anti-Republican journals in the North, and especially in the city of New York.[7]

The southern confederate leaders were over-confident that their northern friends would prevent the Republican administration from using force against the Confederacy. The New Orleans *Picayune* of May 1, wrote:

We are unwilling to believe the telegraphic reports of the total apostasy of the majority of the citizens of the City of New York, who have ever professed to be friends of the South. . . .[8]

Overconfidence also existed in the Confederate government. James G. Blaine, Congressman from Maine who wrote *Twenty Years of Congress,* stated that

> the Confederate Government, . . . had not anticipated the effect of an actual conflict on the people of the North. Until the hour of the assault on Sumter they had every reason for believing that Mr. Lincoln's administration was weak; that it had not a sustaining force of public opinion behind it in the free States; that, in short, Northern people were divided very much on the line of previous party organizations, and that his opponents had been steadily gaining, his supporters as steadily losing, since the day of the Presidential election in November. The Confederates naturally counted much on this condition of Northern sentiment, and took to themselves the comforting assurance that vigorous war could never be made by a divided people. They had treasured all the extreme sayings of Northern Democrats about resisting the march of a Black Republican army towards the South, and offering their dead bodies as obstructions to its progress.[9]

Jefferson Davis believed that all the slave states, including Maryland and Delaware, would eventually join the Confederacy. He was greatly surprised when they stayed with the North after Sumter. He ordered the firing upon Fort Sumter not knowing that the northern allies would join with the Republicans. He felt that he could not permit a foreign power, as he described the United States, to enter a harbor of the Confederacy. There were also internal reasons for his decision to attack Sumter. He was afraid that if he did not demonstrate the strength of the Confederacy it would disintegrate. He had witnessed the attack upon the *Star of the West,* a supply ship of the United States government, which had been fired upon during the month of January 1861, and he heard no outcry. There had been much discussion of this incident and many individuals and newspapers decried this assault upon the United States. Because there was no reaction from the government, many people felt that James Buchanan and the United States Congress might let the South go in peace. However, the firing upon Fort Sumter and the reduction and surrender of the fort was an event of greater magnitude. The Lincoln administration reacted, and the northern people responded with their support.

Jefferson Davis had been warned by Richard Lathers that

> there will be no compromise with Secession if war is forced upon the North. . . . You must not be deceived by the indignant and rather hasty threats made by our Northern Democrats, because of attempted infringements of Southern rights. . . . The first armed demonstration against the integrity of the Union or the dignity of the flag will find these antagonistic partisans enrolled in the same patriotic ranks for the defense of both. . . . Civil war for the destruction of the Union will

bring every man at the North, irrespective of his party or sectional affiliations, to the support of the government and the flag of his country. . . .[10]

Jefferson Davis did not heed this advice.

Immediately after the war, Edward Pollard showed his bitterness when he wrote that the reason the northern Democrats endorsed the war was because they were

> entirely untrustworthy as the friend of the South. . . . It proved the remarkable want of virtue in American politics, common in a certain degree, to all parts of the country.[11]

He never understood that when the South assaulted Fort Sumter it was attacking the United States and that the northern Democrats would rise to defend the nation. He failed to realize that if the South had permitted the peaceful supplying of the fort, the situation would have been different.

Only one southern leader seemed to understand the situation. Robert Toombs, the Secretary of State of the Confederate States of America, argued with President Jefferson Davis that if he permitted the firing upon Fort Sumter

> it is suicide, murder, and you will lose us every friend at the North. You will wantonly strike a hornet's nest . . . now quiet, will swarm out and sting us to death. It is unnecessary; it puts us in the wrong; it is fatal.[12]

No more prophetic statement could have been made.

Abraham Lincoln expected that Confederate forces at Charleston would attack his expedition to supply Fort Sumter. He also knew that the Confederacy claimed the fort and that they would regard this act as an invasion. Lincoln had sent a message to Governor Andrew Curtin of Pennsylvania to meet him in Washington before he sent the expedition to Sumter. At this meeting Lincoln requested that he prepare Pennsylvania for war. Curtin returned to Harrisburg and introduced legislation designed to reform the Pennsylvania militia.

The instructions to the naval commanders who were to supply Fort Sumter were explicit. They included the provision that they were to be ready to defend Fort Sumter if the South assaulted the fort. In a letter written by Gustavus Fox, the Assistant Secretary of the Navy and commander of the expedition to Fort Sumter, on April 17:

> I told the Major [Anderson, commander of Fort Sumter] how anxious the Prest. [President] was that they (S.[outh] C.[arolina]) should stand before the civilized world as having fired upon bread yet they had

made the case much worse for themselves as they knew the Major would leave the 15th, at noon for want of provisions. . . .[13]

Lincoln knew that many people in the North disagreed with his policies of supplying the forts, and many people wanted to let the South depart in peace. Much historical argument has revolved around the question of whether Lincoln "maneuvered" the South into a war by supplying Fort Sumter.

One thing is clear, the support for peaceable secession as well as for other forms of northern secessionist sympathy ended with the attack on Fort Sumter. Lincoln was aware that if he were going to prevent secession he must have the northern people on his side. In a speech in Indianapolis, Indiana, on February 11, he said:

> When the people rise in masses in behalf of the Union and the liberties of their country . . . my reliance will be placed upon you and the people of the United States—and I wish you to remember now and forever, that it is your business, and not mine; that if the union of these States, and the liberties of this people, shall be lost, it is but little to any one man of fifty-two years of age, but a great deal to the thirty millions of people who inhabit these United States, and to their posterity in all coming time. It is your business to rise up and preserve the Union and liberty, for yourselves and not for me. I desire they shall be constitutionally preserved.[14]

The attack upon Fort Sumter did exactly this. Lincoln wrote to Gustavus Fox on May 1, and said:

> You and I both anticipated that the cause of the country would be advanced by making the attempt to provision Fort Sumpter [sic] even if it should fail; and it is no small consolation now to feel that our anticipation is justified by the result.[15]

Lincoln achieved his aim, and the secession movement in the North was dead. It is obvious that had the South not attacked Fort Sumter, the secession movement in the North would have continued to exist and to expand. Lincoln won the first battle of the Civil War, the end of the secession movement in the North—in particular, in the Middle Atlantic states.

APPENDICES

The following Maryland newspapers have been divided according to their views on the question of secession. Their location and the candidate they supported in the election of 1860 are listed after the name of the paper. Where no newspaper exists for the period of the election of 1860, or where the paper began after the election, the designation "no newspaper" is used.

Newspapers that urged Maryland to join the Southern Confederacy
   Montgomery County Sentinel, Rockville, Breckinridge.
   Planter's Advocate, Upper Marlborough, Breckinridge.

Newspapers that supported a central confederacy
   Annapolis Gazette, Annapolis, Bell.
   Baltimore American and Commercial Advertiser, Baltimore, Bell.
   Baltimore County American, Towsontown, Bell.

Newspapers that wanted to permit the South to go in peace
   Baltimore American and Commercial Advertiser, Baltimore, Bell.
   Baltimore County Advocate, Towsontown, no newspaper.
   Baltimore Daily Exchange, Baltimore, Breckinridge.
   Baltimore Republican, Baltimore, no candidate.
   Democratic Alleganian, Cumberland, Douglas.
   Easton Star, Easton, Breckinridge.
   Methodist Protestant, Baltimore, no candidate.
   Southern Aegis, Bel Air, no candidate.
   Sun, Baltimore, no candidate.
   True American, Baltimore, no candidate.

Newspapers that supported the use of coercion
  Civilian and Telegraph, Cumberland, Bell.
  Easton Gazette, Easton, Bell.
  Examiner, Frederick, Bell.
  Herald of Freedom and Torch Light, Hagerstown, Bell.
  Maryland Union, Frederick, Douglas.
  Valley Register, Middletown, Bell.

Newspapers that supported the Union, but did not openly advocate the use of coercion
  Annapolis Gazette, Annapolis, Bell.
  Baltimore Clipper, Baltimore, no candidate.
  Baltimore Evening Patriot, Baltimore, no candidate.
  Cecil Whig, Elkton, Bell.
  National American, Bel Air, Bell.

Newspapers whose position on the question of secession cannot be categorized
  American Sentinel, Westminister, Bell.
  Baltimore Price Current and Weekly Journal, Baltimore, no candidate.
  Cambridge Herald, Cambridge, no candidate.
  Family Journal, Baltimore, no candidate.

APPENDIX B

The following Delaware newspapers have been divided according to their views on the question of secession. Their location and the candidate they supported in the election of 1860 are listed after the name of the paper. Where no newspaper exists for the period of the election of 1860, or where the paper began after the election, the designation "no newspaper" is used.

Newspapers that wanted to permit the South to go in peace
  Delaware Gazette, Wilmington, Democratic.
  Delaware Republican, Wilmington, Lincoln.
  Dover Delawarean, Dover, Breckinridge.
  Smyrna Times, Smyrna, no candidate.

Newspaper that supported the use of coercion
  Georgetown Messenger, Georgetown, no newspaper.

APPENDIX C

The following New Jersey newspapers have been divided according to their views on the question of secession. Their location and the candidate they supported in the election of 1860 are listed after the name of the paper. Where no newspaper exists for the period of the election of 1860, or where the paper began after the election, the designation "no newspaper" is used.

Newspapers that urged New Jersey to join the Southern Confederacy
  Newark Evening Journal, Newark, Breckinridge.
  New Brunswick Times, New Brunswick, Breckinridge.

Newspapers that supported a central confederacy
  Hunterdon Democrat, Flemington, Douglas.
  Monmouth Democrat, Freehold, Douglas.
  New Brunswick Times, New Brunswick, Breckinridge.

Newspapers that wanted to permit the South to go in peace
  Camden Democrat, Camden, Douglas.
  Hunterdon Democrat, Flemington, Douglas.
  Jersey City American Standard, Jersey City, Bell.
  Monmouth Democrat, Freehold, Douglas.
  Mount Holly Herald, Mount Holly, Douglas.
  Newark Daily Advertiser, Newark, Lincoln.
  Newark Evening Journal, Newark, Breckinridge.
  New Jersey Herald, Newton, Breckinridge.
  Paterson Daily True Register, Paterson, Douglas.
  Pioneer, Bridgeton, no newspaper.
  Trenton Daily True American, Trenton, Douglas.

Newspaper that wanted the county to secede if the Republicans compromised
  Ocean Emblem, Toms River, Lincoln.

Newspapers that supported the use of coercion
  Cape May Ocean Wave, Cape May, no newspaper.
  Daily State Gazette and Republican, Trenton, Lincoln.
  Hackettstown Gazette, Hackettstown, no newspaper.
  Jersey City Daily Courier and Advertiser, Lincoln.

Monmouth Herald and Inquirer, Freehold, Lincoln.
Newark Daily Mercury, Newark, Lincoln.
New Brunswick Fredonian, New Brunswick, Lincoln.
New Jersey Mirror, Mount Holly, Lincoln.
Paterson Daily Guardian, Paterson, Lincoln.
Sussex Register, Newton, Lincoln.

APPENDIX D

The following Pennsylvania newspapers have been divided according to their views on the question of secession. Their location and the candidate they supported in the election of 1860 are listed after the name of the paper. Where no newspaper exists for the period of the election of 1860, or where the paper began after the election, the designation "no newspaper" is used.

Newspapers that urged Pennsylvania to join the Southern Confederacy
  The Norristown Register and Montgomery Democrat and Watchman,
    Norristown, Breckinridge.
  Palmetto Flag, Philadelphia, no newspaper.

Newspaper that supported a central confederacy
  Morning Pennsylvanian, Philadelphia, Breckinridge.

Newspapers that wanted to permit the South to go in peace
  Allentown Democrat, Allentown, Douglas.
  Bedford Gazette, Bedford, Douglas.
  Berks and Schuykill Journal, Reading, Lincoln.
  Cambria Tribune, Johnstown, Lincoln.
  Clinton Democrat, Clinton, Douglas.
  Easton Argus, Easton, Lincoln.
  Easton Free Press, Easton, Lincoln.
  Harrisburg Patriot and Union, Harrisburg, Breckinridge.
  M'Kean County Democrat, Smethport, Breckinridge.
  Muncy Luminary, Muncy, Lincoln.
  Pennsylvania Daily Telegraph, Harrisburg, Lincoln.
  Philadelphia Daily News, Philadelphia, Lincoln.
  Philadelphia Inquirer, Philadelphia, Lincoln.
  Selinsgrove Times, Selinsgrove, Democratic.

Newspapers that opposed the use of coercion, but did not openly advocate letting the South go in peace

Compiler, Gettysburg, Democratic.
Easton Sentinel, Easton, Breckinridge.
Erie Observer, Erie, Democratic.
Jeffersonian, West Chester, Democratic.
Lancaster Intelligencer, Lancaster, Douglas.
Montrose Democrat, Montrose, Douglas.
Philadelphia Evening Journal, Philadelphia, Bell.
Public Ledger, Philadelphia, no candidate.
York Gazette, York, Democratic.

Newspapers that supported the use of coercion

Adams Sentinel, Gettysburg, Lincoln.
Agitator, Wellsboro, Lincoln.
Alleghanian, Ebensburg, Lincoln.
Altoona Tribune, Altoona, no candidate.
Beaver Argus, Beaver, Lincoln.
Bedford Inquirer, Bedford, Lincoln.
Bradford Reporter, Towanda, Lincoln.
Cameron Citizen, Smethport, Lincoln.
Daily Express, Lancaster, no candidate.
Daily Pittsburgh Gazette, Pittsburgh, Lincoln.
Erie Weekly Gazette, Erie, Lincoln.
Examiner and Herald, Lancaster, Lincoln.
Gazette, Lewistown, Lincoln.
Genius of Liberty, Uniontown, Democratic.
Hanover Citizen, Hanover, no newspaper (began January 31, 1861, as a Democratic newspaper).
Hanover Spectator, Hanover, no candidate.
Jeffersonian, Stroudsburg, Lincoln.
Lancaster Inquirer, Lancaster, Douglas.
Lebanon Courier, Lebanon, Lincoln.
Lycoming Gazette, Lycoming, Douglas.
M'Kean Miner, Smethport, Lincoln.
Miner's Journal, Pottsville, Lincoln.
Northampton County Journal, Easton, Lincoln.
Pennsylvania Daily Telegraph, Harrisburg, Lincoln.
Post, Pittsburgh, no newspaper.
Potter Journal, Coudersport, Lincoln.

Press, Philadelphia, Douglas.
Raftsman's Journal, Clearfield, Lincoln.
Record of the Times, Wilkes-Barre, Lincoln.
Reporter and Tribune, Washington, Lincoln.
True American, Erie, no newspaper.
Union County Star and Lewisburg Chronicle, Lewisburg, Lincoln.
Warren Mail, Warren, Lincoln.

Newspapers whose position on the question of secession cannot be categorized
  Daily Evening Bulletin, Philadelphia, Lincoln.
  Luzerne Union, Wilkes-Barre, Douglas.
  Philadelphia North American and United States Gazette, Philadelphia, Lincoln.
  Pittsburgh Evening Chronicle, Pittsburgh, no candidate.
  True Democrat, Lewistown, Douglas.

APPENDIX E

The following New York newspapers have been divided according to their views on the question of secession. Their location and the candidate they supported in the election of 1860 are listed after the name of the paper. Where no newspaper exists for the period of the election of 1860, or where the paper began after the election, the designation "no newspaper" is used.

Newspaper that supported a central confederacy
  Albany Atlas and Argus, Albany, Douglas.

Newspapers that wanted to permit the South to go in peace
  Albany Atlas and Argus, Albany, Douglas.
  Albion, New York City, no candidate.
  Bloomville Mirror, Bloomville, no newspaper.
  Brooklyn Daily Eagle, Brooklyn, Breckinridge.
  Cherry Valley Gazette, Cherry Valley, Democratic.
  Corrector, Sag Harbor, Bell.
  Evening Day Book, New York City, Democratic.
  Independent, New York City, Lincoln.
  Long Island Democrat, Jamaica, Douglas.
  National Anti-Slavery Standard, New York City, Lincoln.
  New York Daily News, New York City, Democratic.
  New York Examiner, New York City, no newspaper.

New York Herald, New York City, no candidate.
New York Illustrated News, New York City, no newspaper.
New York Journal of Commerce, New York City, Breckinridge.
New York Leader, New York City, Douglas.
New York Observer, New York City, no candidate.
New York Times, New York City, no candidate.
Niagara Falls Gazette, Niagara Falls, Republican.
Republican, Goshen, Douglas.
Syracuse Daily Courier and Union, Syracuse, Breckinridge.
Times and Courier, Albany, no newspaper.
Troy Daily Arena, Troy, no candidate.
Troy Daily Whig, Troy, Bell.
United States Economist, New York City, no newspaper.
Wilkes' Spirit of the Times, New York City, no candidate.

*Newspapers that opposed the use of coercion, but did not openly advocate
letting the South go in peace*
Irish American, New York City, no newspaper.
New York Chronicle, New York City, no newspaper.
New York Morning Express, New York City, no newspaper.
Plattsburgh Republican, Plattsburgh, Douglas.
Sun, New York City, no candidate.
Sunday Times and Noah's Weekly Messenger, New York City, no
    newspaper.
Utica Daily Observer, Utica, Douglas.

Newspapers that wanted New York City to become a "free city"
New York Daily News, New York City, Democratic.
New York Evening Day Book, New York City, Democratic.
New York Morning Express, New York City, Bell.

Newspapers that supported a "middle position" or "peaceful policy"
American Citizen, Ithaca, Bell.
Corning Democrat, Corning, Douglas.
Elizabethtown Post, Elizabethtown, Douglas.
Newburgh Telegraph, Newburgh, Douglas.
Ovid Bee, Ovid, Douglas.
Steuben Farmers' Advocate, Bath, Douglas.
Tompkins County Democrat, Ithaca, Douglas.
Trumansburg News, Trumansburg, no candidate.

Newspapers that took an ambiguous position that implied that they favored peaceable secession
Binghamton Standard, Binghamton, Lincoln.
Buffalo Daily Courier, Buffalo, Douglas.
Douglass' Monthly, Rochester, Lincoln.

Newspapers that supported the use of coercion
Albany Evening Journal, Albany, Lincoln.
Angelica Reporter, Angelica, Republican.
Auburn Daily Advertiser, Auburn, Lincoln.
Auburn Daily Union, Auburn, Lincoln.
Brooklyn Standard, Brooklyn, Douglas.
Brother Jonathan, New York City, no candidate.
Buffalo Commercial Advertiser, Buffalo, Lincoln.
Buffalo Morning Express, Buffalo, Lincoln.
Century, New York City, no candidate.
Chautauqua Democrat, Jamestown, Lincoln.
Chenango Telegraph, Norwich, Lincoln.
Christian Intelligencer, New York City, no candidate.
Corning Journal, Corning, Lincoln.
Eastern Star Journal, White Plains, Democratic.
Elmira Weekly Advertiser and Chemung County Republican, Elmira, Lincoln.
Evening Express, Rochester, Lincoln.
Evening Post, New York City, Lincoln.
Freeman's Journal, Cooperstown, Republican.
Goshen Democrat, Goshen, no newspaper.
Herkimer County Journal, Little Falls, Lincoln.
Jamestown Journal, Jamestown, Lincoln.
Long Islander, Huntington, Lincoln.
Morning Courier and New York Enquirer, New York City, Lincoln.
New York Commercial Advertiser, New York City, Lincoln.
New York Dispatch, New York City, no candidate.
New York Reformer, Watertown, Lincoln.
New York Spectator, New York City, Republican.
New York Tribune, New York City, Lincoln.
Oneida Weekly Herald and Gazette and Courier, Utica, Lincoln.
Poughkeepsie Eagle, Poughkeepsie, Lincoln.
Queens County Sentinel, Hempstead, Lincoln.
Richmond County Gazette, Stapleton, no candidate.
Rochester Democrat and American, Rochester, Lincoln.
Rochester Union and Advertiser, Rochester, Douglas.

Standard, Montgomery, Lincoln.

Sunday Mercury, New York City, no candidate.

Troy Daily Times, Troy, Lincoln.

Utica Morning Herald and Daily Gazette, Utica, Lincoln.

Waverly Advocate, Waverly, Lincoln.

World, New York City, no candidate.

Yates County Chronicle, Penn Yan, Lincoln.

Yonkers Examiner, Yonkers, Lincoln.

Newspapers that were apolitical

Bible Society Record, New York City.

Christian Advocate and Journal, New York City.

Church Journal, New York City.

Gospel Messenger and Church Record of Western New York, Utica.

Herald of Progress, New York City.

Home Journal, New York City.

New Jerusalem Messenger, New York City.

New York Daily Transcript, New York City.

New York Ledger, New York City.

Northern Christian Advocate, Auburn.

Shipping and Commercial List and New York Price Current, New York City.

Sower: Missionary Record, New York City.

Spirit of the Times, New York City.

NOTES

1. John A. Logan, *The Great Conspiracy: Its Origin and History* (New York: A. R. Hart and Company, 1886), p. 258.

2. *Ibid.*

3. F. N. Boney, *John Letcher of Virginia* (Montgomery: University of Alabama Press, 1966), p. 102.

4. Horace Greeley, *The American Conflict* (Hartford: O. D. Case and Company, 1865), 1:438–39.

5. Jefferson Davis, *The Rise and Fall of the Confederate Government* (New York: D. Appleton and Company, 1912), 1:251–52.

6. *Ibid.,* p. 257.

7. *Ibid.,* pp. 257–58.

8. The author does not discuss New England because it was the traditional opponent of the South and an area that had the greatest number of supporters of the Union. The middle west and the Pacific states had peculiarities of their own that are also separate studies. While specific studies have been made of the Middle Atlantic states as individual states, no study has been written on the region as a whole.

9. *Congressional Globe,* p. 404.

10. *Ibid.,* p. 220.

11. *Ibid.,* p. 110.

1. The spelling of Allegany is that used by the United States Census of 1860 and James W. Thomas and Judge T. J. C. Williams, *History of Allegany County Maryland* (Baltimore: Regional Publishing Company, 1969).

2. Charles B. Clark, *Politics in Maryland During the Civil War* (Chestertown: n.p., 1952), p. 6.

3. Harold R. Manakee, *Maryland in the Civil War* (Baltimore: Maryland Historical Society, 1961), p. 16.

4. Horace Greeley, *The American Conflict* (Hartford: O. D. Case and Company, 1865), 1:420.

5. *The Seventh Census of the United States: 1850* (Washington: 1853), p. 222.

The reason for the increase in the number of slaves in 1850 has never been explained.

6. Katherine A. Harvey, "The Civil War and the Maryland Coal Trade," *Maryland Historical Magazine* 62 (December 1967):363.

7. Ollinger Crenshaw, *The Slave States in the Presidential Election of 1860,* The Johns Hopkins University Studies in Historical and Political Science (Baltimore: The Johns Hopkins University Press, 1945), 63, no. 3:112-13.

8. Ollinger Crenshaw, "Urban and Rural Voting in the Election of 1860," in Eric F. Goldman, ed., *Historiography and Urbanization* (Baltimore: The Johns Hopkins University Press, 1941), p. 58.

9. Philadelphia *Inquirer,* November 20, 1860.

10. *Ibid.*

11. MS. William Wilkins Glenn Diary, February 3, 1861 Glenn Papers (MS 1017), Maryland Historical Society.

12. *Ibid.,* April 17, 1861.

13. David C. Mearns, *The Lincoln Papers* (New York: Doubleday and Company, 1948), 2:398.

14. George L. P. Radcliffe, *Governor Thomas H. Hicks of Maryland and the Civil War,* The Johns Hopkins University Studies in Historical and Political Science (Baltimore: The Johns Hopkins University Press, 1901), p. 12.

15. *Ibid.,* p. 14.

16. *Ibid.,* p. 15.

17. Greeley, *The American Conflict,* p. 461.

18. Henry Wilson, *History of the Rise and Fall of the Slave Power in America* (Boston: James R. Osgood and Company, 1877), 3:185.

19. William F. Brand, *Life of William Rollinson Whittingham* (London: Wells Gardner, Darton and Company, 1883), p. 14.

20. John G. Nicolay, and John Hay, *Abraham Lincoln: A History* (New York: The Century Company, 1909), 4:93.

21. Radcliffe, "Gov. Hicks," p. 31.

22. Roy F. Nichols, *The Disruption of American Democracy* (New York: The Macmillan Company, 1948), p. 455.

23. William B. Hesseltine, *Lincoln and the War Governors* (New York: Alfred A. Knopf, 1948), pp. 108-09.

24. J. Thomas Scharf, *History of Maryland* (Hatboro: Tradition Press, 1967), 3:369.

25. Radcliffe, "Gov. Hicks," p. 20.

26. Thomas H. Hicks to Thomas G. Pratt, Sprigg Harwood, J. L. Franklin, Llewellyn Boyh, and T. Pinkney, November 27, 1860, Thomas H. Hicks, Executive Department, Letter Book, Hall of Records of Maryland, Annapolis, p. 145.

27. *Ibid.,* p. 146.

28. *Ibid.*

29. *Ibid.*

30. *Ibid.,* pp. 146-47.

31. *Ibid.,* pp. 147-48.

32. *Ibid.,* p. 148.

33. Heinrich E. Buchholz, *Governors of Maryland* (Baltimore: William and Wilkins Company, 1908), p. 174.

34. Brand, *Life of Whittingham,* p. 9.

35. Thomas H. Hicks to John J. Crittenden, December 13, 1860, John J. Critten-

den Papers, The Library of Congress (microfilm in possession of the University of Delaware).

36. A. H. Handy to Thomas H. Hicks, December 18, 1860, Hicks, Letter Book, p. 152.

37. Thomas H. Hicks to A. H. Handy, December 19, 1860, Hicks, *Ibid.*, pp. 154–55.

38. Thomas H. Hicks to J. L. M. Curry, January 8, 1861, Hicks, *Ibid.*, pp. 170–73.

39. *The War of the Rebellion: A Compilation of the Official Records of the Union and Confederate Armies* (Washington: United States Government Printing Office, 1899), series 4, vol. 1:38. (Hereafter cited as *O.R.*)

40. MS. Dr. Samuel A. Harrison, "War of the Rebellion in Talbot County," Harrison Collection (MS. 432), Maryland Historical Society, pp. lxxvii–viii.

41. Walter A. Powell, *A History of Delaware* (Boston: The Christopher Publishing House, 1928), p. 252. The *Delmarva Star* of November 5, 1933 printed the letter with a few minor changes, undoubtedly a question of reading Governor Hicks's handwriting. No substantive changes occur between the two accounts.

42. Charles B. Clark, *The Eastern Shore of Maryland and Virginia* (New York: Lewis Historical Publishing Company, 1950), 1:542.

43. Frank Moore, *The Rebellion Record* (New York: G. P. Putnam, 1861), 1, Documents 17–18.

44. Samuel F. Du Pont to Sophie du Pont, January 9, 1861, Samuel F. Du Pont Papers, W9-2235, Eleutherian Mills Historical Library.

45. David C. Mearns, *Lincoln Papers*, 2:371–72.

46. J. M. Lucas to Thomas H. Hicks, January 11, 1861, Thomas H. Hicks Papers, (MS. 1313), Maryland Historical Society.

47. Andrew G. Curtin to Thomas H. Hicks, January 15, 1861, Hicks, Letter Book, pp. 174–75.

48. Thomas H. Hicks to Andrew G. Curtin, January 19, 1861, *Ibid.*, pp. 175–76.

49. Thomas H. Hicks to John J. Crittenden, January 9, 1861, Crittenden Papers, The Library of Congress (microfilm in possession of the University of Delaware).

50. *Maryland State Legislature Documents,* Document F (1861), p. 4.

51. Thomas H. Hicks to General Winfield Scott, January 25, 1861, Hicks, Letter Book, p. 177.

52. *O.R.,* series 4, vol. 1:152.

53. Scharf, *History of Maryland,* 3:383–84.

54. *O.R.,* series 4, vol. 1:151.

55. Thomas H. Hicks to Abraham Lincoln, March 11, 1861, Abraham Lincoln Papers, The Library of Congress (microfilm in possession of the University of Delaware).

56. Thomas H. Hicks to William H. Seward, March 28, 1861, *Ibid.*

57. *Ibid.*

58. *Ibid.*

59. *O.R.,* series 1, vol. 51, pt. 1:317.

60. *Congressional Globe,* p. 741.

61. Philadelphia *Inquirer,* December 4, 1860.

62. *Congressional Globe,* p. 77.

63. *Congressional Globe, Appendix,* p. 297.

64. *Ibid.,* p. 298.

65. *Ibid.,* p. 111.

66. *Ibid.,* p. 282.

67. *Ibid.*

68. *Ibid.*, p. 218.

69. *Ibid.*, p. 220.

70. Upper Marlborough *Planter's Advocate*, December 26, 1860.

71. *Ibid.*

72. *Congressional Globe, Appendix*, p. 150.

73. *Congressional Globe*, p. 220.

74. Samuel S. Cox, *Eight Years in Congress, From 1857–1865: Memoir and Speeches* (New York: D. Appleton and Company, 1865), p. 22.

75. *Congressional Globe, Appendix*, p. 118.

76. Allen Johnson, *Dictionary of American Biography* (New York: Charles Scribner's Sons, 1928), 5:119–20. *Biographical Directory of the American Congress: 1774–1961* (Washington: United States Government Printing Office, 1961), p. 783.

77. *Congressional Globe, Appendix*, p. 182.

78. John P. Kennedy, *The Border States: Their Power and Duty in the Present Disordered Condition of the Country* (1860), p. 21.

79. *Ibid.*, p. 22.

80. *Ibid.*

81. *Ibid.*, pp. 22–23.

82. *Ibid.*, p. 24.

83. *Ibid.*, p. 35.

84. *Ibid.*, p. 35.

85. John P. Kennedy to Gov. Beriah Magoffin, December 25, 1860, John P. Kennedy, Letter Book. George Peabody Department of the Enoch Pratt Free Library, p. 124.

86. *Ibid.*, p. 133.

87. John P. Kennedy to P. C. Pendleton, December 26, 1860, *Ibid.*, p. 135.

88. John P. Kennedy to George S. Bryan, December 27, 1860, *Ibid.*, p. 138.

89. John P. Kennedy to General R. C. Howard, December 28, 1860, *Ibid.*, p. 144.

90. Bishop W. R. Whittingham to John P. Kennedy, January 1, 1861, Letters to John P. Kennedy, George Peabody Department of the Enoch Pratt Free Library.

91. John P. Kennedy to George S. Bryan, January 25, 1861, Kennedy, Letter Book, p. 188.

92. *Ibid.*

93. John P. Kennedy to Philip C. Pendleton, February 10, 1861, *Ibid.*

94. John P. Kennedy to George S. Bryan, March 15, 1861, *Ibid.*, pp. 222–23.

95. John P. Kennedy to Sir Charles Wood, April 6, 1861, *Ibid.*, pp. 237–41.

96. *Ibid.*, pp. 240–41.

97. MS. John P. Kennedy, "Journal," 1859–61, George Peabody Department of the Enoch Pratt Free Library, p. 267.

98. John P. Kennedy, *The Great Drama: An Appeal to Maryland* (Baltimore: n.p., 1861), p. 11.

99. *Ibid.*, p. 14.

100. William H. Collins, *An Address to the People of Maryland* (Baltimore: n.p., 1861), pp. 7–8.

101. Lucius E. Chittenden, *A Report of the Debates and Proceedings in the Secret Sessions of the Conference Convention for Proposing Amendments to the Constitution of the United States* (New York: D. Appleton and Company, 1864), p. 449.

102. *Ibid.*, pp. 405–06.

103. MS. Dr. Samuel A. Harrison, "Journal," (MS 432.1) Maryland Historical Society.

104. Henry W. Thomas and W. Sirus to John J. Crittenden, January 30, 1861, John J. Crittenden Papers.

105. House of Representatives, 36th Congress, 2d. Session; *Report No. 79,* "Alleged Hostile Organization Against the Government within the District of Columbia," p. 34.

106. W. Rogers Hopkins to Gideon Welles, March 9, 1861, Gideon Welles Papers, Manuscript Division, The New York Public Library, Astor, Lenox and Tilden Foundations.

107. J. Thomas Scharf, *History of Western Maryland* (Baltimore: Regional Publishing Company, 1968), 1:194.

108. H. D. Fernandis, *et al.,* "To the People of Hartford," p. 6.

109. B. A. Garlinger to Thomas H. Hicks, January 19, 1861, Thomas H. Hicks Papers, Hall of Records of Maryland.

110. William M. Seabrook, *Maryland's Great Part in Saving the Union,* p. 5.

111. House of Representatives, *Report No. 79,* p. 30.

112. Mearns, *Lincoln Papers,* 2:431-32.

113. *Ibid.,* p. 618.

114. Ulrich B. Phillips, ed., *The Correspondence of Robert Toombs, Alexander H. Stephens, and Howell Cobb, Annual Report of the American Historical Association for the Year 1911* (Washington: American Historical Association, 1913), p. 546.

115. *Ibid.*

116. Levi K. Brown to James Buchanan, November 26, 1860, James Buchanan Papers, The Historical Society of Pennsylvania.

117. *Ibid.*

118. Levi K. Brown to James Buchanan, December 6, 1860, *Ibid.*

119. *Ibid.*

120. Levi K. Brown to James Buchanan, February 3, 1861, *Ibid.*

121. J. Jeffrey Auer, *Antislavery and Disunion, 1858–1861* (New York: Harper and Row, 1963), pp. 169-70.

122. Richard R. Duncan, "Bishop Whittingham, The Maryland Diocese, and the Civil War," *Maryland Historical Magazine,* 61 (December, 1966):330.

123. *Ibid.,* p. 338.

124. Buchholz, *Governors of Maryland,* p. 171.

125. *Ibid.,* p. 149.

126. *Ibid.,* pp. 142, 155-56.

127. Franklin Buchanan to J. A. Pearce, June 26, 1861, James A. Pearce Papers, (MS. 1384), Maryland Historical Society.

128. *Ibid.*

129. *Ibid.*

130. Phillips, *Correspondence of Robert Toombs,* p. 533.

131. Raphael Semmes to John P. Gillis, January 29, 1861. John P. Gillis Papers, Historical Society of Delaware.

132. Upper Marlborough *Planter's Advocate,* April 24, 1861.

133. Montgomery County *Sentinel,* January 4, 1861.

134. Radcliffe, "Gov. Hicks," p. 23.

135. Annapolis *Gazette,* December 13, 1860.

136. *Ibid.,* April 4, 1861.

137. Cumberland *Democratic Alleganian,* December 29, 1860; March 23, 1861. Frederick *Maryland Union,* December 27, 1860.

138. Bel Air *Southern Aegis,* December 1, 1860.

139. MS. A. S. Chambers, "Diary," The New York Historical Society, p. 15.

140. *Ibid.,* p. 27.

141. Baltimore *American and Commercial Advertiser,* April 15, 1861.

142. Howard Swiggett, ed., *John B. Jones, A Rebel War Clerk's Diary* (New York: Old Hickory Bookshop, 1935), 1:14.

143. Nicolay and Hay, *Abraham Lincoln,* 4:119.

144. George Brown, *Baltimore and the Nineteenth of April, 1861* Johns Hopkins University Studies in Historical and Political Science, Extra vol. 3 (Baltimore: N. Murray, 1887), p. 56.

145. *Ibid.,* p. 56.

146. A. S. Chambers, "Diary," pp. 49–50.

147. Brown, *Baltimore and the Nineteenth of April,* p. 57.

148. *Ibid.,* p. 58.

149. *Ibid.*

150. Moore, *Rebellion Record,* 1, Documents: 77.

151. Brown, *Baltimore and the Nineteenth of April,* p. 33.

152. *Ibid.,* p. 63.

153. *Ibid.,* p. 115.

154. *Ibid.,* p. 77.

155. Moore, *Rebellion Record,* 1, Documents: 77.

156. *Ibid.*

157. Thomas H. Hicks to General Kimmell, April 20, 1861, Thomas H. Hicks Papers, Hall of Records of Maryland.

158. Mearns, *Lincoln Papers,* 2:573.

159. *Ibid.*

160. Thomas H. Hicks to General Winfield Scott and William Seward, April 22, 1861, Thomas H. Hicks Papers, Hall of Records of Maryland.

161. *O.R.,* series 1, vol. 2:589–90.

162. Proclamation, April 24, 1861, Executive Papers 1861, Hall of Records of Maryland.

163. *Maryland State Legislature Documents,* (1861), A., p. 6.

164. MS. Alexander Randall Diaries, April 21, 1861, (MS. 652), Maryland Historical Society.

165. Charles Howard to Col. Isaac R. Trimble, April 22, 1861, Isaac R. Trimble Papers, (MS 1449), Maryland Historical Society.

166. Carl Sandburg, *Abraham Lincoln: The War Years* (New York: Harcourt, Brace and Company, 1939), I, p. 233.

167. J. N. Trimble to Charles I. du Pont, May 11, 1861, Ridgely Collection, Hall of Records of Delaware.

168. Harvey, "Civil War and Maryland Coal Trade," p. 364.

169. John A. Steiner, "The Brengle Home Guard," *Maryland Historical Magazine,* 7 (June 1912):196.

170. *Ibid.,* p. 198.

171. Dunbar Rowland, *Jefferson Davis: Constitutionalist: His Letters, Papers, and Speeches* (Jackson, Miss.: Mississippi Department of Archives and History, 1923), V, p. 65.

172. *O.R.,* series 1, vol. 2:773.

173. *O.R.,* series 1, vol. 51, part 2:34–35.

174. Nicholay and Hay, *Abraham Lincoln,* 4:122.

175. *O.R.,* series 2, vol. 1:675.

176. Francis J. Thomas to General Isaac R. Trimble, May 5, 1861, Isaac R. Trimble Papers, (MS. 1449), Maryland Historical Society.

177. *O.R.,* series 1, vol. 2:601–02.

178. MS. Mrs. Benjamin G. Harris Diary, April 21, 29, May 15, 1861, (MS 1585), Maryland Historical Society.

179. *O.R.,* series 1, vol. 2:797.

180. MS. William W. Glenn Diary, Glenn Papers (MS 1017), Maryland Historical Society.

181. Scharf, *History of Maryland,* 3:363.

CHAPTER 3

1. H. Clay Reed, ed., *Delaware: A History of the First State* (New York: Lewis Historical Publishing Company, 1947), 1:165.

2. Harold B. Hancock, *Delaware During the Civil War: A Political History* (Wilmington, 1961), p. 3.

3. *Ibid.,* p. 17.

4. *Ibid.,* pp. 18–19.

5. George P. Fisher to Thurlow Weed, November 19, 1860, Thurlow Weed Papers, University of Rochester.

6. H. W. McColley to Thurlow Weed, November 9, 1860, Thurlow Weed Papers, University of Rochester.

7. Ollinger Crenshaw, *The Slave States in the Presidential Election of 1860,* The Johns Hopkins University Studies in Historical and Political Science (Baltimore: The Johns Hopkins University Press, 1945), 63, no. 3:197.

8. Ollinger Crenshaw, "Urban and Rural Voting in the Election of 1860," in Eric F. Goldman, ed., *Historiography and Urbanization* (Baltimore: The Johns Hopkins University Press, 1941), p. 58.

9. *Ibid.,* p. 66.

10. Horace Greeley, *The American Conflict* (Hartford: O. D. Case and Company, 1865), 1:407.

11. Robert Milligan to Samuel F. Du Pont, April 8, 1861, Samuel F. Du Pont Papers, Eleutherian Mills Historical Library, W9-10754.

12. Hancock, *Delaware During Civil War,* p. 56.

13. *Ibid.,* p. 50.

14. David C. Mearns, *The Lincoln Papers* (Garden City: Doubleday and Company, 1948), 2:352.

15. Georgetown *Messenger,* April 24, 1861.

16. Hancock, *Delaware During Civil War,* p. 51.

17. *Ibid.*

18. *Journal of the House of Representatives of Delaware* (1861), p. 14.

19. *Ibid.*

20. *Ibid.,* p. 15.

21. *Ibid.,* pp. 14–18.

22. Wilmington *Delmarva Star,* November 5, 1933.

23. *Ibid.*

24. *The War of the Rebellion, A Compilation of the Official Records of the*

Union and Confederate Armies (Washington: United States Government Printing Office, 1899), series 3, vol. 1:114. (Hereafter cited as *O.R.*)

25. William Burton, "Proclamation to the Citizens of the State of Delaware," Executive Papers, Hall of Records of Delaware.

26. Greeley, *American Conflict*, 1:461.

27. *O.R.*, series 4, vol. 1:38.

28. *Ibid.*, p. 38.

29. *Ibid.*, series 4, vol. 1:33–34.

30. *Ibid.*, p. 22.

31. *Journal of the Delaware House of Representatives*, 1861, p. 102.

32. *O.R.*, series 4, vol. 1:124.

33. *Ibid.*, pp. 122–23.

34. Edward Ridgely to Mrs. Charles I. du Pont, April 26, 1861, Ridgely Collection, Hall of Records of Delaware.

35. Alexander Johnson to Thomas F. Bayard, February 16, 1861, Thomas F. Bayard Papers, The Library of Congress.

36. *Journal of the Senate of the State of Delaware*, Dover, 1861, p. 315.

37. *Delaware Misc. Documents*, No. 21, Delaware House Journal, 1861.

38. United States House of Representatives, 36th. Congress, 2d. Session, *Report No. 31*, "Disturbed Condition of the Country Report of the Committee of Thirty Three," p. 1.

39. *Ibid.*, p. 2.

40. *Ibid.*, pp. 2–3.

41. *Ibid.*, p. 15.

42. Walter A. Powell, *A History of Delaware* (Boston: The Christopher Publishing House, 1928), pp. 258–59.

43. *Congressional Globe*, p. 14.

44. *Ibid.*

45. *Ibid.*, p. 290.

46. Hancock, *Delaware During Civil War*, p. 42.

47. James A. Bayard to Thomas F. Bayard, December 4, 1860, Thomas F. Bayard Papers, The Library of Congress.

48. *Ibid.*, December 16.

49. *Ibid.*, December 23.

50. *Ibid.*, January 22, 1861.

51. *Ibid.*

52. *Ibid.*, March 9.

53. *Ibid.*, "Condition of the Country" (Washington: n.p.), p. 2.

54. Robert D. Meade, *Judah P. Benjamin: Confederate Statesman* (New York: Oxford University Press, 1943), p. 172.

55. James A. Bayard to Thomas F. Bayard, April 17, 1861.

56. Lucius E. Chittenden, *A Report of the Debates and Proceedings in the Secret Sessions of the Conference Convention for Proposing Amendments to the Constitution of the United States* (New York: D. Appleton and Company, 1864), p. 310.

57. *Journal of the Senate of the State of Delaware*, 1861, p. 261.

58. Henry A. du Pont to Samuel F. Du Pont, April 22, 1861, Henry F. du Pont Collection of Winterthur Manuscripts, Group 8, Series A, Eleutherian Mills Historical Library.

59. William S. Dutton, *Du Pont: One Hundred and Forty Years* (New York: Charles Scribner's Sons, 1951), pp. 91–92.

60. Evelina Bidermann to Henry A. du Pont, January 29, 1861, Henry F. du Pont Papers, WMss Group 8, Series B, Eleutherian Mills Historical Library.

61. Samuel F. Du Pont to William Whetten, February 4, 1861, Samuel F. Du Pont Papers, W9-2250, Eleutherian Mills Historical Library.

62. *Ibid.,* January 5, W9-2232.

63. *Ibid.,* March 26–27, W9-2272.

64. *Ibid.*

65. Samuel F. Du Pont to Henry W. Davis, April 14, 1861, Samuel F. Du Pont Papers, W9-2273, Eleutherian Mills Historical Library.

66. Harold B. Hancock and Norman B. Wilkinson, "A Manufacturer in Wartime: Du Pont, 1860–1865," *Business History Review,* 40 (Summer 1966) :217.

67. Hancock, *Delaware During Civil War,* p. 55.

68. Dover *Delawarean,* January 12, 1861.

69. *Ibid.,* February 16, 1861.

70. Wilmington *Delaware Republican,* January 14, 1861.

71. *Ibid.*

72. *Ibid.,* February 21, 1861.

73. Georgetown *Messenger,* April 24, 1861.

74. *O.R.,* series 1, vol. 2:594.

75. MS. Alexander B. Cooper, "Memoirs of Myself and My Times," p. 24, Historical Society of Delaware.

76. Powell, *A History of Delaware,* p. 258.

77. *Ibid.,* p. 259.

78. Dover *Delawarean,* April 20, 1861.

79. Smyrna *Times,* April 25, 1861.

CHAPTER 4

1. William H. Shaw, *History of Essex and Hudson Counties, New Jersey* (Philadelphia: Everts and Peck, 1884), p. 58.

2. Allen Johnson, ed., *Dictionary of American Biography* (New York: Charles Scribner's Sons, 1928), 20:571.

3. Newark *Daily Advertiser,* September 8, 1860.

4. Alfred M. Heston, *Slavery and Servitude in New Jersey* (Camden: Sinnickson Chew and Sons Company, 1903), p. 6.

5. Francis Basle Lee, *New Jersey as a Colony and as a State* (New York: The Publishing Society of New Jersey, 1902), pp. 35–37.

6. Charles M. Knapp, *New Jersey Politics During the Period of the Civil War and Reconstruction* (Geneva: W. E. Humphrey, 1924), pp. 3–4.

William A. Linn, "Slavery in Bergen County, New Jersey," *Papers and Proceedings of the Bergen County Historical Society,* 4 (1907–08) :28.

7. Marion Thompson Wright, "Negro Suffrage in New Jersey, 1776–1875," *The Journal of Negro History* 33 (April 1948) :178.

8. A. Q. Keasbey, "Slavery in New Jersey," *Proceedings of the New Jersey Historical Society,* Third Series, 5 (1907–08) :83.

9. J. D. B. DeBow, *The Industrial Resources, Etc. of the Southern and Western States* (New Orleans: J. D. B. DeBow, 1853), 2:311.

10. Percival Perry, "The Attitudes of the New Jersey Delegations in Congress on the Slavery Question, 1815–1861" (Master's thesis, Rutgers University, 1939), pp. 258–59.

11. James Scovel, *Three Speeches* (Camden: H. B. Dick, 1870), pp. 42–43.

12. Ulrich P. Phillips, ed., *The Correspondence of Robert Toombs, Alexander H. Stevens, and Howell Cobb, Annual Report of the American Historical Association for the Year 1911* (Washington: American Historical Association, 1913), p. 470.

13. Ollinger Crenshaw, "Urban and Rural Voting in the Election of 1860" in Eric F. Goldman, ed., *Historiography and Urbanization* (Baltimore: The Johns Hopkins University Press, 1941), p. 65.

14. New Brunswick *Times,* December 27, 1860.

15. *Ibid.*

16. *Ibid.*

17. *Ibid.*

18. *Ibid.*

19. New Brunswick *Fredonian,* July 18, 1861.

20. Rodman Price to Appleton Oaksmith, January 26, 1861, Rodman Price Papers, Rutgers, the State University.

21. *Ibid.*

22. John A. Logan, *The Great Conspiracy: Its Origin and History* (New York: A. R. Hart and Company, 1886), pp. 258–59.

23. Howard K. Beale, *The Diary of Edward Bates: 1859–66* (Washington: United States Government Printing Office, 1933), p. 438 n.

24. MS. Charles Perrin Smith, "Personal Reminiscences," New Jersey State Library, p. 196.

25. *Ibid.,* "Chapters from a Journal of Events (Political and Otherwise)," p. 99.

26. *The Political Expressions of Joseph P. Bradley Compiled from Speeches, and Articles Written by Him* (Newark: n.p.), p. 4.

27. Charles S. Olden, "Messages of Hon. Charles S. Olden, Governor of New Jersey with Accompanying Documents" (Trenton, 1861), p. 15.

28. *Ibid.,* pp. 16–19.

29. D. Appleton and Company, *The American Annual Cyclopaedia and Register of Important Events* (New York: D. Appleton and Company, 1862), p. 515.

30. *Minutes of Votes and Proceedings of the Eighty-Fifth General Assembly of the State of New Jersey* (Jersey City, 1861), p. 1207.

31. Robert G. Gunderson, *Old Gentlemen's Convention: The Washington Peace Conference* of 1861 (Madison: University of Wisconsin Press, 1961), p. 38.

32. Jesse L. Keene, "Sectionalism in the Peace Conference of 1861," *The Florida Historical Quarterly* 40 (July 1961):63.

33. Lucius E. Chittenden, *A Report of the Debates and Proceedings in the Secret Sessions of the Conference Convention for Proposing Amendments to the Constitution of the United States* (New York: D. Appleton and Company, 1864), p. 116.

34. *Ibid.*

35. *Ibid.,* p. 182.

36. Gunderson, *Old Gentlemen's Convention,* p. 90.

37. Senator Thomson, *"On Presenting the Resolutions of that State on 'The State of the Union'"* (Washington: n.p., 1861), pp. 6–14.

38. *Ibid.*

39. *Congressional Globe,* p. 396.

40. *Ibid.*

41. *Ibid.*

42. Flemington *Hunterdon Democrat,* April 17, 1861.

43. New Brunswick *Times,* March 14, 1861.

44. *Ibid.*

45. *Ibid.*

46. Trenton *Daily True American,* December 18, 1860.

47. *Ibid.*

48. Howard C. Perkins, *Northern Editorials on Secession* (Gloucester, Massachusetts: Peter Smith, 1942), 2:770.

49. Paterson *Daily Register,* February 11, 1861.

50. Newton *New Jersey Herald,* February 16, 1861.

51. Mount Holly *Herald,* February 28, 1861.

52. Perkins, *Northern Editorials* 1:421.

53. Toms River *Ocean Emblem,* January 30, 1861.

54. *Ibid.,* January 9, 1861.

55. Harold F. Wilson, *The Jersey Shore* (New York: Lewis Historical Publishing Company, 1953), 2:669.

56. Howard Swiggett, ed., *John B. Jones, A Rebel War Clerk's Diary* (New York: Old Hickory Bookshop, 1935), p. 13.

57. John B. Jones, *Secession, Coercion, and Civil War: The Story of 1861* (Philadelphia: T. B. Peterson, 1861), pp. 45–46.

58. *Ibid.,* p. 69.

59. *Ibid.,* p. 189.

60. Smith, "Personal Reminiscences," p. 196.

61. *Ibid.*

62. Newton *New Jersey Herald,* April 20, 1861.

63. New Brunswick *Times,* April 25, 1861.

64. Paterson *Daily True Register,* April 13, 1861.

CHAPTER 5

1. Sylvester K. Stevens, *Pennsylvania: Birthplace of a Nation* (New York: Random House, 1964), pp. 165–66.

2. *Ibid.,* p. 166.

3. Edward R. Turner, *The Negro in Pennsylvania* (Washington: American Historical Association, 1911), pp. 78–79.

4. *Ibid.,* p. 225.

5. *Ibid.,* p. 238.

6. Erwin S. Bradley, *The Triumph of Militant Republicanism: A Study of Pennsylvania and Presidential Politics: 1860–1872* (Philadelphia: University of Pennsylvania Press, 1964), p. 74.

7. *Ibid.,* p. 75.

8. Ollinger Crenshaw, "Urban and Rural Voting in the Election of 1860," in Eric F. Goldman, ed., *Historiography and Urbanization* (Baltimore: The Johns Hopkins University Press, 1941), p. 56.

9. *Ibid.,* p. 65.

10. *Ibid.*

11. *Ibid.*

12. James Buchanan to James Gordon Bennett, December 20, 1860, James Buchanan Papers, The Historical Society of Pennsylvania.

13. John B. Moore, ed., *The Works of James Buchanan* (Philadelphia: J. B. Lippincott Company, 1910), 11:73–74.

14. *Ibid.*, pp. 95–96.

15. *Ibid.*, pp. 109–10.

16. James Buchanan, Message from the President of the United States, 36th. Congress, 2d Session, *Senate Executive Documents, No. 3*, 36th. Congress, 2d Session, pp. 1–2.

17. James Buchanan, *Mr. Buchanan's Administration on the Eve of the Rebellion* (New York: D. Appleton and Company, 1866), p. 129.

18. James Buchanan to General John Dix, March 18, 1861, John Dix Papers, Columbia University Libraries.

19. *Ibid.*, April 19.

20. Fragment of a letter, James Buchanan Papers, The Historical Society of Pennsylvania.

21. Moore, ed., *Works of Buchanan,* 11:22n–23n.

22. *Ibid.*

23. Chauncey F. Black, *Essays and Speeches of Jeremiah S. Black* (New York: D. Appleton and Company, 1885), p. 15.

24. Philip G. Auchampaugh, *James Buchanan and His Cabinet on the Eve of Secession* (Lancaster: Lancaster Press, 1926), p. 107.

25. George E. Reed, ed., *Pennsylvania Archives: Papers of the Governors,* 4th. Series (Harrisburg: The State of Pennsylvania, 1902), 8:286–87.

26. *Ibid.*, p. 287.

27. *Ibid.*, p. 299.

28. *Ibid.*, p. 300.

29. Philip G. Auchampaugh, *Robert Tyler: Southern Rights Champion: 1847–1866* (Duluth: Himan Stein, 1934), p. 307.

30. *Ibid.*, pp. 309–10.

31. *Ibid.*, p. 313.

32. *Ibid.*, pp. 339–40.

33. *Ibid.*, p. 340.

34. *Ibid.*, pp. 340–41.

35. Auchampaugh, *James Buchanan,* pp. 105–06.

36. *Ibid.*, p. 106.

37. *Ibid.*

38. *Ibid.*

39. John W. Forney to J. Alexander Fulton, January 1861, J. Alexander Fulton Papers, Pennsylvania State Archives.

40. Victor E. Piollet to James Buchanan, November 16, 1860, James Buchanan Papers, The Historical Society of Pennsylvania.

41. *Ibid.*

42. Victor E. Piollet to William Bigler, December 14, 1860, William Bigler Papers, The Historical Society of Pennsylvania.

43. *Ibid.*, December 31.

44. John F. Means to William Bigler, January 28, 1861, William Bigler Papers, The Historical Society of Pennsylvania.

45. Bedford *Gazette*, March 1, 1861.

46. Harrisburg *Patriot and Union,* February 25, 1861.

47. Easton *Sentinel,* February 14, 1861.

48. Pittsburgh *Gazette,* December 17, 1860.

49. Philadelphia *North American and United States Gazette,* March 27, 1861.

50. Lancaster *Union,* April 3, 1861.

51. William H. Egle, *Andrew Gregg Curtin: His Life and Services* (Philadelphia: Avil Printing Company, 1895), p. 120.

52. *Ibid.,* pp. 120–21.

53. George P. Donehoo, ed., *Pennsylvania: A History* (New York: Lewis Historical Publishing Company, 1926), 3:1437.

54. Alexander K. McClure, *Old Time Notes of Pennsylvania* (Philadelphia: John C. Winston Company, 1905), 1:449.

55. Egle, *Curtin,* p. 123.

56. Stanton L. Davis, *Pennsylvania Politics, 1860–1863* (Cleveland: Western Reserve University, 1935), pp. 160–61.

57. "Resolutions of the Legislature of the State of Pennsylvania," 36th. Congress, 2d. Session, *House Miscellaneous Documents, no. 24.*

58. *Journal of the Senate of the Commonwealth of Pennsylvania* (Harrisburg, 1861), p. 842.

59. Robert G. Gunderson, *Old Gentlemen's Convention: The Washington Peace Conference of 1861* (Madison: University of Wisconsin Press, 1861), p. 38.

60. Lucius E. Chittenden, *A Report of the Debates and Proceedings in the Secret Sessions of the Conference Convention for Proposing Amendments to the Constitution of the United States* (New York: D. Appleton and Company, 1864), pp. 399–400.

61. *Ibid.,* p. 172.

62. *Ibid.*

63. *Ibid.,* p. 173.

64. Edwin S. Bradley, *Simon Cameron: Lincoln's Secretary of War: A Political Biography* (Philadelphia: University of Pennsylvania Press, 1966), p. 158.

65. Edgar Cowan to Simon Cameron, December 15, 1860, Simon Cameron Papers, The Library of Congress.

66. Charles B. Going, *David Wilmot: Free-Soiler* (New York: D. Appleton and Company, 1924), p. 573.

67. *Congressional Globe,* p. 48.

68. *Ibid.,* p. 48.

69. *Ibid.,* p. 492.

70. *Ibid.,* p. 493.

71. *Ibid.*

72. William Bigler to James Buchanan, April 11, 1861, James Buchanan Papers, Lancaster County Historical Society.

73. *Congressional Globe,* p. 479.

74. *Ibid.,* p. 281.

75. E. Joy Morris to C. C. Lathrop, January 17, 1861, The Historical Society of Pennsylvania Autograph Collection.

76. *Congressional Globe, Appendix,* p. 218.

77. George W. Scranton to his "brother," January 16, 1861, George W. Scranton Papers, Acc. 1250, Eleutherian Mills Historical Library. Scranton appears to have misinterpreted Senator William Seward's speech. Seward was opposed to any compromise with the South.

78. *Congressional Globe,* pp. 696–97.

79. *Ibid.,* p. 909.

80. Philadelphia *Inquirer,* November 8, 1860.

81. Harrisburg *Patriot and Union,* April 9, 1861.

82. *Ibid.,* April 16, 1861.

83. Smethport *McKean County Democrat,* January 17, 1861.

84. *Ibid.,* April 18, 1861.

85. Bedford *Gazette,* March 8, 1861.

86. Clinton *Democrat,* March 21, 1861.

87. Elwyn B. Robinson, "The Press: President Lincoln's Philadelphia Organ,"
The Pennsylvania Magazine of History and Biography 65 (April 1941) :158.

88. Wilkes-Barre *Luzerne Union,* January 16, 1861.

89. Gettysburg *Compiler,* February 25, 1861.

90. Philadelphia *Inquirer,* December 15, 1860.

91. *Ibid.,* December 21, 1860.

92. *Ibid.,* February 28, 1861.

93. Harrisburg *Pennsylvania Daily Telegraph,* January 26, 1861.

94. *Ibid.,* April 5, 1861.

95. Johnstown *Cambria Tribune,* March 29, 1861.

96. Philadelphia *Evening Bulletin,* March 29, 1861.

97. *Ibid.,* April 8, 1861.

98. Philadelphia *North American,* January 12, 1861.

99. *Ibid.,* April 10, 1861.

100. Philadelphia *Public Ledger,* March 11, 1861.

101. McClure, *Old Time Notes,* p. 467.

102. Edward G. Everett, "Contraband and Rebel Sympathizers in Pennsylvania
in 1861," *The Western Pennsylvania Historical Magazine,* 41 (Spring 1958) :37-38.

103. Philadelphia *Inquirer,* February 22, 1861.

104. William Dusinberre, *Civil War Issues in Philadelphia: 1856-1865* (Philadelphia: University of Pennsylvania Press, 1965), p. 103.

105. H. B. Robinson to Hendrick B. Wright, December 3, 1860, Hendrick B.
Wright Papers, Wyoming Historical and Geological Society.

106. John A. Logan, *The Great Conspiracy: Its Origin and History* (New
York: A. R. Hart and Company, 1886), pp. 259-60.

107. Philadelphia *Inquirer,* January 17, 1861.

108. Vincent L. Bradford to James Buchanan, January 3, 1861, James Buchanan
Papers, The Historical Society of Pennsylvania.

109. *Ibid.,* January 25, 1861.

110. Lancaster *Examiner and Herald,* December 12, 1860.

111. J. B. Baker to James Buchanan, January 11, 1861, James Buchanan Papers,
The Historical Society of Pennsylvania.

112. George W. Wharton to James Buchanan, January 10, 1861, *Ibid.*

113. James Campbell to James Buchanan, January 10, 1861, *Ibid.*

114. William B. Reed, *A Paper Containing A Statement and Vindication of
Certain Political Opinions* (Philadelphia: John Campbell, 1862), pp. 6-7.

115. *Ibid.*

116. *Ibid.,* p. 8.

117. Philadelphia *Inquirer,* January 17, 1861.

118. "The Diaries of Sidney George Fisher," *The Pennsylvania Magazine of
History and Biography* 87 (October 1963) :453n.

119. *Ibid.,* 88 (January 1964), p. 70.

120. *Ibid.,* p. 79.

121. Everett, "Contraband and Rebel Sympathizers," p. 39.

122. Chester F. Dunham, *The Attitude of the Northern Clergy Toward the South: 1860–1865* (Toledo: The Gray Company, 1942), p. 74.

123. Philadelphia *Inquirer,* December 28, 1860.

124. George Wilson to James Buchanan, January 4, 1861, James Buchanan Papers, The Historical Society of Pennsylvania.

125. Edwin M. Stanton to James Buchanan, May 6, 1861, *Ibid.*

126. H. B. Robinson to Hendrick B. Wright, April 15, 1861, Hendrick B. Wright Papers, Wyoming Historical and Geological Society.

127. Sidney George Fisher, 88:80–81.

128. *Ibid.,* p. 82.

129. Everett, "Contraband and Rebel Sympathizers," p. 35.

130. M. S. Buckley to Simon Cameron, April 17, 1861, Simon Cameron Papers, The Library of Congress.

131. Everett, "Contraband and Rebel Sympathizers," pp. 30–31.

CHAPTER 6

1. Brother Basil L. Lee, F.S.C., *Discontent in New York City: 1861–1865* (Washington: Catholic University of America Press, 1943), p. 8.

2. Richard Lowitt, *A Merchant Prince of the Nineteenth Century: William A. Dodge* (New York: Columbia University Press, 1954), p. 206.

3. Lee, *Discontent,* p. 16.

4. Edgar J. McManus, *A History of Negro Slavery in New York* (Syracuse: Syracuse University Press, 1966), p. ix.

5. *Ibid.,* p. 4.

6. *Ibid.,* pp. 42–43.

7. *Ibid.,* p. 150.

8. *Ibid.,* p. 154.

9. *Ibid.,* pp. 174–75.

10. *Ibid.,* p. 178.

11. *Ibid.,* p. 172.

12. Sidney D. Brummer, *Political History of New York State During the Period of the Civil War* (New York: Longmans, Green and Company, 1911), pp. 24–36. Stewart Mitchell, *Horatio Seymour of New York* (Cambridge: Harvard University Press, 1938), p. 209.

13. Dwight L. Dumond, *The Secession Movement: 1860–1861* (New York: The Macmillan Company, 1931), pp. 43–44.

14. Brummer, *Political History of New York,* p. 50.

15. Reinhard H. Luthin, *The First Lincoln Campaign* (Cambridge: Harvard University Press, 1944), p. 212.

16. Lee, *Discontent,* p. 4.

17. *Ibid.,* p. 3.

18. *Ibid.,* pp. 3–4.

19. Luthin, *First Lincoln Campaign,* p. 213.

20. *Ibid.,* p. 216.

21. *Ibid.*

22. *Ibid.,* p. 217.

23. *Ibid.,* p. 211.

24. *Ibid.*

25. Brummer, *Political History of New York,* p. 96.

26. Luthin, *First Lincoln Campaign,* p. 217.

27. Brummer, *Political History of New York,* p. 91.

28. Ollinger Crenshaw, "Urban and Rural Voting in the Election of 1860," in Eric F. Goldman, ed., *Historiography and Urbanization* (Baltimore: The Johns Hopkins University Press, 1941), p. 50.

29. *Ibid.,* pp. 55–56.

30. Donald E. Simon, "Brooklyn in the Election of 1860," *The New York Historical Society Quarterly* 51 (July 1967):259.

31. Brummer, *Political History of New York,* p. 98.

32. *Ibid.,* p. 98.

33. Horace Greeley, *The American Conflict* (Hartford: O. D. Case and Company, 1865), 1:388.

34. Albany *Atlas & Argus,* January 25, 1861.

35. DeAlva S. Alexander, *A Political History of the State of New York* (New York: Henry Holt and Company, 1906), 2:354–55.

36. Brummer, *Political History of New York,* pp. 117–19.

37. Brooklyn *Daily Eagle,* February 2, 1861.

38. Greeley, *American Conflict,* p. 393.

39. William B. Weeden, *War Government: Federal and State: 1861–1865* (Boston: Houghton, Mifflin and Company, 1906), p. 21.

40. Brummer, *Political History of New York,* p. 121.

41. Greeley, *American Conflict,* pp. 388–90, 393–94.

42. Alexander, *Political History,* pp. 356–57.

43. Brooklyn *Daily Eagle,* February 2, 1861.

44. Greeley, *American Conflict,* p. 396.

45. New York *Journal of Commerce,* February 2, 1861.

46. August Belmont, *A Few Letters and Speeches of the Late Civil War* (New York: n.p., 1870), p. 29.

47. Irving Katz, *August Belmont: A Political Biography* (New York: Columbia University Press, 1968), p. 88.

48. Belmont, *Letters and Speeches,* p. 24.

49. Mitchell, *Horatio Seymour,* p. 223.

50. Thomas M. Cook and Thomas A. Knox, eds., *Public Record of Horatio Seymour . . . 1856 to 1868* (New York: I. W. England, 1868), p. 26.

51. Samuel J. Tilden, *The Union! Its Dangers! And How They Can Be Averted.* (n.p., 1860), p. 16.

52. Tilden's Speech to the Albany Convention, January 1861. Samuel J. Tilden Papers, Manuscript Division, The New York Public Library, Astor, Lenox and Tilden Foundations.

53. Alexander C. Flick, *Samuel Jones Tilden: A Study in Political Sagacity* (Port Washington: Kennikat Press, Inc., New York, 1963), p. 131.

54. Greeley, *American Conflict,* p. 413.

55. John B. Haskin to Edwin D. Morgan, December 20, 1860, Edwin D. Morgan Papers, New York State Library.

56. Morgan Dix, *Memoirs of John Adams Dix* (New York: Harper and Brothers, 1883) 2:336–37.

57. John Dix to Horatio King, January 3, 1861, Horatio King Papers, The Library of Congress.

58. John A. Dix to William H. Seward, March 15, 1861, William H. Seward Papers, University of Rochester.

59. Dix, *Memoirs of John Adams Dix,* 1:342.

60. *Ibid.,* 1:343–45.

61. Philip S. Foner, *Business and Slavery: The New York Merchants and the Irrepressible Conflict* (Chapel Hill: University of North Carolina Press, 1941), p. 285.

62. Brummer, *Political History of New York,* p. 125.

63. Foner, *Business and Slavery,* pp. 287–88.

64. *Ibid.,* pp. 286–87.

65. Edward McPherson, *The Political History of the United States of America During the Great Rebellion* (Washington: Philip and Solomons, 1865), pp. 42–43.

66. *Ibid.,* p. 43.

67. *Ibid.*

68. Albany *Atlas & Argus,* January 9, 1861.

69. Lee, *Discontent,* p. 19.

70. *DeBow's Review* 30 (February 1861):184–86.

71. Samuel A. Pleasants, *Fernando Wood of New York* (New York: Columbia University Press, 1948), p. 116.

72. John A. Kennedy to Edwin D. Morgan, December 9, 1861, Edwin D. Morgan Papers, New York State Library.

73. Evert A. Duyckinck, *National History of the War for the Union* (New York, n.p., 1861), 1:59–60.

74. Lee, *Discontent,* p. 32.

75. Brummer, *Political History of New York,* pp. 126–27.

76. Julius W. Pratt, "Public Opinion in the East From the Election of Lincoln to the Firing on Sumter," Master of Arts Dissertation for the University of Chicago, 1914.

77. Washington Hunt to Charles S. Ruggles, December 27, 1860, Washington Hunt Papers, New York State Library.

78. Brummer, *Political History of New York,* pp. 17–18.

79. Belmont, *Letters and Speeches,* p. 18.

80. MS. Diary of John Bigelow, 1861, pp. 45–46, Manuscript Division, The New York Public Library, Astor, Lenox and Tilden Foundations.

81. Albany *Evening Journal,* April 11, 1861.

82. MS. Edwin D. Morgan, Annual Message of 1861, Drafts of Messages, p. 72, Edwin D. Morgan Papers, The New York Historical Society.

83. Carl F. Krummel, "Henry J. Raymond and the New York Times in the Secession Crisis, 1860-61," *New York History* 32, no. 4 (October 1951):388–90.

84. New York *Times,* March 21, 1861.

85. New York *Times,* April 11, 1861.

86. Krummel, "Henry J. Raymond," p. 396.

87. David M. Potter, writing in 1941 did not accept the view that Greeley was entirely serious in this matter. He accused Greeley of changing the definition of the term *peaceable secession.* Thomas N. Bonner, on the other hand, writing in 1951, believed that Greeley was sincere about the peaceful secession of the southern states. Greeley himself in his book *The American Conflict,* written during and immediately after the war, does not clear up this confusion. In this book he stressed the use of a convention of all the states to decide upon terms of separa-

tion. He argued that there was a strong sentiment in the North, even among Republicans, that favored the peaceful withdrawal of the slave states.

88. David C. Mearns, *The Lincoln Papers* (New York: Doubleday and Company, 1948), 2:349–50.

89. *Ibid.*

90. *Ibid.*

91. *Ibid.*

92. *Ibid.*

93. James Ford Rhodes, *History of the United States from the Compromise of 1850* (New York: Harper and Brothers, 1895), 3:141.

94. Mearns, *Lincoln Papers,* 2:355.

95. *The War of Rebellion: A Compilation of the Official Records of the Union and Confederate Armies* (Washington: United States Government Printing Office, 1900) Series 4, vol. 1:47. (Hereafter cited as *O.R.*).

96. New York *Tribune,* March 7, 1861.

97. Allan Nevins, *The Evening Post: A Century of Journalism* (New York: Boni & Liveright, 1922), p. 270.

98. William E. Smith, ed., *Carl Russell Fish, The American Civil War* (New York: Longmans, Green and Company, 1937), p. 106.

99. Ezra Cornell to Paul J. Amell, January 8, 1861, Ezra Cornell Papers at DeWitt Historical Society on microfilm at Cornell University Library.

100. Mearns, *Lincoln Papers,* pp. 407–08.

101. *Journal of the Assembly of the State of New York: At Their Eighty-fourth Session* (Albany, 1861), pp. 76–77.

102. *Ibid.*

103. *Journal of the Senate of the State of New York: At Their Eighty-fourth Session* (Albany, 1861), p. 58.

104. *Journal of the Assembly,* pp. 1026–27; *Journal of the Senate,* pp. 608–09.

105. Brummer, *Political History of New York,* pp. 148–49.

106. Lucius E. Chittenden, *A Report of the Debates and Proceedings in the Secret Sessions of the Conference for Proposing Amendments to the Constitution of the United States* (New York: D. Appleton and Company, 1864), pp. 402–03.

107. *Ibid.,* p. 303.

108. Preston King to Thurlow Weed, December 19, 1860, Thurlow Weed Papers, University of Rochester Library.

109. *The Congressional Globe,* p. 341.

110. *Ibid.,* p. 658.

111. *Ibid.,* p. 193.

112. Philadelphia *Inquirer,* March 12, 1861.

113. Alexander, *Political History,* 3:4.

114. *Congressional Globe,* pp. 40–41.

115. *Ibid.*

116. *Ibid.*

117. *Ibid.,* p. 107.

118. *Ibid.,* p. 281.

119. *Congressional Globe, Appendix,* pp. 89–91.

120. *Ibid.*

121. *Ibid.*

122. *Ibid.*

123. *Congressional Globe,* p. 758.

124. *O.R.*, Series 3, vol. 1:72.

125. *Congressional Globe, Appendix*, p. 268.

126. *Congressional Globe*, p. 1101.

127. *Ibid.*, p. 650.

128. *Ibid.*, p. 797.

129. *Ibid.*, pp. 631–32.

130. *Congressional Globe, Appendix*, p. 192.

131. Brummer, *Political History of New York*, p. 102.

132. Richard Lathers to Evert A. Duyckinck, November 28, 1860, Evert Duyckinck Collection, Manuscript Division, The New York Public Library, Astor, Lenox and Tilden Foundations.

133. *Ibid.*

134. Alvan F. Sanborn, *Reminiscences of Richard Lathers* (New York: The Grafton Press, 1907), p. 94.

135. Foner, *Business and Slavery*, p. 231.

136. Lee, *Discontent*, p. 5n.

137. Richard Lather's speech to Jefferson Davis at Montgomery, Alabama, Richard Lathers Papers, The Library of Congress.

138. Foner, *Business and Slavery*, p. 227.

139. *Ibid.*, p. 232.

140. Abram S. Hewitt to Trenton "inter-office," October 26, 1860, Cooper-Hewitt Letter Book, The New York Historical Society, Book 16, p. 381.

141. *Ibid.*, Abram S. Hewitt to Col. E. Houstoun, February 4, 1861, Book 17, pp. 404–05.

142. *Ibid.*

143. Abram S. Hewitt to Charles Knapt, February 16, 1861, Cooper-Hewitt Letter Book, Book 17, pp. 522–23.

144. Peter Cooper to Abraham Lincoln, March 20, 1861, Peter Cooper Papers, Cooper Union Library.

145. Foner, *Business and Slavery*, p. 274.

146. *Ibid.*, p. 290.

147. Lee, *Discontent*, p. 36.

148. Sidney Webster to General Caleb Cushing, December 31, 1860, Caleb Cushing Papers, The Library of Congress.

149. Lee, *Discontent*, p. 35.

150. *Ibid.*, p. 36.

151. *Ibid.*, pp. 34–35.

152. *Ibid.*, p. 35.

153. *Ibid.*

154. Foner, *Business and Slavery*, p. 291.

155. *Ibid.*

156. *Ibid.*, pp. 292–93.

157. Ezra J. Warner, *Generals in Gray* (Baton Rouge: Louisiana State University Press, 1959), pp. 280–81, 194–95.

158. John A. Kennedy to Edwin D. Morgan, January 13, 1861, Edwin D. Morgan Papers, New York State Library.

159. Pratt, "Public Opinion in the East," p. 49.

160. Brummer, *Political History of New York*, p. 145.

161. *Ibid.*, p. 147.

162. John R. Dickinson, *Speeches, Correspondence, Etc., of the Late Daniel S. Dickinson of New York* (New York: G. P. Putnam and Sons, 1867), 2:7.

163. Frank Moore, *The Rebellion Record* (New York: G. P. Putnam, 1861), 1, Documents: 69–70.

164. *Ibid.*, p. 77.

165. Abram S. Hewitt to Messrs. Strickney & Co., April 19, 1861, Cooper-Hewitt Letter Book, The New York Historical Society, Book 18, p. 222.

166. Samuel F. B. Morse to Cornelia P. Goodrich, April 21, 1861, Thomas F. Madigan Collection, Manuscript Division, The New York Public Library, Astor, Lenox and Tilden Foundations.

167. Ulrich B. Phillips, ed., *The Correspondence of Robert Toombs, Alexander H. Stevens, and Howell Cobb, Annual Report of the American Historical Association for the Year 1911* (Washington: American Historical Association, 1913), p. 561.

168. Sidney Webster to Franklin Pierce, April 19, 1861, Franklin Pierce Papers, The Library of Congress.

CHAPTER 7

1. John A. Logan, *The Great Conspiracy: Its Origin and History* (New York: A. R. Hart and Company, 1886), p. 261.

2. Philadelphia *Inquirer* February 9, 1861.

3. Joel T. Headley, *The Great Rebellion: A History of the Civil War in the United States* (Hartford: Hulburt, Williams and Company, 1863), 1:62–63.

4. Morgan Dix, *Memoirs of John Adams Dix* (New York: Harper and Brothers, 1883), 1:345.

5. William Dusinberre, *Civil War Issues in Philadelphia: 1856–1865* (Philadelphia: University of Pennsylvania Press, 1965), p. 122.

6. Carl Sandburg, *Abraham Lincoln: The War Years* (New York: Harcourt, Brace and Company, 1939), 1:219–20.

7. James Buchanan, *Mr. Buchanan's Administration on the Eve of the Rebellion* (New York: D. Appleton and Company, 1866), p. 98.

8. Sidney D. Brummer, *Political History of New York During the Period of the Civil War* (New York: Longmans, Green and Company, 1911), p. 147.

9. James G. Blaine, *Twenty Years of Congress* (Norwich, Conn.: The Henry Bill Publishing Company, 1884), 1:297.

10. Alvin F. Sanborn, *Reminiscences of Richard Lathers* (New York: The Grafton Press, 1907), pp. 160–62.

11. Edward A. Pollard, *The Lost Cause: A New Southern History of the War of the Confederates* (New York: E. B. Treat and Company, 1866), p. 115.

12. Sandburg, *Lincoln*, 1:206.

13. Gustavus A. Fox to Francis P. Blair, Sr., April 17, 1961, Gustavus V. Fox Papers, The New York Historical Society.

14. Roy P. Basler, ed., *The Collected Works of Abraham Lincoln* (New Brunswick: Rutgers University Press, 1953), 4:193–94.

15. Abraham Lincoln to Gustavus V. Fox, May 1, 1861, Gustavus V. Fox Papers, The New York Historical Society.

BIBLIOGRAPHY

MANUSCRIPTS

Frederick A. P. Barnard Papers, Columbia University Libraries.
Thomas F. Bayard Papers, The Library of Congress.
James A. Beaver Papers, Pennsylvania Historical Collections, Pennsylvania State University Library.
John Bigelow Ms. Diary, The New York Public Library.
William Bigler Papers, The Historical Society of Pennsylvania.
Blair Family Papers, The Library of Congress.
J. P. Blanchard Papers, Swarthmore College Peace Collection.
William O. Bourne Papers, The New York Historical Society.
A. W. Bradford Papers, Maryland Historical Society.
Joseph P. Bradley Papers, New Jersey Historical Society.
James Buchanan Papers, The Historical Society of Pennsylvania.
James Buchanan Papers, Lancaster County Historical Society.
James Buchanan Papers, The Library of Congress.
Samuel Calvin Papers, The Historical Society of Pennsylvania.
Simon Cameron Papers, The Library of Congress.
Simon Cameron Papers, Dauphin County Historical Society. (Microfilms in possession of the Pennsylvania State Archives.)
Edward C. Gardiner Collection, The Historical Society of Pennsylvania.
A. S. Chambers Diary and Papers, The New York Historical Society.
Salmon P. Chase Papers, The Historical Society of Pennsylvania.
Alexander B. Cooper, "Memoirs of Myself and My Times," Historical Society of Delaware.
Peter Cooper-Abram S. Hewitt Letter Book, The New York Historical Society.
Peter Cooper Papers, Cooper Union Library.
Cope Papers, Friends Historical Library of Swarthmore College.
Ezra Cornell Papers, DeWitt Historical Society. (Microfilms in possession of Cornell University.)

242

John J. Crittenden Papers, The Library of Congress. (Microfilms in possession of the University of Delaware.)

Caleb Cushing Papers, The Library of Congress.

William M. Davis Papers, The Historical Society of Pennsylvania.

John A. Dix Papers, Columbia University Libraries.

James R. Doolittle Papers, New York City Public Library.

Henry Francis duPont Collection of Winterthur Manuscripts, Eleutherian Mills Historical Library.

Samuel Francis DuPont Papers, Eleutherian Mills Historical Library.

Evert A. Duyckinck Collection, New York Public Library.

Executive Papers, Hall of Records of Delaware.

Fairchild Collection, The New York Historical Society.

Samuel M. Felton Papers, The Historical Society of Pennsylvania.

Hamilton Fish Papers, The Library of Congress.

Gustavus V. Fox Papers, The New York Historical Society.

J. Alexander Fulton Collection, Pennsylvania State Archives.

Henry George Papers, New York Public Library.

John P. Gillis Papers, Historical Society of Delaware.

Margaret C. Griffis Ms. Diaries, Rutgers, the State University Library.

William Wilkins Glenn Papers, Maryland Historical Society.

John M. Gordon Papers, Maryland Historical Society.

William Graves Scrapbook, Maryland Historical Society.

Mrs. Benjamin G. Harris Ms. Diary, Maryland Historical Society.

Dr. Samuel A. Harrison Ms. "Journal," Maryland Historical Society.

Dr. Samuel A. Harrison, "War of the Rebellion in Talbot County," in Harrison Collection, Maryland Historical Society.

Alexander Henry Papers, The Historical Society of Pennsylvania.

Abram S. Hewitt Papers, Cooper Union Library.

Executive Department: Thomas H. Hicks Letter Book, Hall of Records of Maryland.

Thomas H. Hicks Papers, Hall of Records of Maryland.

Thomas H. Hicks Papers, Maryland Historical Society.

The Historical Society of Pennsylvania Autograph Collection.

Reverend Samuel B. How Papers, Rutgers, the State University Library.

Charles Howard Papers, Maryland Historical Society.

Washington Hunt Papers, New York State Library.

John Pendelton Kennedy Journal, Letter Books and Papers, George Peabody Department of the Enoch Pratt Free Library.

Philip C. Kennedy Papers, Columbia University Libraries.

Horatio King Papers, The Library of Congress.

Henry Lane Kendrick Papers, The New York Historical Society.

Richard Lathers Papers, The Library of Congress.

Abraham Lincoln Papers, (Robert Todd Lincoln Collection), The Library of Congress. (Microfilm in possession of the University of Delaware.)

Thomas McHenry Papers, Historical Society of Maryland.

Edward McPherson Papers, The Library of Congress.

Thomas F. Madigan, The New York Public Library.

Ebenezer Meriam Papers, The New York Historical Society.

Edwin D. Morgan Papers, The New York Historical Society.

Edwin D. Morgan Papers, New York State Library.

Charles Olden Papers, Rutgers, the State University Library.

James A. Pearce Papers, Maryland Historical Society.

Franklin Pierce Papers, The Library of Congress.

Rodman M. Price Papers, Rutgers, the State University Library.

Alexander Randall Diaries, Maryland Historical Society.

Ridgely Collection, Hall of Records of Delaware.

William H. H. Ross Papers, Historical Society of Delaware.

George W. Scranton Papers, Eleutherian Mills Historical Library.

William H. Seward Papers, Rochester University Library.

Gerritt Smith Papers, The New York Historical Society.

Robert M. S. Jackson Papers, Pennsylvania State University Library.

"Personal Reminiscences" by Charles Perris Smith, New Jersey State Library.

Thaddeus Stevens Papers, The Library of Congress.

Edward N. Tailer, Jr. Diaries, The New York Historical Society.

Samuel Tilden Papers, New York Public Library.

Isaac R. Trimble Papers, Maryland Historical Society.

Daniel Ullman Papers, The New York Historical Society.

War 1861–1865 Collection, The New York Historical Society.

Ernest H. Wardwell Papers, Maryland Historical Society.

Thurlow Weed Papers, Rochester University Library.

Gideon Welles Papers, New York Public Library.

Andrew D. White Papers, Cornell University Library.

John G. Whittier Papers, Friends Historical Library of Swarthmore College.

John E. Wool Letter Books and Papers, New York State Library.

Hendrick B. Wright Papers, Wyoming Historical and Geological Society, Wilkes-Barre, Pennsylvania.

NEWSPAPERS SEPTEMBER 1860–MAY 1861 PASSIM

Albany *Atlas and Argus.*

Albany *Evening Journal.*

Albany *Times and Courier.*

Altoona *Tribune.*

Angelica (New York) *Reporter.*
Annapolis *Gazette.*
Auburn (New York) *Daily Advertiser.*
Auburn (New York) *Daily Union.*
Auburn (New York) *Northern Christian Advocate.*
Baltimore *American and Commercial Advertiser.*
Baltimore *Clipper.*
Baltimore *Daily Exchange.*
Baltimore *Evening Patriot.*
Baltimore *Family Journal.*
Baltimore *Price-Current and Weekly Journal.*
Baltimore *Sun.*
Bath (New York) *Steuben Farmers' Advocate.*
Beaver (Pennsylvania) *Argus.*
Bedford (Pennsylvania) *Gazette.*
Bedford (Pennsylvania) *Inquirer.*
Bel Air (Maryland) *National American.*
Bel Air (Maryland) *Southern Aegis.*
Binghamton (New York) *Standard.*
Bloomville (New York) *Mirror.*
Bridgeton (New Jersey) *Pioneer.*
Brooklyn *Daily Eagle.*
Brooklyn *Standard.*
Buffalo *Morning Express.*
Cambridge (Maryland) *Herald.*
Cape May (New Jersey) *Ocean Wave.*
Cherry Valley (New York) *Gazette.*
Clearfield (Pennsylvania) *Raftsman's Journal.*
Cooperstown (New York) *Freeman's Journal.*
Corning (New York) *Democrat.*
Corning (New York) *Journal.*
Coudersport (Pennsylvania) *Potter Journal.*
Cumberland (Maryland) *Civilian and Telegraph.*
Cumberland (Maryland) *Democratic Alleganian.*
Dover (Delaware) *Delawarean.*
Easton (Pennsylvania) *Argus.*
Easton (Pennsylvania) *Free Press.*
Easton (Maryland) *Gazette.*
Easton (Pennsylvania) *Northampton County Journal.*
Easton (Pennsylvania) *Sentinel.*
Easton (Maryland) *Star.*
Ebensburg (Pennsylvania) *Alleghanian.*

Elizabethtown (New York) *Post*.
Elkton (Maryland) *Cecil Whig*.
Elmira (New York) *Weekly Advertiser and Chemung County Republican*.
Erie *Observer*.
Erie *Weekly Gazette*.
Flemington (New Jersey) *Hunterdon Democrat*.
Frederick (Maryland) *Examiner*.
Frederick *Maryland Union*.
Freehold (New Jersey) *Monmouth Democrat*.
Freehold (New Jersey) *Monmouth Herald and Inquirer*.
Georgetown (Delaware) *Messenger*.
Gettsyburg *Adams Sentinel*.
Gettysburg *Compiler*.
Goshen (New York) *Democrat*.
Goshen (New York) *Republican*.
Hackettstown (New Jersey) *Gazette*.
Hagerstown (Maryland) *Herald of Freedom and Torch Light*.
Hanover (Pennsylvania) *Citizen*.
Hanover (Pennsylvania) *Spectator*.
Harrisburg *Patriot and Union*.
Harrisburg *Pennsylvania Daily Telegraph*.
Hempstead (New York) *Queens County Sentinel*.
Huntington (New York) *Long Islander*.
Ithaca (New York) *American Citizen*.
Ithaca (New York) *Tompkins County Democrat*.
Jamaica (New York) *Long Island Democrat*.
Jamestown (New York) *Chautauqua Democrat*.
Jamestown (New York) *Journal*.
Jersey City *American Standard*.
Johnstown (Pennsylvania) *Cambria Tribune*.
Lancaster (Pennsylvania) *Daily Express*.
Lancaster (Pennsylvania) *Examiner and Herald*.
Lancaster (Pennsylvania) *Inquirer*.
Lancaster (Pennsylvania) *Union*.
Lebanon (Pennsylvania) *Courier*.
Lewisburg (Pennsylvania) *Union County Star and Lewisburg Chronicle*.
Lewistown (Pennsylvania) *Gazette*.
Lewistown (Pennsylvania) *True Democrat*.
Little Falls (New York) *Herkimer County Journal*.
Lock Haven (Pennsylvania) *Clinton Democrat*.
Middletown (Maryland) *Valley Register*.
Montgomery (New York) *Standard*.

Montrose (Pennsylvania) *Democrat.*
Mount Holly (New Jersey) *Herald.*
Mount Holly (New Jersey) *Mirror.*
Muncy (Pennsylvania) *Luminary and Lycoming County Advertiser.*
Newark (New Jersey) *Daily Advertiser.*
Newark (New Jersey) *Evening Journal.*
New Brunswick (New Jersey) *Fredonian.*
New Brunswick (New Jersey) *Times.*
Newburgh (New York) *Telegraph.*
Newton (New Jersey) *Herald.*
Newton (New Jersey) *Sussex Register.*
New York *Albion.*
New York *Bible Society Record.*
New York *Brother Jonathan.*
New York *Century.*
New York *Christian Advocate and Journal.*
New York *Christian Intelligencer.*
New York *Church Journal.*
New York *Commercial Advertiser.*
New York *Daily News.*
New York *Daily Transcript.*
New York *Daily Tribune.*
New York *Dispatch.*
New York *Evening Day Book.*
New York *Evening Post.*
New York *Family Herald.*
New York *Herald.*
New York *Herald of Progress.*
New York *Home Journal.*
New York *Illustrated News.*
New York *Independent.*
New York *Irish American.*
New York *Journal of Commerce.*
New York *Leader.*
New York *Ledger.*
New York *Morning Courier and New York Enquirer.*
New York *Morning Express.*
New York *National Anti-Slavery Standard.*
New York *New Jerusalem Messenger.*
New York *Observer.*
New York *Shipping and Commercial List and New York Price Current.*
New York *The Sower: Missionary Recorder.*

New York *Spectator.*
New York *Spirit of the Times.*
New York *Sun.*
New York *Sunday Mercury.*
New York *Sunday Times and Noah's Weekly Messenger.*
New York *Times.*
New York *Weekly News.*
New York *Wilkes' Spirit of the Times.*
New York *World.*
Niagara Falls (New York) *Gazette.*
Norwich (New York) *Chenango Telegraph.*
Ovid (New York) *Bee.*
Paterson (New Jersey) *Daily Guardian.*
Paterson (New Jersey) *Daily True Register.*
Penn Yan (New York) *Yates County Chronicle.*
Philadelphia *Daily Evening Bulletin.*
Philadelphia *Inquirer.*
Philadelphia *North American and United States Gazette.*
Philadelphia *Public Ledger.*
Pittsburgh *Daily Gazette.*
Plattsburg (New York) *Republican.*
Pottsville (Pennsylvania) *Miner's Journal and Pottsville General Adver-
tiser.*
Poughkeepsie (New York) *Eagle.*
Rochester *Daily Union and Advertiser.*
Rochester *Democrat and American.*
Rochester *Douglass' Monthly.*
Rochester *Evening Express.*
Rockville (Maryland) *Montgomery County Sentinel.*
Sag Harbor (New York) *Corrector.*
Smethport (Pennsylvania) *Cameron Citizen.*
Smethport (Pennsylvania) *M'Kean County Democrat.*
Smethport (Pennsylvania) *M'Kean Miner.*
Smyrna (Delaware) *Times.*
Stapleton (New York) *Richmond County Gazette.*
Stroudsburg (Pennsylvania) *Jeffersonian.*
Toms River (New Jersey) *Ocean Emblem.*
Towanda (Pennsylvania) *Bradford Reporter.*
Towsontown (Maryland) *Baltimore County Advocate.*
Towsontown (Maryland) *Baltimore County American.*
Trenton *Daily True American.*
Trumansburg (New York) *News.*

Uniontown (Pennsylvania) *Genius of Liberty.*

Upper Marlborough (Maryland) *Planter's Advocate.*

Utica *Gospel Messenger and Church Record of Western New York.*

Utica *Morning Herald and Daily Gazette.*

Utica *Oneida Weekly Herald and Gazette and Courier.*

Warren (Pennsylvania) *Mail.*

Washington (Pennsylvania) *Reporter and Tribune.*

Watertown *New York Reformer.*

Waverly (New York) *Advocate.*

Wellsboro (Pennsylvania) *Agitator.*

Westminister (Maryland) *American Sentinel.*

White Plains (New York) *Eastern Star Journal.*

Wilkes-Barre (Pennsylvania) *Luzerne Union.*

Wilkes-Barre (Pennsylvania) *Record of the Times.*

Williamsport (Pennsylvania) *Lycoming Gazette.*

Wilmington *Delaware Gazette.*

Wilmington *Delaware Republican.*

Wilmington (Delaware) *Delmarva Star,* November 5, 1933.

Yonkers (New York) *Examiner.*

York (Pennsylvania) *Gazette.*

THESES

Perry, Percival. "The Attitudes of the New Jersey Delegation in Congress on the Slavery Question, 1815–1861." Rutgers, the State University, 1939, unpublished Master's thesis.

Pratt, Julius W. "Public Opinion in the East from the Election of Lincoln to the Firing on Sumter." The University of Chicago: Graduate School of Arts and Literature, 1914, unpublished Master's thesis.

White, Stella. "Opposition to the Civil War in Pennsylvania." Pennsylvania State University, 1920, unpublished Master's thesis.

GOVERNMENT DOCUMENTS

Acts of the Eighty-Fourth Legislature of the State of New Jersey and Sixteenth Under the New Constitution. Paterson, 1860.

Acts of the Eighty-Fifth Legislature of the State of New Jersey and Seventeenth Under the New Constitution. Freehold, 1861.

Aggregate Amount of Persons Within the United States in the Year 1810. Washington, 1811.

"Alleged Hostile Organization Against the Government Within the District of Columbia." *House Report,* No. 79, 36 Congress, 2 Session.

Biographical Directory of the American Congress: 1774–1961. Washington, 1961.

Census for 1820. Washington, 1821.

Compendium of the Enumeration of the Inhabitants and Statistics of the United States. Washington, 1841.

The Congressional Globe, Parts I, II and *Appendix.* 36 Congress, 2 Session.

"Disturbed Condition of the Country; Mr. Taylor, Minority Report." *House Report* No. 31, 36 Congress, 2 Session.

Documents of the Assembly of the State of New York. Eighty-Third Session—1860, Albany, 1860.

Documents of the Senate of the State of New York. Eighty-Fourth Session—1861. Albany, 1861.

Fifth Census; or, Enumeration of the Inhabitants of the United States, 1830. Washington, 1832.

Journal of the Assembly of the State of New York at Their Eighty-Third Session. Albany, 1860.

Journal of the Assembly of the State of New York at Their Eighty-Fourth Session. Albany, 1861.

"Journal of the Congress of the Confederate States of America: 1861–65." *Senate Document,* No. 234, 58 Congress, 2 Session.

Journal of the House of Representatives of the State of Delaware, 1861. Wilmington, 1861.

Journal of the House of Representatives of the Commonwealth of Pennsylvania. Harrisburg, 1861.

Journal of the Proceedings of the House of Delegates. Annapolis, 1860.

Journal of the Proceedings of the House of Delegates in Extra Session. Frederick, 1861.

Journal of the Proceedings of the Senate of Maryland. Annapolis, 1860.

Journal of Proceedings of the Senate of Maryland in Extra Session. Frederick, 1861.

Journal of the Senate of the Commonwealth of Pennsylvania. Harrisburg, 1861.

Journal of the Senate of the State of Delaware. Dover, 1861.

Journal of the 16th. Senate of the State of New Jersey. Belvidere, 1860.

Journal of the 17th. Senate of the State of New Jersey. Belvidere, 1861.

Journal of the Senate of the State of New York: At Their Eighty-Third Session. Albany, 1860.

Journal of the Senate of the State of New York: At Their Eighty-Fourth Session. Albany, 1861.

Maryland State Legislature Documents. Frederick, 1861.

"Message from the President of the United States." *Senate Executive Document,* No. 3, 36 Congress, 2 Session.

Minutes of Votes and Proceedings of the Eighty-Fourth General Assembly of the State of New Jersey. Freehold, 1860.

Minutes of Votes and Proceedings of the Eighty-Fifth General Assembly of the State of New Jersey. Jersey City, 1861.

"Petition of the Committee of Thirty-Three," *House Miscellaneous Document*. No. 30, 36 Congress, 2 Session.

Population of the United States in 1860. Washington, 1864.

"Preamble and Resolutions of the Common Council of the City of New York." *House Miscellaneous Document*, No. 15, 36 Congress, 2 Session.

"Report of the Committee of Thirty-Three." *House Report*, No. 31, 36 Congress, 2 Session.

"Resolutions of the Legislature of the State of Delaware." *House Miscellaneous Document*, No. 21, 36 Congress, 2 Session.

"Resolutions of the Legislature of the State of Pennsylvania." *House Miscellaneous Document*, No. 24, 36 Congress, 2 Session.

"Resolutions of the Legislature of the State of South Carolina in Relation to Federal Affairs." *Maryland Legislature Documents*, 1860.

Returns of the Whole Number of Persons Within the Several Districts of the United States. Philadelphia, 1791.

Returns of the Whole Number of Persons Within the Several Districts of the United States. Washington, 1801.

The Seventh Census of the United States: 1850. Washington, 1853.

The War of the Rebellion: A Compilation of the Official Records of the Union and Confederate Armies. 128 vols., Washington, 1880–1901.

OTHER PRINTED MATERIALS

Abrams, Ray H. "*The Jeffersonian,* Copperhead Newspaper." *The Pennsylvania Magazine of History and Biography* 57 (July 1933), pp. 260–83.

Adrain, Garnett B. *State of the Union: Speech of Hon. Garnett B. Adrain, of New Jersey, in the House of Representatives.*

Alexander, DeAlva S. *A Political History of the State of New York*. 3 vols., New York: Henry Holt and Company, 1906.

[Appleton's] *American Annual Cyclopaedia and Register of Important Events*. Vol. 1, New York: D. Appleton and Company, 1862.

American Society for Promoting National Unity. New York: John F. Trow, 1861.

Atkinson, Joseph. *The History of Newark, New Jersey*. Newark: William B. Guild, 1878.

Auchampaugh, Philip G. *James Buchanan and His Cabinet on the Eve of Secession*. Lancaster: Lancaster Press, 1926.

———. *Robert Tyler: Southern Rights Champion: 1847–1866*. Duluth: Himan Stein, 1934.

Auer, J. Jeffery. *Antislavery and Disunion: 1858–1861*. New York: Harper and Row, 1963.

Basler, Roy P., ed. *The Collected Works of Abraham Lincoln*. 9 vols., New Brunswick: Rutgers University Press, 1953–1955.

Bayard, James A. *Condition of the Country.* Washington: H. Polkinhorn, n.d.

Beale, Howard K. *The Diary of Edward Bates: 1859–66.* Washington: United States Government Printing Office, 1933.

Belmont, August. *A Few Letters and Speeches of the Late Civil War.* New York: n.p., 1870.

Benton, Elbert J. "The Movement for Peace Without a Victory During the Civil War." *Collections of the Western Reserve Historical Society.* Cleveland: The Western Reserve Historical Society, 1918.

Bigelow, John. *Letters and Literary Memorials of Samuel J. Tilden.* 2 vols., New York: Harper and Brothers, 1908.

The Biographical Encyclopaedia of New Jersey of the Nineteenth Century. Philadelphia: Galaxy Publishing Company, 1877.

Black, Chauncey F. *Essays and Speeches of Jeremiah S. Black.* New York: D. Appleton and Company, 1885.

Blaine, James G. *Twenty Years of Congress.* 2 vols., Norwich: The Henry Bill Publishing Company, 1884.

Boney, F. N. *John Letcher of Virginia.* Montgomery: University of Alabama Press, 1966.

Bonner, Thomas N. "Horace Greeley and the Secession Movement, 1860–1861." *The Mississippi Valley Historical Review* 38 (December 1951):425–44.

A Book of Cape May, New Jersey. Cape May: The Albert Hand Company, 1937.

Boyd's Business Directory of the State of New Jersey Together with a General Directory of the Citizens of Newark.

Bradley, Erwin Stanley. *Simon Cameron: Lincoln's Secretary of War: A Political Biography.* Philadelphia: University of Pennsylvania Press, 1966.

——————. *The Triumph of Militant Republicanism: A Study of Pennsylvania and Presidential Politics: 1860–1872.* Philadelphia: University of Pennsylvania Press, 1964.

The Political Expressions of Joseph P. Bradley Compiled from Speeches, and Articles written by Him. Newark: Newark Daily Advertiser, n.d.

Brand, William F. *Life of William Rollinson Whittingham.* London: Wells Gardner, Darton and Company, 1883.

Brichford, Maynard J. "Congress at the Outbreak of the War." *Civil War History* 3 (June 1957):153–162.

Brown, George W. *Baltimore and the Nineteenth of April, 1861.* Johns Hopkins University Studies in Historical and Political Science. Extra vol. 3, Baltimore: N. Murray, 1887.

Brummer, Sidney D. *Political History of New York State During the Period of the Civil War.* New York: Longmans, Green and Company, 1911.

Buchanan, James. *Mr. Buchanan's Administration on the Eve of the Rebellion.* New York: D. Appleton and Company, 1866.

Buchholz, Heinrich E. *Governors of Maryland*. Baltimore: William and Wilkins Company, 1908.

Burgess, John W. *The Civil War and the Constitution: 1859–1865*. New York: Charles Scribner's Sons, 1901.

Cale, Edgar B. "Editorial Sentiment in Pennsylvania in the Campaign of 1860." *Pennsylvania History* 4 (October 1937) : 219–34.

Capen, Nathum. *The Indissoluble Nature of the American Union: A Letter to Hon. Peter Cooper*. New York, Boston: A. Williams and Company, 1862.

Carman, Harry J., and Luthin, Reinhard H. *Lincoln and the Patronage*. New York: Columbia University Press, 1943.

Chittenden, Lucius E. *A Report of the Debates and Proceedings in the Secret Sessions of the Conference Convention for Proposing Amendments to the Constitution of the United States*. New York: D. Appleton and Company, 1864.

Clark, Charles B. *The Eastern Shore of Maryland and Virginia*. 3 vols., New York: Lewis Historical Publishing Company, 1950.

———. *Politics in Maryland During the Civil War*. Chestertown: n.p., 1952.

Clayton, W. Woodford. *History of Bergen and Passaic Counties*. Philadelphia: Everts and Peck, 1882.

Cleveland, Henry. *Alexander H. Stephens in Public and Private with Letters and Speeches, Before, During, and Since the War*. Philadelphia: National Publishing Company, 1866.

Collins, William H. *An Address to the People of Maryland*. Baltimore: James Young, 1861.

———. *Third Address to the People of Maryland*. Baltimore: James Young, 1861.

Conlin, Sister Francis Loretto, S.S.J. "The Democratic Party in Pennsylvania from 1856 to 1865," *Records of the American Catholic Historical Society* 48 (1936) :132–83.

Conrad, Henry C. *History of the State of Delaware*. 3 vols., Wilmington: n.p., 1908.

Cook, Thomas M., and Knox, Thomas A., eds. *Public Record of Horatio Seymour . . . 1856 to 1868*. New York: I. W. England, 1868.

Coulter, E. Merton. *The Confederate States of America: 1861–1865*. Baton Rouge: Louisiana State University Press, 1950.

Cox, Samuel S. *Eight Years in Congress, From 1857–1865: Memoir and Speeches*. New York: D. Appleton and Company, 1865.

Crenshaw, Ollinger. *The Slave States in the Presidential Election of 1860*. The Johns Hopkins University Studies in Historical and Political Science. 63, no. 3, Baltimore: The Johns Hopkins University Press, 1945.

———. "Urban and Rural Voting in the Election of 1860." In Goldman, Eric F., *Historiography and Urbanization*. Baltimore: The Johns Hopkins University Press, 1941.

Cunz, Dieter. "The Maryland Germans in the Civil War." *Maryland Historical Magazine* 36 (December 1941) :394–419.

Current, Richard N. *Lincoln and the First Shot*. Philadelphia: J. B. Lippincott Company, 1963.

Curtis, George T. *Life of James Buchanan*. 2 vols., New York: Harper and Brothers, 1883.

Davis, Jefferson. *The Rise and Fall of the Confederate Government*. 2 vols., New York: D. Appleton and Company, 1912.

Davis, Stanton Ling. *Pennsylvania Politics, 1860–1863*. Cleveland: Western Reserve University, 1935.

De Bow, J. D. B. *The Industrial Resources, Etc., of the Southern and Western States*. 3 vols., New Orleans: J. D. B. De Bow, 1853.

De Bow's Review 30, Enlarged Series 5, New Orleans: J. D. B. De Bow, 1861.

"The Diaries of Sidney George Fisher." *The Pennsylvania Magazine of History and Biography* 76 (January 1952) :49–90; (April 1952): 177–220; 87 (October 1963) :431–53; 88 (January 1964) :70–93.

Dickinson, John R. *Speeches, Correspondence, Etc., of the Late Daniel S. Dickinson of New York*. New York: G. P. Putnam and Sons, 1867.

Dix, Morgan. *Memoirs of John Adams Dix*. 2 vols., New York: Harper and Brothers, 1883.

Dodd, William E. *Jefferson Davis*. New York: Russell and Russell, 1966.

Dodds, A. John. "Honest John Covode." *The Western Pennsylvania Historical Magazine* 16 (August 1933) :175–82.

Donald, David. *Charles Sumner and the Coming of the Civil War*. New York: Alfred A. Knopf, 1961.

Donehoo, George P., ed. *Pennsylvania: A History*. New York: Lewis Historical Publishing Company, 1926.

Dumond, Dwight L. *The Secession Movement: 1860–1861*. New York: The Macmillan Company, 1931.

Duncan, Bingham. "New Castle in 1860–61: A Community Response to a War Crisis." *The Western Pennsylvania Historical Magazine* 24 (December 1941) :251–60.

Duncan, Richard R. "Bishop Whittingham, the Maryland Diocese, and the Civil War." *Maryland Historical Magazine* 61 (December 1966): 329–47.

Dunham, Chester F. *The Attitude of the Northern Clergy Toward the South: 1860–1865*. Toledo: The Gray Company, 1942.

Dusinberre, William. *Civil War Issues in Philadelphia: 1856–1865*. Philadelphia: University of Pennsylvania Press, 1965.

Dutton, William S. *Du Pont: One Hundred and Forty Years*. New York: Charles Scribner's Sons, 1951.

Duyckinck, Evert A. *National History of the War for The Union*. New York: Johnson, Fry and Company, 1861–65.

Dyer, Frederick H. *A Compendium of the War of the Rebellion*. 3 vols., New York: Thomas Yoseloff, 1959.

BIBLIOGRAPHY

Effross, Harris I. "Origins of Post-Colonial Counties in New Jersey." *Proceedings of the New Jersey Historical Society* 81 (April 1963): 103–122.

Egle, William H. *Andrew Gregg Curtin: His Life and Services.* Philadelphia: Avil Printing Company, 1895.

———. *An Illustrated History of the Commonwealth of Pennsylvania.* Harrisburg: De Witt C. Goodrich and Company, 1876.

Eiselen, Malcolm R. *The Rise of Pennsylvania Protectionism.* Philadelphia, n.p., 1932.

Eliot, Ellsworth. *West Point in the Confederacy.* New York: G. A. Baker and Company, 1941.

Elmer, Lucius Q. C. *The Constitution and Government of the Province and State of New Jersey.* Newark: Martin R. Dennis and Company, 1872.

Everett, Edward G. "Contraband and Rebel Sympathizers in Pennsylvania in 1861." *The Western Pennsylvania Historical Magazine* 41 (Spring 1958): 29–40.

———. "Pennsylvania Newspapers and Public Opinion, 1861–1862." *The Western Pennsylvania Historical Magazine* 44 (March 1961): 1–11.

Fein, Isaac M. "Baltimore Jews During the Civil War." *American Jewish Historical Quarterly* 51 (December 1961): 67–96.

Fernandis, H. D., *et al. To the People of Hartford.* n.p.

Fielder, Herbert. *A Sketch of the Life and Times and Speeches of Joseph E. Brown.* Springfield: Springfield Printing Company, 1883.

Fite, Emerson D. *The Presidential Campaign of 1860.* New York: The Macmillan Company, 1911.

The Five Cotton States and New York; or, Remarks upon the Social and Economical Aspects of the Southern Political Crisis: n.p., 1861.

Flick, Alexander C., ed. *History of the State of New York.* 10 vols., New York: Columbia University Press, 1933–1937.

———. *Samuel Jones Tilden: A Study in Political Sagacity.* Port Washington: Kennikat Press, Inc., 1963.

Foner, Philip S. *Business and Slavery: The New York Merchants and the Irrepressible Conflict.* Chapel Hill: University of North Carolina Press, 1941.

Foster, John Y. *New Jersey and the Rebellion.* Newark: M. R. Dennis and Company, 1868.

Frasure, Carl M. "Union Sentiment in Maryland: 1859–1861." *Maryland Historical Magazine* 24 (September 1929): 210–24.

French, General Samuel G. *Two Wars: An Autobiography.* Nashville: Confederate Veteran, 1910.

"A Friendly Enemy." *Woodstown First National Bank Almanac and Year Book.* Woodstown: n.p., 1918.

Fulton, Cecil G., Jr., ed. *"It Happened in Western Pennsylvania": Some*

Excerpts from the Memoirs, Diaries, etc. of J. Alexander Fulton, Esq., n.p., 1862.

Going, Charles B. *David Wilmot: Free-Soiler.* New York: D. Appleton and Company, 1924.

Greeley, Horace. *The American Conflict.* 2 vols., Hartford: O. D. Case and Company, 1864–66.

Gunderson, Robert G. *Old Gentlemen's Convention: The Washington Peace Conference of 1861.* Madison: University of Wisconsin Press, 1961.

Halstead, Murat. *Caucuses of 1860: A History of the National Political Conventions.* Columbus: Follett, Foster and Company, 1860.

Hancock, Harold B. *Delaware During the Civil War: A Political History.* Wilmington: Historical Society of Delaware, 1961.

Hancock, Harold B., and Wilkinson, Norman B. "A Manufacturer in Wartime: Du Pont, 1860–1865." *Business History Review* 40 (Summer 1966) :213–36.

Harmon, George D. "The Pennsylvania Clergy and the Civil War." *Pennsylvania History* 6 (April 1939) :86–102.

Harper, Robert S. *Lincoln and the Press.* New York: McGraw-Hill Book Company, 1951.

Harvey, Katherine A. "The Civil War and the Maryland Coal Trade." *Maryland Historical Magazine* (December 1967), pp. 361–80.

Headley, Joel T. *The Great Rebellion: A History of the Civil War in the United States.* 2 vols., Hartford: Hurlbut, Williams and Company, 1863–66.

Henry, Allan J., ed. *The Life of Alexis Irenee du Pont.* 2 vols., Philadelphia: William F. Fell Company, 1945.

Heslin, James J. "Peaceful Compromise in New York City, 1860–1861." *The New York Historical Society Quarterly* 44 (October 1960): 349–62.

Hesseltine, William B. *Lincoln and the War Governors.* New York: Alfred A. Knopf, 1948.

————. *Three Against Lincoln: Murat Halstead Reports the Caucuses of 1860.* Baton Rouge: Louisiana State University Press, 1960.

Heston, Alfred M. *Slavery and Servitude in New Jersey.* Camden: Sinnickson Chew and Sons Company, 1903.

Hibben, Paxton. *Henry Ward Beecher: An American Portrait.* New York: The Press of the Readers Club, 1942.

Honeyman, A. Van Doren. *Northwestern New Jersey.* 5 vols., New York: Lewis Historical Publishing Company, 1927.

Johannsen, Robert W., ed. *The Letters of Stephen A. Douglas.* Urbana: University of Illinois Press, 1961.

Johnson, Allen, and Malone, Dumas, eds. *Dictionary of American Biography.* 20 vols., New York: Charles Scribner's Sons, 1928–37.

Johnston, Elma L. *The Significance of Trenton's 250th. Anniversary.* Trenton: The Kenneth W. Moore Company, 1929.

Jones, John B. *Secession, Coercion, and Civil War, the Story of 1861.* Philadelphia: T. B. Peterson, 1861.

Katz, Irving. *August Belmont: A Political Biography.* New York: Columbia University Press, 1968.

Keasbey, A. Q. "Slavery in New Jersey." *Proceedings of the New Jersey Historical Society* 4 (January–April 1907):90–96; (May–October 1907):147–154; 5 (January 1908):12–20; (April 1908):79–85.

Keene, Jesse L. "Sectionalism in the Peace Convention of 1861." *The Florida Historical Quarterly* 40 (July 1961):53–81.

Kennedy, John P. *The Border States: Their Power and Duty in the Present Disordered Condition of the Country.* n.p., 1860.

———. *The Great Drama; An Appeal to Maryland.* Baltimore: John D. Toy, 1861.

———. *Political and Official Papers.* New York: G. P. Putnam and Sons, 1872.

Kettell, Thomas P. *Southern Wealth and Northern Profits.* New York: George W. and John A. Wood, 1860.

Klein, Philip S. *President James Buchanan: A Biography.* University Park: Pennsylvania State University Press, 1962.

Knapp, Charles M. *New Jersey Politics During the Period of the Civil War and Reconstruction.* Geneva: W. E. Humphrey, 1924.

Knoles, George H. *The Crisis of the Union: 1860–1861.* Baton Rouge: Louisiana State University Press, 1965.

Koehler, Leroy J. *The History of Monroe County, Pennsylvania During the Civil War.* East Stroudsburg: Monroe County Historical Society, 1950.

Krummel, Carl F. "Henry J. Raymond and the New York Times in the Secession Crisis, 1860–1861." *New York History* 32 (October 1951): 377–98.

Kull, Irving, ed. *New Jersey: A History.* 6 vols., New York: American Historical Society, Inc., 1930–32.

Layton, C. S. *Speech at a Union Meeting held at Georgetown, Sussex County, Delaware, Tuesday, May 7, 1861.* Wilmington: Henry Eckel, 1861.

Lee, Brother Basil L. *Discontent in New York City: 1861–1865.* Washington: Catholic University of America Press, 1943.

Lee, Francis B. *New Jersey as a Colony and as a State.* 4 vols., New York: The Publishing Society of New Jersey, 1902–03.

Lee, Guy C. *The True History of the Civil War.* Philadelphia: J. B. Lippincott Company, 1903.

Legrand, John C. *Letter to Hon. Reverdy Johnson, on the Proceedings at the Meeting, Held at Maryland Institute, January 10th. 1861.* Baltimore: Murphy and Company, 1861.

Linn, William A. "Slavery in Bergen County, New Jersey." *Papers and Proceedings of the Bergen County Historical Society* 4 (1907–08): 23–40.

Logan, John A. *The Great Conspiracy: Its Origin and History*. New York: A. R. Hart and Company, 1886.

Long, Durward. "Alabama's Secession Commissioners." *Civil War History* 9 (March 1963) :55–66.

Lord, Daniel. *The Effect of Secession Upon the Commercial Relations Between the North and South and Upon Each Section*. London: H. Stevens, 1861.

Lore, Charles B. "The Life and Character of George P. Fisher." *Papers of the Historical Society of Delaware* 36 (1902).

Lowitt, Richard. *A Merchant Prince of the Nineteenth Century: William A. Dodge*. New York: Columbia University Press, 1954.

Luthin, Reinhard H. *The First Lincoln Campaign*. Cambridge: Harvard University Press, 1944.

McClure, Alexander K. *Old Time Notes of Pennsylvania*. 2 vols., Philadelphia: John C. Winston Company, 1905.

McCormick, Richard P. *The History of Voting in New Jersey: A Study of the Development of Election Machinery: 1664–1911*. New Brunswick: Rutgers University Press, 1953.

McCulloch, Hugh. *Men and Measures of Half a Century*. New York: Charles Scribner's Sons, 1889.

McElroy, Robert. *Jefferson Davis: The Unreal and the Real*. 2 vols., New York: Harper and Brothers, 1937.

Mack, Edward C. *Peter Cooper: Citizen of New York*. New York: Duell, Sloan and Pearce, 1949.

McKelvey, Blake, ed. *Rochester in the Civil War*. Rochester: Rochester Historical Society, 1944.

McManus, Edgar J. *A History of Negro Slavery in New York*. Syracuse: Syracuse University Press, 1966.

McMaster, John B. *A History of the People of the United States, from the Revolution to the Civil War*. 8 vols., New York: D. Appleton and Company, 1883–1913.

———. *A History of the People of the United States During Lincoln's Administration*. New York: D. Appleton and Company, 1927.

McPherson, Edward. *The Political History of the United States of America During the Great Rebellion*. Washington: Philip and Solomons, 1865.

McSherry, James, and James, Bartlett B. *History of Maryland*. Baltimore: The Baltimore Book Company, 1904.

Manakee, Harold R. *Maryland in the Civil War*. Baltimore: Maryland Historical Society, 1961.

Martyn, Carlos. *William E. Dodge: The Christian Merchant*. New York: Funk and Wagnalls, 1890.

Matthews, Sidney T. "Control of the Baltimore Press During the Civil War." *Maryland Historical Magazine* 36 (June 1941) :150–70.

Meade, Robert D. *Judah P. Benjamin: Confederate Statesman*. New York: Oxford University Press, 1943.

Mearns, David C. *The Lincoln Papers.* 2 vols., Garden City: Doubleday and Company, 1948.

Miller, Alphonse B. *Thaddeus Stevens.* New York: Harper and Brothers, 1939.

Milton, George F. *The Eve of Conflict: Stephen A. Douglas and the Needless War.* Boston: Houghton Mifflin Company, 1934.

Mitchell, Stewart. *Horatio Seymour of New York.* Cambridge: Harvard University Press, 1938.

Moore, Frank. *The Rebellion Record.* 12 vols., New York: G. P. Putnam, and D. Van Nostrand, 1862–1868.

Moore, John B. *The Works of James Buchanan.* 12 vols., Philadelphia: J. B. Lippincott and Company, 1908–11.

Message of His Excellency Edwin D. Morgan to the Legislature of the State of New York: January 2, 1861. Albany: C. Van Benthuysen, 1861.

Mulford, William C. *Historical Tales of Cumberland County, New Jersey.* Bridgeton: Evening News Company, 1941.

Myers, C. Maxwell. "The Influence of Western Pennsylvania in the Campaign of 1860." *The Western Pennsylvania Historical Magazine* 24 (December 1941) :229–50.

Myers, William S. "Governor Bradford's Private List of Union Men in 1861." *Maryland Historical Magazine* 7 (March 1912) :83–89.

————. *The Story of New Jersey.* 5 vols., New York: Lewis Historical Publishing Company, 1945.

The National Cyclopaedia of American Biography. 51 vols., New York: J. T. White, 1893–1970.

Nevins, Allen. *Abram S. Hewitt: With Some Account of Peter Cooper.* New York: Harper and Brothers, 1935.

————, and Robertson, James I., and Wiley, Bell I., eds. *Civil War Books: A Critical Bibliography.* 2 vols. Baton Rouge: Louisiana State University Press, 1969.

————, and Thomas, Milton H., eds. *The Diary of George Templeton Strong: The Civil War: 1860–1865.* New York: The Macmillan Company, 1952.

————. *The Evening Post: A Century of Journalism.* New York: Boni and Liveright, 1968.

New Jersey Statutes Annotated. St. Paul: West Publishing Company, 1940.

Nicholay, John G., and Hay, John. *Abraham Lincoln: A History.* 10 vols., New York: The Century Company, 1890.

Nichols, Isaac T. *Historic Days in Cumberland County, New Jersey: 1855–1865.* Bridgeton: n.p., 1907.

Nichols, Roy F. *The Disruption of American Democracy.* New York: The Macmillan Company, 1948.

Olden, Charles S. *Message of Hon. Charles S. Olden, Governor of New Jersey, With Accompanying Documents.* Trenton: n.p., 1861.

————. *Message of His Excellency Charles S. Olden, Governor of New Jersey, Delivered to the Extra Session of the Legislature Convened April 30, 1861.* Trenton: n.p., 1861.

Parker, Joel. *The Right of Secession.* Cambridge: Welch, Bigelow and Company, 1861.

Parks, Joseph H. "John Bell and Secession." *The East Tennessee Historical Society's Publications* 16 (1944):30–47.

Perkins, Howard C. "The Defense of Slavery in the Northern Press on the Eve of the Civil War." *The Journal of Southern History* 9 (November 1943):501–31.

————. *Northern Editorials on Secession.* 2 vols., Gloucester: Peter Smith, 1964.

Pershing, B. F. "Senator Edgar A. Cowan: 1861–1867." *The Western Pennsylvania Historical Magazine* 4 (October 1921):224–33.

Phillips, Ulrich B., ed. *The Correspondence of Robert Toombs, Alexander H. Stevens, and Howell Cobb. Annual Report of the American Historical Association for the Year 1911,* vol. 2, Washington: American Historical Association, 1913.

Platt, Hermann K. *Charles Perrin Smith: New Jersey Political Reminiscences.* New Brunswick: Rutgers University Press, 1965.

Pleasants, Samuel A. *Fernando Wood of New York.* New York: Columbia University Press, 1948.

Podmore, Harry J. *Trenton, Old and New.* Trenton: The Kenneth W. Moore Company, 1927.

Pollard, Edward A. *The Lost Cause: A New Southern History of the War of the Confederates.* New York: F. B. Treat and Company, 1866.

————. *Southern History of the War.* 2 vols., New York: Charles B. Richardson, 1866.

Potter, David M. "Horace Greeley and Peaceable Secession." *The Journal of Southern History* 7 (May 1941):145–59.

————. *Lincoln and His Party in the Secession Crisis.* New Haven: Yale University Press, 1942.

Powell, Walter A. *A History of Delaware.* Boston: The Christopher Publishing House, 1928.

Prowell, George R. *The History of Camden County.* Philadelphia: L. J. Richards and Company, 1886.

Radcliffe, George L. P. *Governor Thomas H. Hicks of Maryland and the Civil War.* The Johns Hopkins University Studies in Historical and Political Science, Baltimore: The Johns Hopkins University Press, 1901.

Randall, James G. *The Civil War and Reconstruction.* Boston: D. C. Heath and Company, 1953.

————. *Constitutional Problems Under Lincoln.* New York: D. Appleton and Company, 1926.

————. *Lincoln: The Liberal Statesman.* New York: Dodd, Mead and Company, 1947.

————, and Current, Richard N., *Lincoln the President*. 4 vols., New York: Dodd, Mead and Company, 1945.

The Record of the Democratic Party: 1860–1865.

Reed, George E., ed. *Papers of the Governors*. Pennsylvania Archives, Fourth Series, vol. 8, Harrisburg: The State of Pennsylvania, 1902.

Reed, H. Clay, ed. *Delaware: A History of the First State*. 3 vols., New York: Lewis Historical Publishing Company, 1947.

Reed, William B. *A Paper Containing a Statement and Vindication of Certain Political Opinions*. Philadelphia: John Campbell, 1862.

Rembert, W. Patrick. *Jefferson Davis and His Cabinet*. Baton Rouge: Louisiana State University Press, 1944.

Rhodes, James Ford. *History of the United States from the Compromise of 1850*. 7 vols., New York: Harper and Brothers, 1893–1906.

Richardson, James D. *A Compilation of the Messages and Papers of the Presidents: 1789–1897*. 10 vols., Washington: United States Congress, 1898–99.

Robinson, Elwyn B. "The Press: President Lincoln's Philadelphia Organ." *The Pennsylvania Magazine of History and Biography* 65 (April 1941):157–70.

Rowland, Dunbar. *Jefferson Davis: Constitutionalist: His Letters, Papers and Speeches*. 10 vols., Jackson: Mississippi Department of Archives and History, 1923.

Russ, William A., Jr. "Franklin Weirick: 'Copperhead' of Central Pennsylvania." *Pennsylvania History* 5 (October 1938):245–56.

Russel, Robert R. *Economic Aspects of Southern Sectionalism: 1840–1861*. New York: Russell and Russell, 1960.

Russell, William H. *My Diary: North and South*. 2 vols., London: Bradbury and Evans, 1863.

Sanborn, Alvan F. *Reminiscences of Richard Lathers*. New York: The Grafton Press, 1907.

Sandburg, Carl. *Abraham Lincoln: The Prairie Years*. 2 vols., New York: Harcourt, Brace and Company, 1926.

————. *Abraham Lincoln: The War Years*. 4 vols., New York: Harcourt, Brace and Company, 1939.

Speech of Hon. Willard Saulsbury of Delaware on the Resolution Proposing to Expel the Hon. Jesse D. Bright, Delivered in the United States Senate, January 29th., 1862. Washington: n.p., 1862.

Scharf, J. Thomas. *History of Maryland*. 3 vols., Hatboro: Tradition Press, 1967.

————. *History of Western Maryland*. 2 vols., Baltimore: Regional Publishing Company, 1968.

Schermerhorn, William E. *The History of Burlington, New Jersey*. Burlington: Press of Enterprise Publishing Company, 1927.

Scott, Kenneth. "Candidate Lincoln in the New York Press." *The New York Historical Society Quarterly* 43 (January 1959):5–37.

Scovel, James M. *Three Speeches by James M. Scovel*. Camden: H. B. Dick, 1870.

Seabrook, William M. *Maryland's Great Part in Saving the Union*. n.p., 1913.

Secret Correspondence Illustrating the Condition of Affairs in Maryland. Baltimore: n.p., 1863.

Seyfert, A. G. "A Page of Lancaster County History, During Civil War Times." *Papers Read Before the Lancaster County Historical Society* 31 (October 1927) :111–17.

Shaw, William H. *History of Essex and Hudson Counties New Jersey*. 2 vols., Philadelphia: Everts and Peck, 1884.

Sherwin, Oscar. *Prophet of Liberty: The Life and Times of Wendell Phillips*. New York: Bookman Associates, 1958.

Sickler, Joseph S. *The History of Salem County New Jersey*. Salem: Sunbeam Publishing Company, 1937.

Simon, Donald E. "Brooklyn in the Election of 1860." *The New York Historical Society Quarterly* 51 (July 1967) :249–62.

Smith, William, ed., Fish, Carl R. *The American Civil War*. New York: Longmans, Green and Company, 1937.

Sommer's Newspaper Manual. Newark: Frederick N. Sommer, 1903.

Sprague, Abram P., ed. *Speeches, Arguments and Miscellaneous Papers of David Dudley Field*. 3 vols., New York: D. Appleton and Company, 1884–90.

Sprague, Dean. *Freedom Under Lincoln*. Boston: Houghton Mifflin Company, 1965.

Spruance, John S. *Delaware Stays in the Union*. Newark: University of Delaware Press, 1955.

Stampp, Kenneth M. *And the War Came: The North and the Secession Crisis: 1860–1861*. Chicago: University of Chicago Press, 1964.

Steiner, Bernard C. "James Alfred Pearce." *Maryland Historical Magazine* 19 (March 1924) :13–29.

———. *Life of Henry Winter Davis*. Baltimore: John Murphy Company, 1916.

Steiner, John A. "The Brengle Home Guard." *Maryland Historical Magazine* 7 (June 1912) :196–200.

Stevens, Lewis T. *The History of Cape May County, New Jersey*. Cape May: Lewis T. Stevens, 1897.

Stevens, Sylvester K. *Pennsylvania: Birthplace of a Nation*. New York: Random House, 1964.

Strode, Hudson. *Jefferson Davis: American Patriot: 1808–1861*. New York: Harcourt, Brace and Company, 1955.

———. *Jefferson Davis: Confederate President*. New York: Harcourt, Brace and Company, 1959.

Swanberg, W. A. *Sickles: The Incredible*. New York: Charles Scribner's Sons, 1956.

Swiggett, Howard, ed. *John B. Jones, A Rebel War Clerk's Diary*. 2 vols., New York: Old Hickory Bookshop, 1935.

Tansill, Charles C. *The Congressional Career of Thomas Francis Bayard: 1869–1885*. Washington: Georgetown University Press, 1946.

———. *The Foreign Policy of Thomas F. Bayard: 1885–1897*. New York: Fordham University Press, 1940.

Thomas, James W., Williams, T. J. C. *History of Allegany County Maryland*. 2 vols., Baltimore: Regional Publishing Company, 1969.

Speech of Senator Thomson of New Jersey, on Presenting the Resolutions of the State on "The State of the Union." Washington: n.p., 1861.

Tilden, Samuel J. *The Union! Its Dangers! And How They Can Be Averted*. 1860.

Turner, Edward R. *The Negro in Pennsylvania*. Washington: American Historical Association, 1911.

Tyler, Lyon G. *The Letters and Times of the Tylers*. 2 vols., Richmond: Whittet and Shepperson, 1885.

Tyson, Raymond W. "Henry Winter Davis: Orator for the Union." *Maryland Historical Magazine* 58 (March 1963) :1–19.

Urquhart, Frank J. *A History of the City of Newark, New Jersey*. New York: Lewis Historical Publishing Company, 1913.

Vaira, Louis. "Some Aspects of Pittsburgh's Industrial Contributions to the Civil War." *The Western Pennsylvania History Magazine* 6 (January 1923) :9–20.

Walker, Edwin R. *et al. A History of Trenton: 1679–1929*. Princeton: Princeton University Press, 1929.

Warner, Ezra J. *Generals in Gray*. Baton Rouge: Louisiana State University Press, 1959.

Weeden, William B. *War Government: Federal and State: 1861–1865*. Boston: Houghton, Mifflin and Company, 1906.

The Weekly Southern Spy. 1, no. 1. Baltimore, 1861.

Westervelt, Frances A. *History of Bergen County, New Jersey: 1630–1923*. New York: Lewis Historical Publishing Company, 1923.

Wilson, Harold F. *The Jersey Shore*. 3 vols., New York: Lewis Historical Publishing Company, 1953.

Wilson, Henry. *History of the Rise and Fall of the Slave Power in America*. 3 vols., Boston: James R. Osgood and Company, 1873–77.

Wilson, W. Emerson. *Delaware in the Civil War*. Dover: Civil War Centennial Commission of the State of Delaware, 1962.

Wilson, Woodrow. *Division and Reunion: 1829–1909*. New York: Longmans, Green and Company, 1910.

Wolstoncraft, Joseph B. "Western Pennsylvania and the Election of 1860." *The Western Pennsylvania History Magazine* 6 (January 1923): 25–38.

Woodburn, James A. *The Life of Thaddeus Stevens*. Indianapolis: Bobbs-Merrill Company, 1913.

Wooster, Ralph A. "The Membership of the Maryland Legislature of 1861." *Maryland Historical Magazine* 56 (March 1961):94–102.

————. *The Secession Conventions of the South.* Princeton: Princeton University Press, 1962.

Wright, Marion T. "Negro Suffrage in New Jersey, 1776–1875." *The Journal of Negro History* 33 (April 1948):168–98.

————. "New Jersey Laws and the Negro." *The Journal of Negro History* 28 (April 1943), pp. 156–99.

INDEX

Abell, A. S., 61
Abolition, 34, 99
Abolitionists, 16, 76, 99, 185, 199, 209
Adrain, Garnett B., 19, 112, 113
Adrain Resolutions, 19, 43, 112, 144, 189, 190
Alabama, 18, 30, 34, 82, 98, 119, 130, 135, 184, 196
Albany, N.Y., 170, 174, 175, 178, 180, 190, 203; newspapers in, 167, 170, 178, 180, 181–82, 198, 218–20
Albany *Atlas and Argus,* 167, 178, 180, 198, 218, 219
Albany *Evening Journal,* 181–82, 220
Albany Regency, 167, 171, 180, 203
Albany *Statesman,* 170
Albany *Times and Courier,* 219
Alexander, William C., 106
Allentown *Democrat,* 216
Altoona *Tribune,* 217
American party, 17, 28, 44, 103, 107, 110, 170, 171, 180, 188, 192
American Railway Review, 177
American Society for Promoting National Unity, 197–98, 203
Angelica *Reporter,* 220
An Address to the People of Maryland, 51
Annapolis, Md., 45, 53, 54, 66, 67; newspapers in, 57, 59–60, 213–14
Annapolis *Gazette,* 57, 59–60, 213–14
A Rebel War Clerk's Diary, 119
Auburn *Daily Advertiser,* 220
Auburn *Daily Union,* 220
Auburn *North Christian Advocate,* 221

Baker, J. B., 157
Baltimore, Md., 21, 22–23, 27, 28, 38–39, 40, 41, 51, 52, 74, 206; congressmen from, 44, 45, 46; Democratic convention in, 18, 24, 76, 101, 127, 168; election of 1860 in, 25–26; newspapers in, 27, 58, 60–62, 213–14; post-Sumter, 62, 65, 67, 68–71, 71–73; secessionist activities in, 54–55, 56
Baltimore *American and Commercial Advertiser,* 61, 213
Baltimore and Ohio Railroad, 22, 38
Baltimore *Clipper,* 62, 214
Baltimore *Daily Exchange,* 27, 60–61, 213
Baltimore *Evening Patriot,* 61, 214
Baltimore *Family Journal,* 61, 214
Baltimore *Methodist Protestant,* 213
Baltimore *Price Current,* 61, 214
Baltimore *Republican,* 62, 213
Baltimore *Sun,* 61–62, 213
Baltimore *The True Union,* 62
Baltimore *True American,* 213
Bates, David M., 90
Bates, Edward, 24, 177
Bath *Steuben Farmers' Advocate,* 219
Bayard, James A., 78, 79, 92, 95; election of 1860, 75–76; views on secession, 88–90, 96
Bayard, Thomas F., 78, 91; letters to, 78, 84, 88; militia company of, 79, 90; views on secession, 95, 96
Beauregard, General P. G. T., 161
Beaver *Argus,* 217
Bedford *Gazette,* 149, 216
Bedford *Inquirer,* 217
Bel Air *National American,* 60, 214
Bel Air *Southern Aegis,* 60, 213
Bell, John, 76, 171, 207; election of 1860 and, 18, 24–26, 77, 102, 129,

169–70; newspaper supporters of, 59–62, 118, 199; supporters of, 45, 46, 64, 76, 91, 169
Belmont, August, 167, 168, 173–74, 181
Benjamin, Judah, 89
Bennett, James Gordon, 129, 169
Bidermann, Evelina, 91
Bigler, William, 104, 111, 127, 136, 141, 142, 142–44
Binghamton, N.Y., 167, 220
Binghamton Standard, 220
Black, Jeremiah S., 132–33, 135, 137
Blair, Samuel S., 145
Bloomingburg, N.Y., 193
Bloomville Mirror, 218
Border States, The, 46, 107, 174
Border War: A Tale of Disunion, 119–20
Bradford Reporter, 217
Bradford, Vincent L., 157, 161
Bradley, Joseph P., 107
Brady, James T., 168, 169
Breckinridge, John C., 78, 91, 172, 175, 176; Democratic convention and, 18, 24, 75–76, 127; election of 1860 and, 25–26, 77, 96, 102, 129, 168–69, 206; newspaper supporters of, 58–62, 92, 114, 116, 121, 135, 148–49
Bridgeton Pioneer, 117, 215
Bridgeville, Dela., 90
Briggs, George, 192
Bronson, Greene C., 187, 196
Brooklyn, N.Y., 170, 178, 194, 200, 201; newspapers in, 173, 218, 220
Brooklyn Daily Eagle, 173, 218
Brooklyn Standard, 220
Brower, John M., 198
Brown, George W., 63–65, 68
Brown, John, 18
Bryan, E. B., 100
Bryant, William Cullen, 181, 184
Buchanan, Franklin, 57–58
Buchanan, James, 16, 55, 56, 58, 61, 127, 128, 134, 135, 137, 143, 144, 153, 157, 160, 168, 175, 176, 186, 210; Lecompton policy of, 17–18, 105, 142, 192; views on secession, 129, 130–32, 133, 142, 161, 209
Buckley, M. S., 162
Buffalo, N.Y., 170, 172; newspapers in, 170, 220
Buffalo Commercial Advertiser, 170, 220
Buffalo Daily Courier, 220
Buffalo Morning Express, 220

Burlington, N.J., 119
Burnett, L. W., 105
Burr, C. Chauncey, 106
Burton, William, 79–80, 81, 90, 94, 96, 97, 207; letter from Thomas H. Hicks, 32, 34, 80–81, 85; southern commissioners and, 82–84
Butler, Benjamin F., 66, 67, 70, 71

California, 16
Cambridge Herald, 59, 214
Camden Democrat, 117, 215
Camden, N.J., 101; newspapers in, 117, 215
Cameron, Simon, 36, 66, 128; Secretary of War, 71, 81, 94, 162, 191; United States Senator, 141–42
Campbell, D. C., 83
Campbell, James H., 147, 157
Cape May Ocean Wave, 117, 215
Carter, Luther C., 192
Carson, William, 90
Cassidy, Lewis C., 127
Cassidy, William, 167
Catonsville, Md., 52
Central confederacy, 15–16, 19, 20, 208, 213, 215, 216, 218; in Delaware, 80–81, 85, 87–88, 96–97; Thomas H. Hicks's support of the, 30, 31, 34, 35, 36, 37–38, 40, 80, 207; John P. Kennedy's plan for a, 46–52; in Maryland, 39, 42, 44, 52, 59–61; in New Jersey, 104, 113–18, 120–21, 123, 206; in New York, 198, 204; in Pennsylvania, 148, 156, 162
Chambers, A. S., 61, 63
Charleston, S.C., 100–101, 149, 151, 157, 167; Democratic convention in, 18, 24, 76, 127, 168
Chase, Salmon P., 159
Cherry Valley Gazette, 218
Chicago, Ill., 18, 24, 101, 148, 149
Cincinnati platform, 24, 76, 127
Clark, Daniel, 19, 40, 41
Clay, Clement C., 130
Clearfield, Pa., 136, 218
Clearfield Raftsman's Journal, 218
Clinton Democrat, 149, 216
Clinton, George W., 172–73
Clopton, David, 82
Cobb, Howell, 58
Cochrane, John, 167, 189
Collins, William, 51–52
Colonization Society, 24, 100
Committee of Thirteen, 18

Committee of Thirty-Three, 18, 41, 42, 86, 96, 112, 113, 145, 188, 192, 194
Compromise of 1850, 17
Conkling, Roscoe, 173, 192–93
Constitutional Union party, 54, 187, 207; convention of, 24, 76; election of 1860 and the, 18, 24, 25, 76–77, 102, 129, 169
Contee, Captain, 32
Cooper, Alexander B., 94
Cooper, Peter, 197, 203
Cooper, Samuel, 99
Cooperstown *Freeman's Journal,* 220
Copperheads, 106
Cornell, Ezra, 185
Corning *Democrat,* 219
Corning, Erastus, 167
Corning *Journal,* 220
Corwin, Thomas, 27
Coudersport *Potter Journal,* 217
Covode, John, 128
Cowan, Edgar, 139, 141, 142
Cox, Samuel S., 44
Cagger, Peter, 167
Crittenden compromise, 19, 104, 151, 188, 192; supporters in: Delaware, 85–87, 89, 90, 91; Maryland, 38, 40, 44–45; New Jersey, 108, 111; New York, 173; Pennsylvania, 135, 136, 143, 144, 155
Crittenden, John J., 18, 32, 36, 37, 39, 53, 142, 174, 187
Cumberland *Civilian & Telegraph,* 25, 60, 214
Cumberland *Democratic Alleganian,* 60, 213
Curry, Jabez L. M., 33–34
Curtin, Andrew, 36, 67, 110, 128, 138–39, 140, 162, 211
Curtis, George W., 155
Cushing, Caleb, 200

Davis, Henry Winter, 26, 41, 45–46, 91
Davis, Jefferson, 14, 15, 55, 69, 135, 196, 201, 206, 210–11
Dayton, William L., 107
DeBow's Industrial Resources, 100
DeBow's Review, 178–79
Delaware, 13, 15, 16, 74–97, 98, 114, 120, 162, 210; governor of, 28, 32, 34, 38. *See* Hicks, Thomas H.
Delaware legislature, 75, 77, 81, 88, 96, 97, 207; southern commissioners and, 80, 82–86; Washington Peace Conference report of, 90.

Democratic party, 16, 17, 106, 202–5, 209–11; election of 1860 and the, 18, 24–26, 75–77, 101–3, 126–29, 147–50, 167–71; supports secession, 13, 55–56, 96, 123, 129–37, 154, 156–58, 160, 163, 171–76, 180, 197–98
Dickinson, Daniel S., 167, 168, 203
Dickinson, Henry, 80, 82–83
Dimmick, William H., 144
Dix, John A., 68, 131, 175–76, 195, 208–9
Douglas, Stephen A., 17, 127; election of 1860 and, 24–25, 77, 102, 127, 169–70, 206; Democratic convention and, 17, 18, 24, 75–76, 101–2, 167–68; newspaper supporters of, 60, 62, 113–16, 118, 135, 149–50, 177, 180, 199
Douglass, Frederick, 199
Douglass' Monthly, 199, 220
Dover, Dela., 76, 79, 87, 90, 92–93, 95; newspapers in, 92, 93, 95, 214
Dover *Delawarean,* 92, 93, 95, 214
Dred Scott decision, 17, 38
E. I. DuPont de Nemours & Company, 74, 92, 94
duPont, General Henry, 91
duPont, Henry A., 90–91
DuPont, Samuel F., 35, 78, 91, 92

Easton (Md.) *Gazette,* 59, 214
Easton (Md.) *Star,* 58, 213
Easton, Pa., 136, 154, 161; newspapers in, 148, 152, 161, 216–17
Easton (Pa.) *Argus,* 216
Easton (Pa.) *Free Press,* 152, 216
Easton (Pa.) *Northampton County Journal,* 217
Easton (Pa.) *Sentinel,* 148, 161, 217
Ebensburg *Alleghanian,* 217
Election of 1860, 206, 207, 210; in Delaware, 75–77, 91, 92, 93, 94, 96; in Maryland, 24–26, 58–62; in New Jersey, 101–3, 114, 116–17; in New York, 167–71, 181, 182, 189, 192, 199, 200, 204; in Pennsylvania, 127–29, 147, 150, 154
Elizabethtown *Post,* 219
Elkton *Cecil Whig,* 60, 214
Ellet, Henry, 99
Elmira, N.Y., 43, 220
Elmira *Weekly Advertiser and Chemung County Republican,* 220
Erie, Pa., 125, 217–18
Erie *Observer,* 217
Erie *True American,* 218

Erie *Weekly Gazette,* 217

Everett, Edward, 207

Field, David Dudley, 181, 187

Fillmore, Millard, 46, 87, 107, 169–70, 181, 196

Fisher, George P., 76, 77, 95

Fisher, Sidney George, 159, 161

Fitzhugh, George, 178–79

Flemington *Hunterdon Democrat,* 113, 114, 215

Florence, Thomas B., 144

Florida, 18

Forney, John W., 127, 135

Forsyth, John, 201

Fort Delaware, 78, 79, 119

Fort Sumter, 13, 15, 40, 65, 108, 112, 119, 130, 131, 143, 182, 183, 189; the effect of the firing upon, 14, 22, 50–51, 58–62, 68, 72, 79, 81, 87, 89–92, 94–97, 108, 109, 114–16, 121–24, 135, 140, 146, 148–50, 152–53, 160–63, 174, 175, 176, 186, 191, 198, 202–5, 208–12

Foster, Henry D., 128

Fowler, Isaac V., 167

Fox, Gustavus, 211, 212

Franklin, Thomas E., 140

Frederick *Examiner,* 60, 214

Frederick, Md., 44, 57, 66, 67, 69; newspapers in, 60, 214

Frederick *Maryland Union,* 60, 214

Freehold, N.J., 118–19; newspapers in, 113–14, 116, 215

Freehold *Monmouth Democrat,* 113, 114, 116, 215

Frelinghuysen, Frederick T., 110

Fremont, John C., 17, 170

Fugitive Slave Law, 16, 51, 80, 126, 182, 188

Fulton, J. Alexander, 135

Georgetown, Dela., 78, 79, 87; newspapers in, 94, 214

Georgetown *Messenger,* 79, 94, 214

Georgia, 18, 30, 34, 37, 38, 57, 83, 84, 101, 179, 196

Gettysburg *Adams Sentinel,* 217

Gettysburg *Compiler,* 150, 217

Gist, William H., 37

Glenn, William Wilkins, 27, 72

Glenwood, Pa., 145

Goodrich, John Z., 110

Goshen *Democrat,* 220

Goshen *Republican,* 219

Greeley, Horace, 22–23, 28, 81–82, 181,

187; views on Democrats, 171, 173; views on secession, 14, 183–84, 205

Green, John, 85

Greensburg, Pa., 142

Grimshaw, Dr. A. H., 78

Grow, Galusha A., 128, 145, 147

Guthrie, James, 127

Hackettstown *Gazette,* 117, 215

Hagerstown *Herald of Freedom and Torch Light,* 60, 214

Handy, A. H., 32–33

Hanover *Citizen,* 150, 217

Hanover *Spectator,* 217

Harpers Ferry, 18, 69

Harris, James M., 41, 44–45

Harris, Mrs. Benjamin G., 71–72

Harrisburg, Pa., 136, 137, 138, 154, 211; newspapers in, 148, 152, 216–17

Harrisburg *Patriot and Union,* 148, 216

Harrisburg *Pennsylvania Daily Telegraph,* 152, 216, 217

Harrison, Dr. Samuel A., 53

Haskin, John B., 175, 192

Hempstead *Queens County Sentinel,* 220

Henry, Alexander, 155–56, 158

Henry, Joshua, 169

Herkimer County Journal, 220

Herndon, William H., 184

Hewitt, Abram S., 196, 203

Hickman, John, 144–45

Hicks, Thomas H., 24, 26, 45, 48, 52–53, 54, 55, 56, 71, 88, 91; post-Sumter, 63–68; views on secession, 26–40, 59, 60, 80, 207

Hilliard, Henry W., 98

Hoboken, N.J., 102

Hollidaysburg, Pa., 145

Holt, Joseph, 179

Holt, W., 131

Houston, John W., 90

Houstoun, Colonel E., 197

How, Samuel B., 100

Howard, Benjamin C., 49, 52–53

Howard, Charles, 68

Hudson Valley, 16, 166, 169, 193, 199, 205, 206

Hughes, Francis W., 14

Hughes, George W., 41, 43–44

Humphrey, James, 188, 194

Hunt, Washington, 180

Hunter, Robert M. T., 24, 76

Huntington *Long Islander,* 220

Illinois, 17, 19, 27, 99, 114

Indiana, 99, 144
Indiana, Pa., 141
Ithaca, N.Y., 193, 219
Ithaca *American Citizen,* 219
Ithaca *Tompkins County Democrat,* 219

Jamaica *Long Island Democrat,* 218
James, Amaziah B., 187
Jamestown *Chautauqua Democrat,* 220
Jamestown *Journal,* 220
Jersey City, N.J., 102, 105; newspapers in, 117, 215
Jersey City *American Standard,* 117, 215
Jersey City *Daily Courier and Advertiser,* 215
Johnson, Alexander, 85
Johnson, Alex B., 172
Johnson, Bradley T., 69
Johnson, Philip, 161
Johnson, Reverdy, 38, 52
Johnstown *Cambria Tribune,* 152, 216
Jones, John B., 61, 89, 119–21, 122

Kane, Marshal, 64, 70
Kansas, 17, 18, 105, 133, 187, 192
Kansas-Nebraska Bill, 17
Keitt, L. M., 13
Kelly, William, 169
Kennedy, Anthony, 40
Kennedy, Philip, 49
Kennedy, John A., 179, 201, 202
Kennedy, John Pendleton, 26, 40, 46–51, 52, 56, 107, 174
Kentucky, 18, 34, 48, 97, 114
Kernan, Francis, 186
Kerrigan, James, 200–201
Killinger, John W., 146
King, Horatio, 176
King, Preston, 187–88
Kittanning *Mentor,* 135
Knights of the Golden Circle, 49
Know Nothing party, 17, 28, 107
Kunkel, Jacob M., 41, 44

Lamar, Gazaway B., 201, 204
Lancaster, Pa., 140, 145; newspapers in, 137, 150, 217
Lancaster *Daily Express,* 217
Lancaster *Examiner and Herald,* 217
Lancaster *Inquirer,* 150, 217
Lancaster *Intelligencer,* 217
Lancaster *Union,* 137
Lathers, Richard, 194–95, 196, 210–11
Lebanon, Pa., 146, 217

Lebanon *Courier,* 217
Lecompton constitution, 17, 112, 127, 128, 133, 142, 144, 192
Letcher, John, 13, 14, 69, 70
Lewisburg *Union County Star and Lewisburg Chronicle,* 218
Lewistown *Gazette,* 217
Lewistown *True Democrat,* 150, 218
Lincoln, Abraham, 13, 16, 24–27, 29, 30, 39, 55, 70, 71, 72, 97, 114, 131–32, 136, 138, 144, 150, 163, 179, 182, 184, 199, 205, 207, 209–12; appointed by, 141, 146, 188; call for troops by, 62, 90, 95, 131, 202, 204; election of 1860, 18, 20, 31, 76–77, 101–2, 109, 128, 167–71, 174–75, 201; letters to, 36, 39, 64, 78, 183, 185, 197; newspaper support for, 93, 115, 117; no compromise by, 19, 107, 181
Logan, John A., 13
Loomis, A. W., 140
Louisiana, 14, 18, 41, 80, 178
Lovell, Mansfield, 201–2
Lowe, Enoch L., 57, 64
Lucas, Josiah M., 36
Lycoming *Gazette,* 150, 217
Lyons, Lord, 66

McClure, Alexander K., 154
McKenty, Jacob K., 144
McMichael, Morton, 153, 159
McPherson, Edward, 147
Magoffin, Governor Besiah, 48
Maryland, 13, 15, 21–73, 79, 96, 125, 126, 162, 163, 207; secession of, 83, 85, 88–89, 90, 91, 97, 114, 120, 210
Maryland Institute, 38
Maryland legislature, 24, 28, 43, 45, 48, 52; not permitted to meet, 29, 30–32, 34–35, 38, 40, 54–56, 59, 207; post-Sumter, 67, 69–71
Massachusetts, 200
May, Henry, 71
Methodists, 56
Mexican War, 16, 43
Middletown *Valley Register,* 60, 214
Milford, Dela., 79, 87, 90
Milton, Pa., 141
Mississippi, 14, 18, 32–33, 80, 82–83
Missouri, 24, 34, 38, 97, 114, 151, 188
Missouri Compromise, 16, 17, 129, 181, 189, 192
Monmouth *Herald and Inquirer,* 216
Montgomery *Standard,* 221
Montgomery, William, 145

Monticello, 179
Montrose *Democrat,* 217
Moore, Andrew B., 82
Moore, John A., 82
Moorhead, James K., 160
Morgan, Edwin D., 169, 175, 179, 182, 187
Morris, Edward J., 145–46, 146–47
Morris, Isaac C., 19, 42
Morse, Samuel F. B., 197–98, 203
Mount Holly *Herald,* 116, 215
Mount Holly *New Jersey Mirror,* 216
Mozart Hall, 167, 168, 169, 171, 179–80, 201
Muncy *Luminary,* 152, 216

Newark, Dela., 79, 86
Newark, N.J., 98, 102, 105, 118, 122; newspapers in, 103, 105, 113, 115, 118, 215–16
Newark *Daily Advertiser,* 105, 115, 118, 215
Newark *Daily Mercury,* 216
Newark *Evening Journal,* 103, 113, 118, 215
New Brunswick, N.J., 100; newspapers in, 103, 113–15, 122, 215–16
New Brunswick *Fredonian,* 216
New Brunswick *Times,* 103, 113, 114–15, 122, 215
Newburgh *Telegraph,* 219
New Castle, Dela., 76, 90, 91
New England, 13, 14, 47–48, 87, 148, 149, 165
New Hampshire, 19
New Jersey, 13, 15, 16, 89, 98–124, 178, 197, 207; in a central confederacy, 38, 49, 134, 206; congressmen from, 19, 111–13; secession of, 14, 135, 162
New Jersey legislature, 103, 108, 108–9, 111, 123, 124
New Orleans, La., 160, 196, 209
Newton *New Jersey Herald,* 116, 121, 215
Newton *Sussex Register,* 216
New York *Albion,* 218
New York *Bible Society Record,* 221
New York *Brother Jonathan,* 220
New York Central Railroad, 167, 178
New York *Century,* 220
New York Chamber of Commerce, 198, 199, 203
New York *Christian Advocate and Journal,* 221

New York *Christian Intelligencer,* 220
New York *Chronicle,* 219
New York *Church Journal,* 221
New York City, 16, 104, 164–66, 185, 187, 199–202, 204–5, 206, 209; congressmen from, 175, 188–92; election of 1860 in, 167–70, 199; free city of, 16, 174, 176–80, 190, 201, 204; merchants of, 130, 164–65, 170, 178, 181, 194–98, 200, 201, 203–4, 205; newspapers in, 14, 104, 129, 157, 167, 169, 173, 177, 178, 179, 181, 182, 184, 198, 199, 200, 202, 205, 218–21; post-Sumter in, 202–4; state legislators from, 185–87
New York *Commercial Advertiser,* 220
New York *Daily Transcript,* 221
New York *Daily News,* 167, 173, 178, 198, 218, 219
New York *Dispatch,* 220
New York *Evening Day Book,* 178, 198, 202, 218, 219
New York *Evening Post,* 184, 220
New York *Examiner,* 218
New York *Express,* 177, 178, 198, 219
New York *Herald,* 129, 167, 169, 177, 178, 191, 200, 219
New York *Herald of Progress,* 221
New York *Home Journal,* 221
New York *Illustrated News,* 219
New York *Independent,* 218
New York *Irish American,* 219
New York *Journal of Commerce,* 150, 173, 179, 219
New York *Leader,* 177, 219
New York *Ledger,* 221
New York legislature, 166, 177, 185–87
New York *Morning Courier and New York Enquirer,* 220
New York *National Anti-Slavery Standard,* 218
New York *New Jerusalem Messenger,* 221
New York *Observer,* 219
New York *Shipping and Commercial List and New York Price Current,* 221
New York *Sower: Missionary Record,* 221
New York *Spectator,* 220
New York *Spirit of the Times,* 221
New York (state), 13, 14, 15, 16, 20, 27, 117, 120, 130, 164–205, 206, 207,

209; in a central confederacy, 38, 48, 104–5, 114, 151

New York *Sun,* 219

New York *Sunday Mercury,* 221

New York *Sunday Times and Noah's Weekly Messenger,* 219

New York *Times,* 181, 182, 205, 219

New York *Tribune,* 14, 104, 157, 184, 220

New York *United States Economist,* 219

New York *Wilkes' Spirit of the Times,* 219

New York *World,* 221

Niagara Falls *Gazette,* 219

Nixon, John T., 113

The Norristown Register and Montgomery Democrat and Watchman, 216

North Carolina, 34, 114, 135

Norwich *Chenango Telegraph,* 220

O'Conor, Charles, 175, 195

Odessa, Dela., 79

Ogdensburg, N.Y., 187

Ohio, 38, 99, 111, 114

Olden, Charles S., 106, 107–8, 109, 111, 118, 122

"Opposition party" (New Jersey), 101, 106

O'Sullivan, John, 175

Ould, Robert, 58

Ovid *Bee,* 219

Packer, William F., 126, 133–34, 163

Palmer, George W., 194

Palmer, Robert M., 139

Parker, Judge Amasa J., 171–72

Parker, Joel, 106

Paterson *Daily Guardian,* 216

Paterson *Daily True Register,* 116, 118, 122, 215

Pearce, James A., 40, 41, 57

Pennington, William, 45, 102, 112

Pennsylvania, 13, 15, 16, 64, 66, 69, 96, 105, 117, 125–63, 207; in a central confederacy, 48, 49, 52, 61, 104, 114; election of 1860 in, 20, 169; governor of, 36, 38, 111, 211. *See* Curtin, Andrew

Pennsylvania legislature, 126, 139–40, 163

Penn Yan, *Yates County Chronicle,* 221

Pensacola, Fla., 14

People's party (Delaware), 76, 77, 87

People's party (Pennsylvania), 127, 141

Perry, Nehemiah, 98, 102

Personal liberty laws, 16, 108, 112, 126, 136, 148, 196

Perth Amboy, N.J., 103, 104

Phelps, Royal, 130

Philadelphia, Pa., 74, 78, 85, 103, 119, 120, 125, 126, 138, 142, 163, 209; attitude toward secession in, 154–60, 162, 206; congressmen from, 144–46, 147; election of 1860 in, 126–27; 129; newspapers in, 26, 105, 106, 137, 148, 150–54, 155, 156, 159, 160, 216–18; post-Sumter in, 90, 135, 161–62; state legislators from, 139–40

Philadelphia *Daily Evening Bulletin,* 153, 218

Philadelphia *Daily News,* 152, 216

Philadelphia *Evening Journal,* 217

Philadelphia *Inquirer,* position on secession, 151–52, 216; quoted, 26, 41, 105–6, 155, 156, 160

Philadelphia *North American and United States Gazette,* 137, 153, 159, 218

Philadelphia *Palmetto Flag,* 154, 161, 216

Philadelphia *Morning Pennsylvanian,* 129, 148, 156, 216

Philadelphia *Press,* 150, 218

Philadelphia *Public Ledger,* 154, 217

Pierce, Franklin, 17, 157, 206

Pikesville Arsenal, 67

Pine Street meeting, 194–96

Piollet, Victor E., 135–36

Pittsburgh, Pa., 125, 128, 129, 140, 154–60, 162; newspapers in, 137, 217–18

Pittsburgh *Evening Chronicle,* 218

Pittsburgh *Daily Gazette,* 137, 217

Pittsburgh *Post,* 217

Plattsburgh, N.Y., 194, 219

Plattsburgh *Republican,* 219

Pollock, James, 141

Popular sovereignty, 17, 112, 196

Pottsville *Miner's Journal,* 217

Poughkeepsie *Eagle,* 220

Pratt, Thomas G., 30, 57

Presbyterians, 159–60

Price, Rodman, 14, 104, 105, 106

Pryor, Roger A., 19, 44, 72

Quakers, 99, 100, 107, 120, 126, 160, 166

Raymond, Henry J., 181, 182–83, 205

Reading, Pa., 127, 128, 129, 216
Reading *Berks and Schuylkill Journal,*
216
Reed, William B., 156, 157
Reformed Protestant Dutch Church of
North America, 100
Republican party, 13, 17–18, 27, 36,
114, 121, 122, 135, 136, 137, 141, 172,
175, 187, 196, 201, 202, 209, 210;
convention of 1860, 18, 24, 76, 101–2;
election of 1860, 24–26, 76–77, 102–3,
127–29, 167, 169–71, 176; newspaper
supporters of, 14, 117–18, 148–54, 199;
New York, 181–85, 187–89, 192–94,
205; opposed compromise, 19, 107,
111, 147, 183–85, 187–88, 192–93, 194;
Pennsylvania congressmen, 141–44,
144–47; views on secession, 20, 107–
11, 112, 113, 123, 138–39, 139–40,
158–59, 163
Reynolds, Edwin R., 192
Reynolds, John H., 192
Richmond, Va., 18, 101, 135, 168, 189
Richmond, Dean, 167, 168
Ridgeley, Edward, 84
Ridgeley, Henry, 90
Riggs, Jetur R., 111–12, 113
Robinson, H. B., 156, 161
Rochester, N.Y., 170, 220
Rochester *Democrat and American,* 220
Rochester *Evening Express,* 220
Rochester *Union and Advertiser,* 220
Rockville *Montgomery County Sentinel,*
59, 213
Rodney, George B., 90
Ross, William H., 78
Russell, William H., 201
Rynders, Isaiah, 200, 201

Sag Harbor *Corrector,* 218
Saulsbury, Willard, 75, 77, 84, 87–88,
92, 96
Scharf, J. Thomas, 54, 72–73
Scott, T. Parkin, 70
Scott, General, 37, 39, 66, 70
Scovel, James, 101
Scranton, George W., 146
Scranton, Pa., 146
Seaford, Dela., 78
Sedwick, Charles B., 193
Selinsgrove *Times,* 216
Semmes, Raphael, 58
Sennifer, Lieutenant, 162
Seward, William, 146, 181, 182, 183;

letters to, 39, 66, 176; position on se-
cession, 188
Seymour, Horatio, 14, 167, 168, 172, 174
Sickles, Daniel, 177, 189–91, 204
Slavery, 16–20, 37, 107, 117, 128, 145,
159, 181, 188, 192, 193, 196, 206;
Delaware 75, 77, 83, 84, 90, 96–97;
Maryland, 21–25, 28–29, 33; New
Jersey, 99–101, 118, 120, 123; New
York, 164, 165–66; Pennsylvania,
125–26
Smethport *Cameron Citizen,* 217
Smethport *McKean County Democrat,*
149, 216
Smethport *McKean Miner,* 217
Smith, Charles Perrin, 106, 121
Smith, George Rush, 139–40
Smith, Gerrit, 185, 209
Smith, Gustavus W., 201–2
Smyrna *Times,* 79, 92, 95–96, 214
South Carolina, 13, 18, 25, 37, 46, 77,
79, 80, 87, 100, 101, 103, 127, 130,
131, 132, 135, 151, 154, 157, 186,
194, 195, 211
The Southern Monitor, 119
Stanton, Edwin, 161
Stapleton *Richmond County Gazette,*
220
Star of the West, 151, 210
State Conference Convention, 38–39
States-Rights Convention, 62
Steiner, John A., 69
Stephens, Alexander H., 101
Steuart, George H., 69
Stevens, Thaddeus, 145, 147
Stewart, James A., 41, 42
Stockton, Robert F., 110, 122
Story of Disunion, 89
Stowe, Harriet Beecher, 17
Stratton, John L. N., 113
Stroudsburg *Jeffersonian,* 217
Syracuse, N.Y., 168, 170, 193; news-
papers in, 219
Syracuse *Daily Courier and Union,* 219

Tammany Hall, 167, 168, 169, 171,
202–3
Tariff, 22, 24, 73, 76, 102, 128, 182
Ten Eyck, John C., 111
Tennessee, 18, 34, 114
Texas, 14, 18
Thayer, James S., 172
Thirteenth Amendment, 99
Thomas, Francis, 57

Thomas, Philip F., 57
Thomson, John R., 111
Tilden, Samuel J., 172, 174–75, 175
Toms River *Ocean Emblem,* 117, 118, 215
Toombs, Robert, 101, 211
Townsend, Samuel, 76
Towsontown *Baltimore County Advocate,* 60, 213
Towsontown *Baltimore County American,* 60, 213
Tremain, Lyman, 172
Trenton, N.J., 106, 122, 118; newspapers in, 105, 115–16, 118, 122, 215
Trenton *Daily State Gazette and Republican,* 215
Trenton *Daily True American,* 105, 115–16, 118, 122, 215
Trimble, Isaac R., 68
Troy, N.Y., 170; newspapers in, 219, 221
Troy *Daily Arena,* 219
Troy *Daily Times,* 221
Troy *Daily Whig,* 219
Trumansburg *News,* 219
Tyler, Robert, 127, 129, 134–35, 156, 161, 162

Uncle Tom's Cabin, 17
Uniontown *Genius of Liberty,* 150, 217
United States Census, 15, 22, 23, 58, 91, 98, 100, 113, 147, 198
United States Congress, 16, 18–20, 37, 66, 86, 108, 130, 131, 133, 204, 210; Delaware delegation in, 86–90; Maryland delegation in, 40–44, 71; New Jersey delegation in, 101, 111–13; New York delegation in, 181, 187–94, 200; Pennsylvania delegation in, 141–47, 163
United States House of Representatives, 41, 43, 45, 53–54, 57, 76, 86, 87, 102, 112
United States Naval Academy, 53
United States Senate, 40, 41, 86, 87, 110
Upper Marlborough's *The Planter's Advocate,* 59, 213
Utica, N.Y., 170, 219, 220, 221
Utica *Daily Observer,* 219
Utica *Gospel Messenger and Church Record of Western New York,* 221
Utica *Morning Herald and Daily Gazette,* 221
Utica *Oneida Weekly Herald and Gazette and Courier,* 220

Van Wyck, Charles H., 193
Vaux, Richard, 127
Virginia, 27, 31, 35, 39, 41, 49, 74, 75, 91, 143, 174; central confederacy and, 34, 38, 90, 114; legislature's call for a peace conference, 19, 52, 109; secession of, 13–14, 40, 45, 51, 69, 70, 72, 78, 83, 85, 89, 97, 207
Wall, James W., 106
Walworth, Reuben H., 172
Warren *Mail,* 218
Washburne, Elihu B., 27
Washington, D.C., 20, 39, 43, 62, 68, 69, 70, 76, 94, 95, 98, 179, 195, 198, 211; Peace Conference in, 19, 108, 140; seizure of, 53–54, 136; Virginia taking, 35, 36
Washington Peace Conference, 19, 85, 108–11; Delaware delegation in, 90; Maryland delegation in, 49, 52–53; New Jersey delegation in, 109–11, 122; New York delegation in, 187; Pennsylvania delegation in, 140–41
Washington *Reporter and Tribune,* 218
Watertown *New York Reformer,* 220
Waverly *Advocate,* 221
Webster, Daniel, 138
Webster, Edwin H., 30, 41, 42–43, 46
Webster, Sidney, 200, 204
Weed, Thurlow, 77, 181, 182, 183, 187, 188, 205
Wells, Alfred, 193–94
Wellsboro *Agitator,* 217
West Chester *Jeffersonian,* 161, 217
Westminister *American Sentinel,* 60, 214
Wharton, George W., 157
Whetten, William, 91
Whig party, 16, 17, 24, 28, 41, 76, 171, 181
Whiteley, William G., 76, 79, 86, 87, 96
White Plains, *Eastern Star Journal,* 220
White, Thomas, 141
Whittingham, Bishop William R., 49, 56
Wild Western Scenes, 120
Wilkes-Barre *Luzerne Union,* 150, 218
Wilkes-Barre *Record of the Times,* 218
Wilmington, Dela., 74, 79, 85, 86, 87, 88, 90, 94, 96; election of 1860 in, 76–77; newspapers in, 92, 94, 214; secessionist activities in, 78
Wilmington *Delaware Gazette,* 92, 94, 214
Wilmot, David, 139, 140, 141, 142
Wilson, George, 160

Wise, Henry A., 35, 36
Wood, Benjamin, 167
Wood, Fernando, 167, 201, 202, 203;
    election of 1860, 168, 170; free city,
    16, 174, 176–80, 190, 204
Woodward, George W., 14, 135, 156
Wool, John E., 185

Wright, Ambrose R., 34, 37, 38
Wright, Edwin R. V., 105
Wright, Hendrick B., 156, 161
Wright, William, 98, 101

Yonkers *Examiner,* 221
York *Gazette,* 217